A Natural History of
F E R N S

A Natural History of
FERNS

Robbin C. Moran

Timber Press

To Lee & Cirri

Drawings by Haruto M. Fukuda and photographs by Robbin C. Moran unless otherwise indicated.

Preceding page, reconstruction of *Phlebopteris smithii*, the oldest (late Triassic) fossil species of Matoniaceae.

Published in 2004 by

Timber Press, Inc.
The Haseltine Building
133 S.W. Second Avenue, Suite 450
Portland, Oregon 97204, U.S.A.

www.timberpress.com

Reprinted with corrections 2005

Printed in China
Jacket and text designed by Susan Applegate

Library of Congress Cataloging-in-Publication Data

Moran, Robbin Craig, 1956–
    A natural history of ferns / Robbin C. Moran.
        p. cm.
    Includes bibliographical references and index.
    ISBN 0-88192-667-1 (hardback)
    1. Ferns. I. Title.
    QK522.M67 2004
    587'.3—DC22   2004001299

A catalogue record for this book is also available from the British Library.

CONTENTS

FOREWORD

Oliver Sacks

Wittgenstein once wrote that a book should consist of examples. *A Natural History of Ferns* is such a book, and it presents its subject in the form of 33 delightful and learned essays, written by Robbin Moran. It is our good fortune that Robbin, one of the world's great experts on ferns and curator of ferns at the New York Botanical Garden, also happens to be an engaging writer. Many of the chapters here are entirely new, and others have been enlarged and updated from essays originally published in the *Fiddlehead Forum*, a journal published by the American Fern Society for fern lovers and amateurs, and so they are designed to be accessible not just to professional botanists and students, but to a much wider audience. Readers of the *Fiddlehead Forum* never know what Robbin Moran will write about next—his essays might range from the mythological Scythian lamb one month to the logarithmic spirals of fiddleheads the next—but they can always be sure of a delightful adventure into the world of ferns, combining the scholarly and the personal with a charming naturalness and ease. Robbin is interested in everything (not just ferns!) and can make any topic fascinating—a gift he shares with the late Stephen Jay Gould.

One can open this book at any point, for the essays in it are each autonomous and independent. But they are also richly interconnected, and organized into six general categories: the life cycle of ferns, their classification, their special forms of adaptation, their geography and ecology, their more than 300-million-year history, and, not least, their many uses and roles in human society. *A Natural History of Ferns* brings to life, in a way no textbook or systematic treatment could ever do, the entire natural history of ferns, a superarching sense of their fascination and beauty, and their place in the world.

We travel a lot with Robbin, in this book: to La Paz, in Bolivia, to the tepuis in Venezuela, to Costa Rica (where he teaches and conducts field research every summer), to Taiwan (where he finds an old woman collecting adder's-tongue ferns to make tea), and to Lake Kalgaard, in Jutland, where he hunts mud-dwelling quillworts, fascinating "living fossils" allied to the giant scale trees of the Carboniferous age (and, like them, capable of breathing through their roots).

We move, too, through time, on these journeys. There is a marvelous chapter on the giant scale trees, the lepidodendrons, so vivid that we seem to be living with them in the age of the great coal-forming swamps. We voyage to the Permian, when the world is getting much drier, and the lush Carboniferous flora is dying out; through the Mesozoic, with its "fern prairies" and its open forests, carpeted with dipterids and Matoniaceae—ferns which almost became extinct with the rise of flowering plants and tall trees, which cast a deep shade on the forest floor. Toward the end of the Mesozoic, in the Cretaceous, we see the emergence and evolution of the polypodiaceous ferns, the fern "equivalent" of mammals, which emerged soon afterwards in the Tertiary. Finally, we see the famous "fern spike," the virtual recolonization of the earth by ferns after the catastrophic mass extinctions of 65 million years ago.

Everywhere in *A Natural History of Ferns* there is enthusiasm as well as deep knowledge, acquired over a lifetime of fieldwork and study, as well as that "feeling for the organism," for the forms and lives of animals and plants which E. O. Wilson calls biophilia. Describing the radical new classifications of plants which DNA analysis has made possible, Robbin writes, "there has never been a more exciting time to be a systematist."

We all tend to think of ferns as graceful plants with spreading fronds, and pay little heed to the humble, often liverwort-shaped little gametophytes, the hidden generation from which they spring. One of the many charms of *A Natural History of Ferns* is the respect it pays to the unregarded little gametophyte. Robbin Moran is entranced by them, and compares the independently living gametophytes of the filmy fern *Trichomanes* to "tiny pads of green steel wool," and the Appalachian gametophytes to "finely chopped lettuce."

Such gametophytes can be almost impossible for the untrained eye to spot, and Robbin describes how, as a student, he spent 2 years searching for them in an area where they were said to be plentiful, but never saw a single one. Finally, having gone back to study them in libraries and herbarium specimens, he returns to the field, only to discover, with his newly honed eye, millions of them in the same terrain he had previously scrutinized. *A Natural History of Ferns* is full of such charming, honest admissions, of ferns not recognized at first, of mechanisms not understood or misunderstood—but these misrecognitions and misunderstandings are, for a scholar, a fertile stimulus to research and learning. An observation or experience comes first: seeing the strange red ochre, the ferruginous mud, which clusters around the roots of quillworts; or the way in which scaly polypodies curl up and wither as they dry yet revive unharmed with the next rain; or the incredible toughness of tree ferns, whose trunks resist rotting, and may disable chain saws—such experiences stimulate, bewilder, puzzle, demand research, experiment, investigation, and understanding.

So in each of these chapters there is also a journey of mental exploration, and it is here that the book moves from the level of description—passionate, detailed, wondering description, which is the essence of natural history—to the search for patterns, for mechanisms, for deep understanding. *A Natural History of Ferns* not only represents science writing at its best, but it is a delightful adventure into the world of one of our foremost botanists; it is stimulating, enthralling, a beautiful companion for any fern lover.

Oliver Sacks is the author of *Awakenings, The Man Who Mistook His Wife for a Hat,* and *Oaxaca Journal*

P R E F A C E

First, I have a slight confession to make: the title of this book is not completely accurate. Although about ferns, the book is also about lycophytes, a group of vascular plants that, like ferns, possesses vascular tissue and reproduces by liberating spores. Lycophytes comprise the club mosses (*Lycopodium, Huperzia, Lycopodiella,* and *Phylloglossum*), *Selaginella,* and *Isoetes.* Because ferns and lycophytes disperse by spores and share other similarities of the life cycle, they are often referred to collectively as pteridophytes to distinguish them from seed plants, which consist of the gymnosperms and flowering plants. I considered using *pteridophytes* in the title, but how many people would buy a book titled *A Natural History of Pteridophytes?*

This book is not a field guide to the identification of ferns and lycophytes—there are plenty of those available. Instead, it picks up where field guides leave off, examining the biology of these plants—how they grow and develop, reproduce and disperse, adapt and evolve. It takes a look at what ferns and lycophytes do in the wild, how they interact with their environment, and what their fossil history tells of their past. It also includes examples of how they affect the lives of people.

I hope the book will interest fern specialists and general readers alike. It brings together much information that, even for specialists, is hard to obtain and widely scattered throughout the botanical literature. It can be readily understood by anyone who has taken an introductory biology course, and for those who have not, unfamiliar terms are defined in the text where first used, and there is also a glossary.

Many of the chapters are based on articles originally published in the *Fiddlehead Forum*, the bulletin of the American Fern Society, and one (Chapter 13) was published in the *Pteridologist*, the bulletin of the British Fern Society. These chapters have been updated to include more recent events and research, and they have been revised, sometimes extensively, to integrate them with other chapters.

ACKNOWLEDGMENTS

Upon completing a work such as this, it is humbling to contemplate my debt to others. I realize how much poorer the work would have been if I had to go it alone. I thank John and Carol Mickel, and Cindy Johnson-Groh, editors of the *Fiddlehead Forum*, for their help in reviewing and editing the original articles. I also appreciate the encouragement from Oliver Sacks and Kenneth R. Wilson to write a new book, one that expands those first articles and adds new chapters.

This book relies heavily on illustrations, and I thank Haruto M. Fukuda for his care in preparing many of the drawings. All drawings are by him unless otherwise indicated.

Many people from around the world have generously shared their knowledge about ferns with me and reviewed chapters of this book. I deeply appreciate their collegiality and willingness to help: Brad Boyle (tropical ecology), Gillian Cooper-Driver (*Pteridium*, fern chemistry), Peter Crane (paleobotany), John Earl (*Marsilea*, thiaminase), Joseph Ewan (history of botany), Donald Farrar (independent gametophytes), Else Marie Friis (paleobotany), Luis Gómez (pteridophytes), Judy Garrison Hanks (spores), Jim Harbison (thin-film interference), Cindy Johnson-Groh (pteridophytes), Paul Kenrick (paleobotany), Johanna H. A. van Konijnenburg-van Cittert (fossil Dipteridaceae and Matoniaceae), Cheng-meng Kuo (Taiwanese ferns), Thomas Lammers (island biogeography, Juan Fernández Islands), David Lee (iridescent ferns), David Lellinger (pteridophytes), Carol Mickel (editorial help), John Mickel (pteridophytes), John Milburn (sporangial dehiscence; cavitation), Cirri Moran (editorial help), Scott Mori (tropical biology), Michael Nee (seed plants), Benjamin Øll-gaard (pteridophytes, especially Lycopodiaceae), James Peck (fern ecology), Tom Ranker (hybridization, polyploidy), Erika Rohrbach (editorial help), Peter Room (*Salvinia molesta*, biological control), Oliver Sacks (cycads, ferns, history of botany), Judith Skog (paleobotany), Alan Smith (fern systematics, biogeography), Elizabeth Socolow (ferns, Shakespeare), Brian Sorrell (*Isoetes*, from physiological ecology), Dennis Stevenson (systematics of ferns and lycophytes), Tod Stuessy (island biogeography, Juan Fernández Islands), Michael Sundue (fern taxonomy), W. Carl Taylor (*Isoetes*), Barry Thomas (paleobotany), Hanna Tuomisto (tropical fern ecology), Florence Wagner (pteridophytes), Warren H. Wagner, Jr. (pteridophytes), Paul Wolf (molecular systematics of ferns), and George Yatskievych (pteridophytes).

I especially acknowledge Timber Press, whose efforts throughout the publication process have made this a much better book. Finally, I thank the members of the New York Chapter of the American Fern Society. The chapter's monthly meetings from October to May, held at the New York Botanical Garden, gave me with the opportunity to present some of the material here and sharpen my ideas. The membership's enthusiasm for ferns—and indeed all kinds of plants—and their willingness to listen was a big help.

THE LIFE CYCLE OF FERNS

I

In Search of the Fern Seed

In Shakespeare's *Henry IV*, Falstaff, Prince Hal, and Poins scheme to rob a rich merchant on his way to London in the dark hours of the early morning. Because they need help with the heist, one of Falstaff's henchmen tries to persuade another thief to join them. He says to the thief, "We steal as in a castle, cock-sure; we have the receipt of fern-seed, we walk invisible," to which the thief replies, "Nay, by my faith, I think you are more beholding to the night than to fern-seed for your walking invisible" (act 2, scene 1, lines 95–98).

What do the thieves mean by *fern seed?* Anyone who has taken a botany course knows that ferns do not have seeds; instead, they disperse by tiny dust-like spores. Did people in Shakespeare's day believe that ferns had seeds? And what is this about walking invisible?

In 1597 when *Henry IV* was written and first performed, the belief that ferns had seeds was common. To be sure, no one had ever seen a fern seed, but how could ferns—or any plant, for that matter—reproduce without such propagules. Therefore, the reasoning was that ferns *must* have seeds. "The views of those who believe all plants have seeds are founded on very reasonable conjectures," wrote Joseph Pitton de Tournefort, a celebrated French botanist, in 1694.

But sometimes the conjectures went too far. The early herbalists, for example, claimed that fern seed had to be invisible because no one had ever seen it. Furthermore, they asserted that it conferred invisibility to the bearer, that if you held the fern seed, you walked invisible. They also specified that the seed could only be collected at midnight on St. John's Eve (Midsummer's Night Eve, June 23), the exact moment it fell from the plant, during the shortest night of the year. You could catch it by stacking twelve pewter plates beneath a fern leaf; the seed would fall through the first eleven plates and be stopped by the twelfth. If you came up empty-handed, it was because goblins and fairies, roaming freely that one night of the year, had snatched the seed as it fell, much as Puck, Oberon, and the other fairies caused mischief, some of it botanical, in Shakespeare's *A Midsummer Night's Dream.*

Of course, not everyone believed all this about invisibility, but they did believe that ferns had seeds. The only problem was, what *was* the fern seed? Many early botanists suspected it was the dust liberated from the dark spots or lines (the sori) on the underside of the fern leaf (Figure 2 and Plate 19). Other botanists thought that this dust was not seed but instead equivalent to pollen that impregnated a female organ somewhere on the plant.

The first person to investigate fern dust scientifically was Marcello Malpighi, the Italian anatomist. In the late 1600s he focused his microscope on the curious dark spots or lines on the undersides of fern leaves. He observed that the spots or lines resolved into hundreds of tiny "globes" or "orbs" (the sporangia), each encircled by a thick, segmented band, the annulus (Figure 1). Inside the orbs sat the dust, which ap-

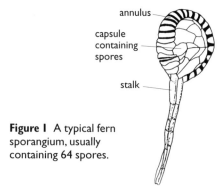

annulus

capsule
containing
spores

stalk

Figure 1 A typical fern sporangium, usually containing **64** spores.

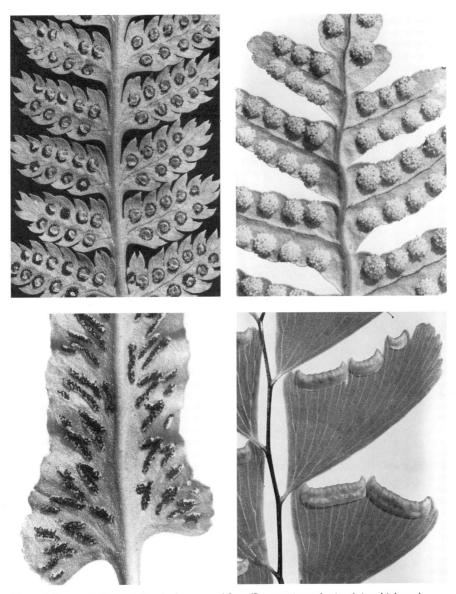

Figure 2 Fern sori. Upper left, spinulose wood fern (*Dryopteris carthusiana*), in which each sorus is covered by a thin indusium that protects the sporangia beneath. Upper right, common polypody (*Polypodium virginianum*), in which the sori lack a protective covering, or indusium. Lower left, walking fern (*Asplenium rhizophyllum*), in which sori are elongated along the veins; the thin, membranous indusium is starting to shrink and be pushed aside by the developing sporangia. Lower right, maidenhair fern (*Adiantum pedatum*), in which the indusium is formed by the margin of the blade, a so-called false indusium. Photographs by Charles Neidorf.

peared as round or bean-shaped bodies. He noted that the dust was hurled out of the orb by the catapult-like action of the annulus. Nearly half a century later, Malpighi's observations were confirmed and elaborated by Nehemiah Grew, an English microscopist. But the observations of neither man solved whether the dust was equivalent to pollen or seed.

Even the great Swedish botanist Carl Linnaeus was puzzled about the nature of fern dust. In a letter written in 1737 to Swiss botanist Albrecht von Haller, he said, "this powder seen under a microscope, exactly agrees with the dust of the anthers in other plants." But one month later he said, "[I know] nothing about the imperfect tribes of plants [mosses and ferns] and must confess my ignorance whether what I see is seed, or dust of the anthers." In 1751, however, he changed his mind and asserted that the dust was the true fern seed. Despite his flip-flopping, Linnaeus was sure about one thing: ferns *have* seeds.

Uncertainty reigned until 1794 when John Lindsay, a British surgeon, proved that ferns reproduced from their dust. He discovered this while stationed in Jamaica, where he noticed hundreds of young ferns arising on freshly exposed soil after rains. With a microscope, he examined the soil in the hope of finding a fern seed but was unsuccessful. Undaunted, he decided to sow some of the dust. (For some unknown reason, fern gametophytes abound on *freshly* exposed soil, generally less than 3 years old since exposure. Of course, the gametophytes from which the young ferns grow are easier to find on exposed soil because they are not obscured by vegetation, but there is something peculiar about freshly exposed soil that promotes their growth. Even if the soil is kept free of vegetation, particularly mosses and grasses, fern gametophytes will become fewer over time. To find fern gametophytes in the field, look for freshly exposed soil along trails, under tipped-up tree bases, along roadsides, and on landslides.)

Lindsay gathered the dust from several weedy ferns and sprinkled it over soil in a flowerpot. He placed the pot in a window of his room, watered it daily, and every day or two examined a small portion of the soil with his microscope. Lindsay (1794) describes what happened:

> I could always readily distinguish the dust or seeds from the mould, but observed no alteration till about the 12th day after sowing, when

many of the small seeds, represented at 6 in the annexed plate [Figure 3], had put on a greenish colour, and some were pushing out their little germ, like a small protuberance, the rudiment of the new fern, as at 8. This little protuberance gradually enlarged, and successively put on the appearances at 9, 10, and 11. They had acquired small roots, and the remains of the little seeds were still discernible where the roots of the infant plant commenced. Although the young ferns were now very conspicuous by the microscope, the naked eye could see nothing but a green appearance on the surface of the mould, as if it were covered with some very small moss: this was the numberless young plants from the quantity of the seed sown. In some weeks this moss began to appear to the naked eye like small scales, as at 13, which gradually enlarged, as at 14: they were generally of a roundish figure, somewhat bilobate, but sometimes more irregular; they were of a membranous substance, like some of the small *lichens* or liverworts, for which they might readily be mistaken, and of a dark green colour. At last there arises from this membrane a small leaf, different from it in

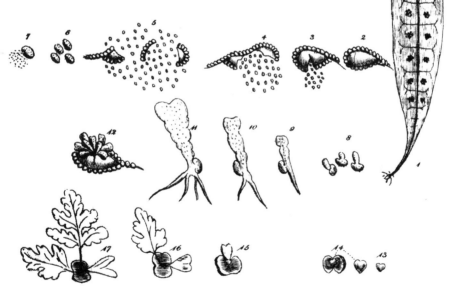

Figure 3 The plate from John Lindsay's 1794 article, describing the development of a spore into a mature fern, *Microgramma lycopodioides* (it has no common name), a species widespread in tropical America. The three young leaves on bottom left (15–17) are from another, unknown species of fern.

19

colour and appearance, as at 15, and shortly after another still more different, as at 16. Now each succeeding leaf grows larger than the last, till they attain the full size, and are complete in all the parts and discriminating characters of their respective species.

Clearly, Lindsay thought he had seen a full-sized fern develop from a mote of fern dust. He felt certain that the dust *is* the true fern seed.

A busy medical practice kept Lindsay from making further observations, until one day he received a letter from Sir Joseph Banks, president of the Royal Society of London and scientific advisor to the Royal Botanic Gardens, Kew. Banks asked Lindsay to collect Jamaican plants, especially ferns, and send them to England for cultivation. Lindsay wrote back that given the risk of transporting green ferns over such a great distance, he would send some of their seeds instead. Banks must have been flabbergasted that Lindsay claimed knowledge of the true fern seed. He wrote back that if Lindsay could furnish the means of making ferns grow from seed, he would be given the credit of having made a valuable discovery, one that Banks would communicate to the Linnean Society.

Lindsay sent Banks the seeds along with instructions for their sowing. The result was pteridological history. Thanks to Lindsay's information, gardeners in England learned to propagate ferns from spores, and they passed this knowledge to colleagues in other countries. Ferns began to enrich greenhouses, gardens, and parks around the world. Furthermore, the horticulturists at Kew began raising ferns sent from far corners of the British Empire. They amassed the world's largest and richest collection of living ferns—a distinction held to this day (the Kew collection is important scientifically as well as horticulturally). James Edward Smith, a pteridologist and one of England's leading botanists, commemorated Lindsay for his discovery by naming a genus of tropical ferns after him: *Lindsaea.*

Yet Lindsay's observations raised more questions. Are the "membranes" or "scales" he observed equivalent to the seed leaves or cotyledons of flowering plants? If the dust were equivalent to seeds, where are the pollen-producing anthers? (The pollen, of course, would be necessary to "stimulate" the development of the seed.) How and when did pollination take place?

20

We smile at these questions today, knowing that ferns do not produce seeds, but they were valid questions to botanists in the 1700s and early 1800s. It was not until 1844 that Karl von Nägeli, a Swiss botanist, steered questions about fern seed in the right direction. By focusing his microscope on the undersurfaces of the prothalli (the membranes or scales that Lindsay originally reported), von Nägeli saw minute globose bumps, which he called papillae, containing dark, spiral filaments. He noticed that when the papillae were wet, they burst at the tip and released the spiral filaments, which began to wiggle and swim away (Figure 4). He knew that similar papillae and filaments had been found in mosses and liverworts, where they are called antheridia, in allusion to the anther of the flower. Thus, Nägeli adopted the name antheridia for the papillae he saw on fern prothalli. But where did the spiral filaments swim?

This question was answered in 1848 by Michael Jérôme Leszczyc-Suminski, a Polish count with a botanical bent (Domanski 1993). He found that the spiral filaments swam to another kind of papilla also located on the undersurface of the prothalli. This type of papilla, which we now call an archegonium, is flask-shaped with a long neck and a single large cell at the base (Figure 4). When the sperm swam to the archegonium, they wiggled downward between the neck cells and penetrated the large basal cell. After penetration, this cell (now known to be an egg cell) developed into an embryonic fern with roots, stem, and leaves. This baby plant eventually grows into a mature fern with spore-bearing leaves.

What developed from Leszczyc-Suminski's observations was the picture of fern reproduction still taught today. The spores (fern dust) are produced on the undersides of the leaves in sporangia. They are liberated from a sporangium, land on a suitable substrate, and germinate. They grow into prothalli (Plate 1), which bear the sex organs—archegonia and antheridia—that produce eggs and sperm, respectively (the prothalli of some ferns produce only one kind of sex organ or the other). Sperm are released from an antheridium when water is present and swim to an archegonium and fertilize the egg (the archegonium may be on the same prothallus as the antheridium or on a neighboring one). The resulting cell, the zygote, develops into an embryo with stem, roots, and leaves. This embryo grows by elongating and widening its stem, pro-

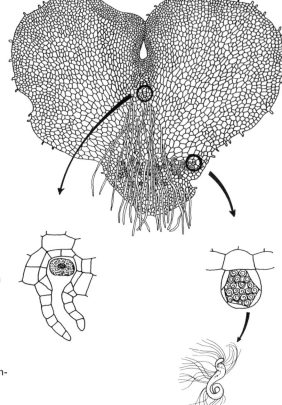

Figure 4 The underside of a typical fern gametophyte. The hair-like structures at the base are rhizoids, which anchor the gametophyte to the substrate. At left is an archegonium, containing an egg cell (shaded). At right is an antheridium, containing sperm cells that are coiled (with enlargement of a swimming sperm shown).

ducing successively larger leaves until a spore-bearing leaf eventually appears (Plate 6). At this point the process is complete.

The time it takes to complete the life cycle varies among ferns. Some, like tree ferns, complete it in 2–3 years—a long time. The fastest life cycle known is that of the water sprite (*Ceratopteris*, Figure 18), which under optimal conditions can be completed in as little as a month.

This sequence of events is known as the fern life cycle—the bugbear of many introductory botany students. It has two distinct phases, or generations. The first is called the gametophyte generation because it produces gametes, or sex cells. The second is called the sporophyte generation because it produces the spores. The gametophyte is the prothallus, and the sporophyte is the plant we typically think of as a fern—

22

the one with roots, stems, and leaves. Each generation develops from a single cell: the gametophyte from a spore, the sporophyte from a zygote.

There is a distinction between these two generations that is often dimly understood. The gametophyte is the sexual generation because it produces the sex cells, the egg and sperm. In contrast, the sporophyte is the asexual generation because it produces asexual spores; it does *not* produce sex cells. The next time you spot a leafy fern, luxuriating in the wild, remember that it is an asexual being, one that cannot engage in sex. We tend to equate, erroneously, our own bodies with those of fern sporophytes. But unlike plants, humans and other animals produce their gametes directly by meiosis; we have no intervening gametophytic (sexual) stage that produces gametes by mitosis. (The early history of ideas about sexual reproduction in plants and animals, especially how it reflects prevailing social attitudes about sex, is traced by Farley 1982.)

But returning to the fern seed, botanists today realize that spores and seeds are completely different structurally. A spore consists of a single cell and contains no preformed embryonic parts. In contrast, a seed typically has of hundreds or thousands of cells, forming an embryo and a specialized tissue that stores food: the endosperm. All this is enclosed in a usually tough, multicellular outer wall: the seed coat. Moreover, spores and seeds differ in what they give rise to. A fern spore gives rise to the prothallus of the gametophyte generation; a seed, to the baby plant of the new sporophyte generation.

The differences between spores and seeds seem to us so great that we are astonished to learn that early botanists seriously considered spores as seeds. But our astonishment is only proof that botany has progressed. Nowadays, it is the belief in the fern seed that walks invisible.

THE LIFE CYCLE OF FERNS

2

Spore Shooting

"¡Ay Profesor!" exclaims Jasivia González, peering through her dissecting microscope. *"¡Venga acá! ¡Les veo moviéndose!"* (Come here! I see them moving!) I hurry over to the lab table where Jasivia is working. Beneath her microscope lies a fresh, green fern pinnule from whose surface are furiously hopping dozens of spores, all of which I can see clearly, backlit by the stage illuminator. The spores leap more than an inch into the air and then arch downward. It is like watching popcorn popping.

Through the microscope I observe the action up close. Hundreds of tiny globose sporangia fill the field of view, and some have split transversely and are slowly bending their top half backward, filled with a charge of spores like a catapult being readied for action (Figure 5). Suddenly a movement too fast for the eye to follow, but I notice that the sporangium has flicked forward to its original position, and a second later brown spores tumble to a stop on the microscope stage. I have seen this action many times before, yet it never ceases to amaze me. It is the process of sporangial dehiscence, the splitting of the sporangial capsule and the discharge of spores—a process I like to refer to as "spore shooting."

By now several students have gathered around, eager to take a look at what is going on. They are part of a group of fifteen students taking my pteridology course at the National Herbarium in La Paz, Bolivia. After looking through the microscope, they ask how spore shooting happens. My answer, however, must be a bit complicated. It involves explaining the structure of a fern sporangium and how it interacts with the physical and chemical properties of water.

A typical fern sporangium consists of a thin stalk on top of which is attached a globose capsule measuring about $1/128$ inch (0.25 mm) in diameter. The wall of the capsule is one cell layer thick and therefore thin, fragile, and translucent. But along the top, one row of cells stands out from the rest. This row, called the annulus, is darker and encircles two-thirds of the capsule (Figures 2 and 5). Its cells are thickened on the inner and radial walls but have thin, flexible outer walls. The dark radial walls impart a segmented appearance to the annulus, and for this reason when students see the annulus for the first time they usually say it resembles a *gusanito* (little worm). In the front of the capsule, the annulus gives way to two transversely elongated cells called the stomium (mouth).

During spore shooting the annulus functions by taking advantage of the physical and chemical properties of water. These properties arise from water's polarity, which is created by each water molecule's carrying a slight negative charge near the oxygen atom and a slight positive charge near the hydrogen atoms. The oppositely charged regions of different water molecules attract to form a weak, short-lived hydrogen bond. This attraction accounts for the cohesive properties of water—its tendency to stick together even though it is liquid. The slight pull created by the cohesion of water molecules is what supports the weight of an insect as it scurries across the surface of a pond. The insect does not sink because it is not heavy enough to break the cohesive forces at the water's surface.

Polarity also accounts for another property of water: adhesion, the ability to cling to charged surfaces. Adhesion can be demonstrated by partially filling a glass with water. If you look at the side of the glass where it meets the water surface, you see a tiny crescent of water that has crept up the side. This crescent, called the meniscus, results from the adhesion of water to the glass. In plants, adhesion is important because water is strongly attracted to cellulose, a charged molecule that is the most abundant constituent of plant cell walls—walls such as those of the annulus. Adhesion is what makes some substances such as wood wettable, and others such as wax unwettable.

How do cohesion and adhesion interact with the shape of the annulus cells to shoot the spores? What happens is perhaps best explained by analogy with a simple experiment first done in 1850 by Pierre Berthelot, a French chemist. He took a glass capillary tube with thick walls, filled it with water, then sealed it at both ends so that the tube contained only water and a tiny air bubble. He gently warmed the tube to 86°F (30°C), expanding the water and forcing the air bubble into solution, resulting

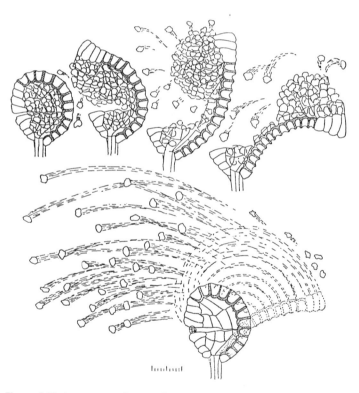

Figure 5 Various stages of spore shooting in a sporangium of the Christmas fern (*Polystichum acrostichoides*). The annulus is the thickened row of cells along the top. Upper left shows the beginning of dehiscence, with a transverse split forming between the two stomium (mouth) cells. Bottom shows spore discharge brought about by cavitation (breaking) of the water column in each annulus cell. Scale, 1 mm (about 1/32 inch). From Slosson (1906).

in the tube's being completely filled with water. Next, he let the tube cool. During cooling, the water column inside the tube contracted, and because the water adhered to the glass, it pulled inward on the walls of the tube, causing a narrowing of the tube that Berthelot could actually measure with a micrometer.

At this point, the water column in the glass capillary tube is stretched, or under tension. The force of cohesion holds the water column together, and the force of adhesion attracts the water to the walls of the glass tube. While these forces are pulling inward, they are opposed—and thus tension is created—by the elastic force of the glass wall's returning to its original (wider) width upon cooling. The situation is unstable; the more the tube cools and the water column within contracts, the greater the tension. Finally, a point is reached at which the forces of adhesion and cohesion of the water column are overcome by the elastic force of the glass wall. Suddenly, the water column breaks, or cavitates. The forces pulling inward on the glass wall are gone, and the wall springs back to its original diameter. Some of the latent energy in the distorted glass wall is converted into sound energy as the wall reverberates. This can be heard as a metallic click.

The same forces interact in spore shooting. At the start of the process, before the sporangial capsule dehisces, each cell of the annulus is filled with water. Each cell is like a water-filled, glass capillary tube. The water coheres in each cell to form a short column; it also adheres to the cellulose cell walls of each annulus cell. Water evaporates from the thin outer wall of the annulus cell. This contracts the water column inside the cell, just as the water column contracted inside the cooling capillary tube. Through adhesion, the contracting water column pulls the cell walls inward. Here, however, the situation deviates from Berthelot's capillary tube because of the shape of the annulus cell. The cell's flexible outer wall is drawn inward by the contracting (and adhering) water column, and the dark, rigid radial walls are pulled toward each other (Figure 6). This deformation, occurring in each cell along the length of the annulus, bends the entire annulus backward (Figure 5).

The bending annulus strains the front of the capsule and splits the

Figure 6 Forces act on an annulus cell as it dries. As the water inside the cell evaporates through the thin outer wall, the water column inside the cell contracts and pulls the thin wall inward (shown by the downward-pointing arrow), pulling the thick (shaded) radial walls toward each other. This force is opposed by the elastic tendency of the cell walls to return to their original position (the two lateral arrows).

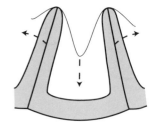

two stomium cells (Figure 5). As water continues to evaporate and bends the annulus even farther backward, the split spreads laterally through the sides of the capsule. (Note that dehiscence, the actual splitting open of the sporangial capsule, is gradual and does not immediately discharge the spores.) After the capsule dehisces, the annulus continues to flex backward until it assumes the shape of an inverted U. The upper half of the capsule forms a small cup filled with a charge of spores ready to be shot out (a few spores usually remain in the bottom cup formed by the basal half of the capsule). The sporangium is now primed.

At this point, most of the water has evaporated from the annulus cells so that the remaining water inside the cells is tightly stretched. The forces of cohesion and adhesion hold the column together *and* to the sides of the annulus cells, but the opposing elastic force of the cell walls tends to rip it apart (Figure 6). Finally, a point is reached at which the elasticity of the annulus cell walls overcomes the forces of adhesion and cohesion, and the water column cavitates. Gone is the force pulling inward on the cell walls, and the walls spring back to their original position. This causes the entire annulus to fling forward to its original C-shaped position—just like the walls of Berthelot's capillary tubes sprang back to their original diameter with a resounding click. The charge of spores held in the upper cup are flung into the air, caught by the wind, and carried away. (Excellent descriptions of spore dispersal in bryophytes and fungi can be found in the classic works on the subject by Ingold, 1939 and 1965.)

Just as cavitation of the water column in Berthelot's capillary tube results in a sound, so too does the cavitation of water in an annulus cell. The sound is too faint to be heard but can be detected with special equipment. John Milburn, a plant physiologist at the University of New England in Australia, and his postgraduate student Kim Ritman studied sound from cavitating annulus cells of fern sporangia and in the conducting vessels of trees (cavitation in the xylem disrupts the flow of water and is a serious physiological problem for trees). They found that the small jolt from a single cavitated annulus cell usually upsets the equilibrium in the remaining annulus cells, causing their simultaneous cavitation and shooting the spores (Ritman and Milburn 1990). In other words, the first cell acts like the primer of an explosive that detonates the main charge.

Spore shooting has also been studied using concentrated solutions of either table sugar (sucrose) or glycerol. A fully hydrated sporangium is placed in a solution of known concentration and then observed to see whether spore shooting occurs. Because the strength of the solution is known, the force that causes cavitation of the water column can be calculated. Researchers have found that the force required is 200–300 atmospheres of pressure, or 3000–4500 pounds per square inch (1400–2000 kg/cm^2)! (This study method might seem paradoxical. If cavitation depends on water evaporating from annulus cells, how can it occur in liquids? Actually, dry air and concentrated aqueous solutions produce the same effect of withdrawing water from the annulus cells. In concentrated solutions, the water moves by osmosis from inside the cell, where it is in high concentration, to the outside, where it is in lower concentration. The result is the same as in dry air: water is lost from inside the cell, and the annulus bends backward until cavitation occurs.)

Demonstrating spore shooting within liquids, as opposed to dry air, has two advantages. First, in dry air, spore discharge is often so violent that the sporangial capsules are torn loose from their stalks and tumble away. Viewing the process in a liquid stabilizes the sporangium so that it can be seen during and after spore discharge. Second, after cavitation a vacuum bubble (or near-vacuum bubble, because some water vapor is present) forms within each annulus cell. This bubble cannot be seen when the sporangium is in dry air, but in a liquid the bubble appears as a blackish sphere (Figure 7).

Figure 7 A sporangium after spore discharge. Within each annulus cell is a bubble formed after cavitation of the water column.

"¡Así es como lo hacen!" (So that's how it's done!) exclaim the students—that is, those whose minds have not turned into a television test pattern after listening to my long explanation. But most are still with me because spore shooting has grabbed their attention. It has excited them about ferns and stimulated their curiosity about these plants. That is why I demonstrate spore shooting during the first lab of my pteridology courses.

3

Sporadic Results

A few years ago I walked into the fern herbarium at the New York Botanical Garden, selected a specimen of the spinulose wood fern (*Dryopteris carthusiana*), and proceeded to estimate the number of spores produced by a single leaf. I first counted the number of sori on the leaf: 7134. I then multiplied this number by the average number of sporangia per sorus, which was 16, and the result was 114,144 sporangia. Because each sporangium contains 64 spores, the total number of spores produced by the leaf was 7,305,216. Not bad for a leaf only 25 inches (60 cm) long!

This calculation illustrates that, in general, ferns produce *a lot* of spores. And as you might expect from the quantities in which they are produced, spores play an important role in the biology of ferns. They are also curious and beautiful structures as seen under a microscope, coming in a variety of sizes, shapes, and colors.

All fern spores are extremely small. Even the largest ones are only about the size of a sand grain or the head of a pin—a distinction that goes to the female spores (which produce archegonium-bearing prothalli) of *Selaginella* and *Isoetes*, measuring only $1/32$ inch (1 mm) long. Most spores range from 30 to 50 μm long (a micrometer, μm, is one-thousandth of a millimeter, or 0.00004 inch). Individual spores of this size are extremely hard to see, but when viewed en masse they appear as a fine powder.

When examined under a microscope, spores can be seen to come in two basic shapes: bean-shaped (Figure 9) and globose-tetrahedral (Figure 10). These shapes result from the different ways the cell walls orient themselves during meiosis, the kind of cell division that gives rise to the spores (Figure 8). After a spore mother cell divides by meiosis, the resulting four spores are stuck together in a tetrad. They soon separate, but each carries a scar where it was attached to the other spores in the tetrad. In bean-shaped spores the scar is a short, straight line on the concave side (Figure 9), and in globose-tetrahedral spores the scar is Y-shaped (Figure 10). Because bean-shaped spores have a single scar they are called monolete, and tetrahedral spores with their three short lines are called trilete. The lines represent a weakness in the cell wall through which the spore contents protrude upon germination. (The beauty and diversity of fern spores as revealed by photos taken with the scanning electron microscope can be seen in Tryon and Tryon 1982, Tryon and Lugardon 1991, and Tryon and Moran 1997.)

Fern spores have two protective layers, and these layers account for much of the spore's external form and beauty. The inner layer, or exospore, is secreted by the living contents of the cell, whereas the outer

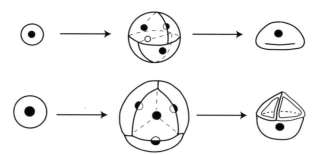

Figure 8 The two basic shapes of fern spores, monolete (top) and trilete (bottom), and how they form during meiosis. Left, spore mother cell. Middle, tetrad stage after meiosis (note the different orientations of the cell walls). Right, a single spore separated from the tetrad. The block dot in the center of each cell represents the nucleus. After Øllgaard and Tind (1993).

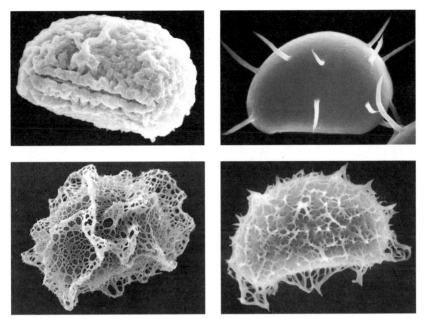

Figure 9 Monolete, bean-shaped spores. Upper left, *Paesia anfractuosa,* from tropical America; the straight groove is the scar where the spore was joined to other spores in the tetrad. Upper right, spleenwort (*Asplenium volubile*) from Colombia. Lower left, *Lomariopsis hederacea,* from Gabon; photograph by Judy Garrison Hanks. Lower right, deer's-tongue fern (*Elaphoglossum rufum*) from tropical America; photograph by John Mickel.

 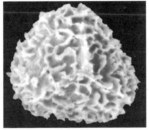 

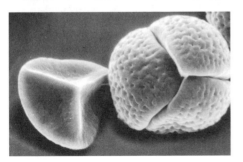

Figure 10 Trilete, globose-tetrahedral spores. Lower left, a fir moss (*Huperzia reflexa*) from tropical America; at right is a tetrad. Other spores shown are from ferns. Upper left, *Lonchitis hirsuta,* from tropical America. Center, *Hemionitis tomentosa,* from tropical America. Upper right, *Anemia* sp. from Mexico. Photographs by John Mickel.

layer, or perispore, is deposited from the outside and represents the disintegrated remains of a nutritive layer of cells in the sporangium. In some ferns the perispore is barely noticeable because it is extremely thin and adheres tightly to the exospore (Figure 10). In other ferns the perispore is loosely attached, highly elaborated, and ornamented with folds, knobs, or spines. Sometimes the perispore is wing-like and perforated, appearing doily-like; in others it is spiny, resembling a bur or caltrop (Figure 9).

Most ferns and lycophytes produce only one kind of spore and are termed homosporous. Others produce two kinds or spores, male and female, and are termed heterosporous. Of the approximately 300 genera of ferns and lycophytes worldwide, only 7 are heterosporous: *Azolla, Isoetes, Marsilea, Pilularia, Regnellidium, Salvinia,* and *Selaginella.* In these genera the female spores are much larger than the male spores, usually 10–20 times larger in diameter (Figure 11). Why the difference?

Female spores need to store copious amounts of food. Unlike the spores of homosporous ferns, female spores of heterosporous ferns germinate and develop into gametophytes *within* the spore wall, not outside it. This condition, called endosporic, exposes little surface area of the female gametophyte so that photosynthesis (if it were present, which it is not) would not suffice to manufacture enough food for the gametophyte and, after fertilization, the growing embryo. Thus female spores must store food, which necessitates a larger size. The male spores are small because they are ephemeral. They produce the sperm, liberate it, then die. They have no need for stored food.

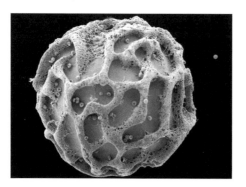

Figure 11 Heterospory in a spike moss (*Selaginella exaltata*) from Ecuador. The female spore (left) is huge compared to the male spores (on the right is one not stuck to the female spore). Photograph by Judy Garrison Hanks.

Besides size and shape, fern spores differ in color. Most are brown or black, as in the wood fern family (Dryopteridaceae) and thelypteris family (Thelypteridaceae). But a few groups have yellow or green spores. Yellow spores characterize the polypody family (Polypodiaceae), and a good species in which to see this is the commonly cultivated golden polypody (*Phlebodium aureum*). Its spores are bright yellow and impart their color to the entire sorus (the "golden" in its name, however, refers to the rhizome scales, not the spores). Green spores contain the photo-synthetic pigment chlorophyll and occur in about 7% of ferns world-wide. Some familiar ferns with green spores are the osmundas, filmy ferns (Hymenophyllaceae), ostrich fern (*Matteuccia struthiopteris*), and the sensitive fern (*Onoclea sensibilis*). The horsetails or scouring rushes (*Equisetum*) also have green spores.

Functionally, green spores differ from nongreen ones in two ways: they are viable for shorter periods but germinate faster (Lloyd and Kle-kowski 1970). Green spores usually remain viable for a few days to a few months, whereas nongreen ones remain so for 3 to many years. Fur-thermore, green spores usually germinate 1–3 days after sowing, whereas nongreen spores take their time, germinating at a more leisurely pace, usually 10–20 days after sowing. Green spores remain metabolically ac-tive, unlike brown or black spores, which go dormant. Because they re-main active, green spores constantly use their stored food, and when it is gone, they lack the energy to germinate. This accounts for their short viability. Their continuous metabolic activity also means that they can germinate as soon as conditions are favorable. They do not waste time breaking dormancy.

Dormancy in nongreen spores, however, has some advantages. It al-lows spores that have been washed into the darkness of the soil to remain viable for many years. These ungerminated underground spores form a spore bank, a long-term storage reservoir of a population's spores. These spores might one day be brought to the surface by the activities of bur-rowing animals, or falling trees that uproot at their base and form a tip-up mound, or erosion. At the surface, the spores germinate—a response triggered by light—and develop into gametophytes that in turn pro-duce sporophytes after fertilization. Thus new plants can be added to populations by spores that have lain dormant in the soil bank (Dyer and Lindsay 1992, Haufler and Welling 1994, Raghaven 1992).

Buried spores can contribute to future populations another way. They can be induced to germinate—something that normally happens only in light—by hormones secreted by mature, usually female prothalli on the soil surface. These hormones, called antheridiogens, are washed or diffuse into the soil where they stimulate buried spores to germinate. The spores develop into dwarf prothalli studded with antheridia (normally, antheridia form only on older, more well developed prothalli). When there is enough water in the soil, the antheridia burst and release their sperm, and these swim upward toward the larger female prothalli on the soil surface—the same prothalli that released the antheridiogens. So buried spores can contribute to a population's gene pool (Chiou and Farrar 1997, Yatskievych 1993).

Unlike most ferns, the spores of some ferns and lycophytes germinate *only* in the dark. Examples are the grape ferns (*Botrychium*), adder's-tongues (*Ophioglossum*), and club mosses (*Lycopodium*). Their spores germinate in the darkness of the soil and develop into prothalli underground. The prothalli are generally whitish or tan, having no need for chlorophyll, a pigment useless without light. Subterranean prothalli are often fleshy and carrot- or potato-shaped, usually as long as 3/8 inch (1 cm), and have embedded in their tissues a symbiotic fungus that absorbs nutrients from the soil and translocates these to the plant. Little is known about subterranean prothalli; they are rarely seen.

All spores—especially those that germinate underground—contain stored food in the form of oils. In fact, the spores of some species contain so much oil that they may ignite. This is particularly true of the spores of *Lycopodium*, whose spores were an ingredient in flash powder early days of photography. Their oiliness also repels water, and early apothecaries kept jars of *Lycopodium* spores to coat pills to prevent them from sticking. Nowadays, *Lycopodium* spores are used commercially to dust latex surgical gloves to prevent them from sticking together (Balick and Beitel 1988).

(As a grand finale to lectures about ferns and lycophytes, I usually ignite some *Lycopodium* spores. I place about a teaspoon of spores in the crease of a folded sheet of smooth paper, hold the paper about 2 feet (60 cm) above a lit match, and pour. The falling spores sizzle and burst into a yellow flame with occasional flecks of blue. If that does not grab people's attention, I take a cup of water and coat the water's surface with *Lycopodium* spores. I push my index finger into the water and withdraw it. The finger comes out completely dry, demonstrating the oiliness and hydrophobic properties of the spores. To get enough spores to do these tricks, collect 50–100 strobili and place them between two sheets of smooth paper. In a day or two the sporangia will have dried and dehisced, releasing their spores, which look like a yellow powder. Remove the strobili from the paper, tapping them if necessary to dislodge any spores still in the sporangia, then fold the paper lengthwise. Using the crease in the paper as a guide, pour the spores into a vial for storage.)

One last thing about fern spores: they are *not* villains in hay fever. That malady is caused primarily by pollen from wind-pollinated flowering plants. Allergies to pollen result from the reaction of our immune system to proteins on the surface of the pollen grains. These proteins signal the pollen to germinate if they are compatible with proteins on the stigma, the pollen-receiving tip of the seed-producing organ. If proteins of the pollen and stigma are incompatible, then the pollen does not germinate or, if it does, the subsequent growth of the pollen tube (which contains the sperm) is irregular or incomplete and fertilization does not occur. This protein recognition system prevents cross-fertilization between different species of flowering plants. In ferns, however, there are no flowers, no stigmas, no surface proteins, and consequently, no hay-fever-causing spores. This is good. After all, given their beauty and importance, fern spores are nothing to sneeze at.

THE LIFE CYCLE OF FERNS

4

The Asexual Revolution

"Of all sexual aberrations," wrote French symbolist poet Rémy de Gourmont, "perhaps the most peculiar is chastity." Although he was referring to people, de Gourmont could have said the same about ferns. Sexual reproduction, which involves the fusion of gametes (egg and sperm), is normal for ferns, just as it is for most plants and animals. But some ferns are abnormal—chaste, if you will—because they reproduce entirely asexually by a method called apogamy, "without gametes." This method of reproduction imparts some peculiar characteristics to those ferns that have it.

To appreciate how peculiar apogamy is, it is necessary to review the sexual life cycle of a typical fern described in detail in Chapter 1. The cycle consists of two alternating phases or generations: sporophyte and gametophyte. Each begins from a single cell: the sporophyte from a zygote (fertilized egg cell) and the gametophyte from a spore. The sporophyte is the most familiar generation because it forms the plants we commonly see—the one with roots, stems, and leaves. Early in development each sporangium contains 16 spore mother cells. These divide by meiosis, each forming four daughter cells, for a total of 64 spores. During meiosis the spore mother cells replicate their chromosomes once but divide twice. The result is spores with only half the chromosome number of the parent plant, a condition called haploid. Spores are liberated from the sporangium and, if all goes well, land on a suitable substrate and germinate. Each develops into a prothallus, which in most ferns is small, heart-shaped, and flattened. This represents the gametophyte generation of the life cycle, a generation that few are familiar with it because of its small size. The lower surface of the prothallus bears the sex organs—archegonia and antheridia—and these produce the egg and sperm, respectively. When wetted, the antheridia burst and release their sperm, which swim to the archegonia and fertilize the eggs. Because a haploid sperm plus a haploid egg equals a diploid zygote, the diploid condition—the original condition of the plant that produced the spore—is now restored. From the diploid zygote develops a new sporophyte.

The apogamous life cycle differs from this typical sexual one because it lacks fusion of gametes; it is asexual. Instead of producing 64 haploid spores per sporangium, apogamous ferns produce, by a glitch in meiosis, 32 *diploid* spores per sporangium. When sown, these spores germinate and develop into smaller than normal prothalli, and instead of producing sex organs, they vegetatively proliferate a tiny plantlet consisting of a root, stem, and leaf. As the plantlet grows, the prothallus withers away, and the plantlet then assumes an independent life of its own. When large enough, it sends forth spore-bearing leaves, and these in turn produce apogamous (diploid) spores, at which point the apogamous life cycle is complete.

The apogamous life cycle is merely a fancy form of vegetative propagation, akin to dividing a plant's stem and replanting both halves, or detaching bulblets from a mature leaf and planting them to make new individuals. The only difference is that in apogamy the propagating part of the plant is a single-celled diploid spore.

About 5–10% of fern species worldwide are apogamous. In Japan, where the fern flora is well studied, 13% of fern species are apogamous. Apogamy is more frequent in some ferns than in others, being especially common in spleenworts (*Asplenium*), lip-ferns (*Cheilanthes*), wood ferns (*Dryopteris*), holly ferns (*Cyrtomium*), brakes (*Pteris*), and cliff brakes

(*Pellaea*). On the other hand, it is noticeably absent from some groups, even large ones such as theylpterids (*Thelypteris*), chain ferns (*Blechnum*), and tree ferns (Cyatheaceae and Dicksoniaceae).

Apogamy is especially common in ferns that grow in dry habitats such as deserts, chaparral, and exposed cliff faces. In these environments apogamy offers two advantages. First, there is no need for water in reproduction because apogamous ferns lack swimming sperm (and the eggs that would need to be fertilized). Second, the prothalli of apogamous ferns mature faster than those of sexually reproducing ferns. Because the prothallus stage is present only briefly during the life cycle, it stands less chance of its dying from desiccation. Although apogamy is frequent in ferns of dry habitats, some apogamous species, such as the northern beech fern (*Phegopteris connectilis*) and black wood fern (*Dryopteris cycadina*), grow in moist forests. The advantage of apogamy in such habitats is unknown.

Another peculiarity of apogamous ferns is that nearly 75% contain three or more sets of chromosomes in their cells instead of the normal two, a condition called polyploidy. Most contain three sets of chromosomes, that is, they are triploid. Familiar examples of North American triploid ferns are some of the black-stemmed spleenworts (*Asplenium monanthes* and *A. resiliens*), purple cliff brake (*Pellaea atropurpurea*), slender lip-fern (*Cheilanthes feei*), and star-scaled cloak fern (*Astrolepis sinuata* var. *sinuata*). Among cultivated ferns, examples include the variegated brake (*Pteris cretica* var. *albolineata*), Fortune's holly fern (*Cyrtomium fortunei*), and shaggy wood fern (*Dryopteris atrata*).

Because these ferns are triploid, they *must* be apogamous to reproduce by spores; they cannot reproduce sexually. The reason is the way the chromosomes behave during meiosis. During spore formation only two chromosome sets of the triploid can pair; the third set remains unpaired. The chromosomes in the paired set separate and move into the daughter cells, each daughter cell receiving one of each kind of chromosome. But the chromosomes in the unpaired set are distributed unequally to the daughter cells. For example, one cell might receive 10 chromosomes from the unpaired set, another 16, and so on. This imbalance results is spore abortion—the spores cannot germinate and appear irregular, misshapen, and usually blackened (Figure 12). Apogamy avoids this problem because it omits the meiotic step that involves chromosome pairing. As a result, the triploid ferns that reproduce apogamously produce viable spores.

Viable spores can be picked up by air currents and dispersed over long distances—one way that ferns extend their geographic distribution. In general, apogamous ferns have wider geographic distributions compared to their sexually reproducing relatives. For instance, the smooth cliff brake (*Pellaea glabella*) consists of two races, one a sexually reproducing diploid (two sets of chromosomes) and the other an apogamously reproducing tetraploid (four sets of chromosomes). The diploid gave rise to the tetraploid by the process of chromosome doubling, or polyploidy (Gastony 1988). The two races are indistinguishable to the naked eye; their habit, size, and blade division all appear the same. Yet the sexually reproducing diploid has a much narrower range, found only in southeastern Missouri where it is relatively rare. In contrast, the apogamous tetraploid is widespread and common throughout much of eastern United States (Figure 13). Similar range differences are found in closely related sexual versus apogamous species in genera such as copper ferns (*Bommeria*), brakes (*Pteris*), star-scaled cloak ferns (*Astrolepis*), and comb ferns (*Pecluma*).

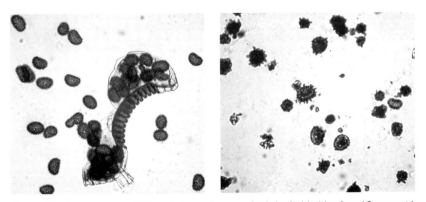

Figure 12 Normal spores (left) and aborted spores (right) of a bladder fern (*Cystopteris*).

Apogamous ferns are "abnormal" in the sense that they are chaste in a world that where sexual reproduction is the norm. They also differ from many of their sexually reproducing relatives by a tendency to predominate in dry habitats, have duplicated sets of chromosomes, and exhibit relatively wide ranges. Nevertheless, it might be better—more politically correct—to refer to them as "ferns with an alternative lifestyle."

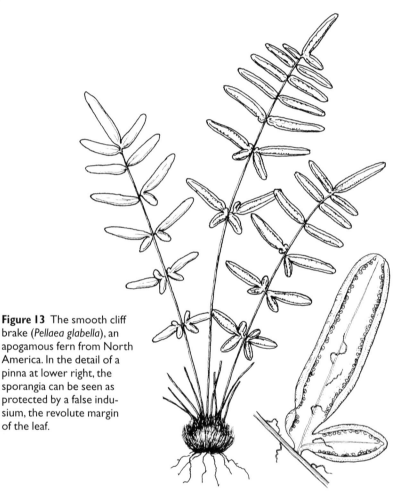

Figure 13 The smooth cliff brake (*Pellaea glabella*), an apogamous fern from North America. In the detail of a pinna at lower right, the sporangia can be seen as protected by a false indusium, the revolute margin of the leaf.

THE LIFE CYCLE OF FERNS

5

Reproduction by Buds

The life of most fern gametophytes is short and nasty. This is illustrated by a story once told to me by Donald Farrar, a pteridologist and botany professor at Iowa State University. One day in mid-July Don was hiking along a trail at the Woodman Hollow Nature Preserve in central Iowa when he spotted some plants belonging to a species being studied by a graduate student in his department. Don decided to mark the location of the plants so that they could be easily relocated. He grabbed a fist-sized rock—one of many along the trail—and put it in a plastic sandwich bag that he then placed near the trail. In mid-October he relocated the bag and withdrew the rock—it was covered with hundreds of glistening fern gametophytes. Yet he could not find *any* gametophytes on the rocks along the trail, even though those rocks had presumably received the same dusting of fern spores. What happened? Did the spores on the rocks along the trail fail to germinate? Did they germinate and were the resulting gametophytes eaten by insects, snacked on by snails, finished off by fungi, or desiccated by dry weather? One thing seems clear: hundreds of spores or gametophytes failed to develop or had had a short life.

This story shows that sexual reproduction can be risky business. It makes sense that ferns have some kind of backup, something to rely on when attempts to reproduce by spores and gametophytes fail. One such backup system is vegetative budding—buds produced on roots, stems, or leaves.

In eastern North America the most common bud-producing fern is the bulblet bladder fern (*Cystopteris bulbifera*), a species that grows in rock crevices or on talus slopes. Its buds appear as pea-like outgrowths on the lower surface of the leaf midribs (Figure 14), and they can be so numerous that their weight causes the leaf to droop. When mature, the buds fall readily, even at the slightest touch. I remember how frustrating it was as a beginning botanist when I collected specimens of this fern in a plastic bag, only to find that at the end of day, when I withdrew the fern from the bag, all the buds had fallen off. In the wild the buds work their way into rock crevices or under boulders where they take root and develop into new plants. Judging by the abundance of the bulblet bladder fern around rock outcrops, its reproduction by buds is highly successful.

Unlike the bulblet bladder fern, the buds on most other ferns do not drop from the leaf. They remain attached until the leaf senesces, at which time the base of the petiole weakens and the rest of the leaf gradually reclines to the soil surface where the bud can take root. In ferns with this kind of bud, it is common to find new plantlets on the ground still attached to the old, decaying parent leaves. If one follows the midrib of these decaying leaves, they can usually be traced to the stem that produced them. Generally, buds that remain attached develop

Figure 14 Bulblets on the lower surface of the bulblet bladder fern (*Cystopteris bulbifera*).

slowly while the leaf is mature and grow rapidly, producing more leaves with larger blades, after the leaf starts to die. Ferns with buds that remain attached can produce them anywhere on the leaf, although for a given species they are usually borne in a specific location. For instance, they always develop at the base of the blade in some species of *Doryopteris* and *Hemionitis* (including the widely cultivated *H. arifolia*). Those species of *Tectaria* and *Diplazium* with buds usually bear them along the midribs of leaves or leaflets, either above or below. This is also the location in which buds are borne in one of the most widely cultivated bud-bearing ferns, the mother fern (*Asplenium bulbiferum*), which may bear hundreds of tiny buds on a single leaf (Figure 15). Sometimes buds occur only at the tips of leaves, as in many species of *Danaea*, a tropical American fern, and in certain paddle ferns (*Elaphoglossum*, Figure 16).

Figure 15 The mother fern (*Asplenium bulbiferum*), a widely cultivated tropical species, bears many buds (three indicated by arrows) on the upper surface of its leaves. Above, detail of a bud. Modified from Hoshizaki and Moran (2001).

An unusual location for leaf budding occurs in the oriental chain fern (*Woodwardia orientalis*). Its buds form on the upper surface of the leaf at a point exactly above where the sori form on the lower surface. The formation of the bud inhibits the development of the sorus beneath; if a bud does not develop, the sorus develops normally. A large leaf can be studded with hundreds of buds bearing tiny spatulate leaves (Figure 17).

Buds are produced along the leaf margins in the water sprite (*Ceratopteris pteridoides,* Figure 18), a fern commonly cultivated in aquariums. This fern floats because its enlarged petioles are composed of buoyant, spongy, air-filled tissue called aerenchyma. Its buds proliferate while

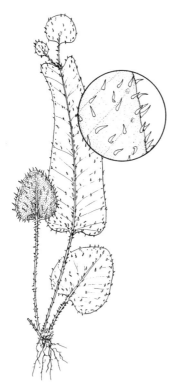

Figure 16 A paddle fern (*Elaphoglossum proliferans*) from Costa Rica with a bud at the tip of its leaf. The enlargement shows details of scales on the leaf. From Mickel (1985).

Figure 17 Buds on the oriental chain fern (*Woodwardia orientalis*), from Taiwan.

46

still attached to the leaves, and the new bud-produced plantlets in turn form buds on their leaves, and so on, leading to a series of leaves attached to leaves. Anyone who has grown this fern in an aquarium knows how quickly it can spread across the water's surface by this method of vegetative reproduction.

Some ferns produce buds on long, whip-like leaf tips, a condition known as flagellate or cirrhate. The buds are borne either singly at the very tip or at several places along the prolonged apex. Presumably the advantage of having an elongated leaf tip is that it establishes the buds far from the parent plant where competition will be less. In some ferns the whip-like tip is formed by an extension of the rachis lacking any green blade tissue—a naked rachis such as that of the trailing maidenhairs (*Adiantum caudatum* and *A. lunulatum*, Figure 19) and certain spleenworts (*Asplenium cirrhatum, A. prolongatum,* and *A. uniseriale*). In other ferns the elongated bud-bearing apex has a green wing or highly reduced pinnae, as in *Bolbitis heteroclita*, a widely cultivated fern from Asia, and *B. portoricensis*, native to the American tropics (Figure 20).

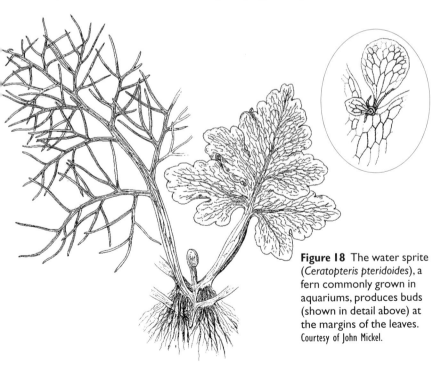

Figure 18 The water sprite (*Ceratopteris pteridoides*), a fern commonly grown in aquariums, produces buds (shown in detail above) at the margins of the leaves. Courtesy of John Mickel.

Several species of spleenworts (*Asplenium mannii, A. stoloniferum, A. stolonipes,* and *A. triphyllum*) bear buds at the top of elongated petioles. These may be four to five times the length of the petioles of the non-bud-bearing leaves. As they lengthen, the petioles arch over the soil and eventually touch down and produce a bud. Beyond this bud, the petiole turns into a rachis that develops a typical green blade (Figure 21).

Buds are produced at the *base* of the petioles in the ray spiked ferns (*Actinostachys*) and curly grass ferns (*Schizaea*). As soon as buds are formed, they develop short stems that send up more leaves, and these leaves produce buds on their petioles, and so on. After this process reiterates several times, the fern assumes a bunched or clump-like growth habit. All its leaves appear to emanate from the same stem, but dissection of the clump reveals that the petioles actually arise from many separate petiolar buds.

Petiolar buds of a slightly different kind are found in many species of cup ferns (Dennstaedtiaceae) and lindsaeas (Lindsaeaceae). These buds

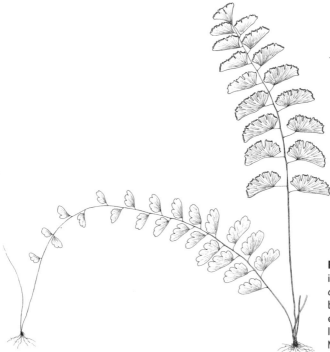

Figure 19 The trailing maidenhair (*Adiantum lunulatum*), bearing a bud at the end of its long, whiplike leaf apex. From Mickel and Beitel (1988).

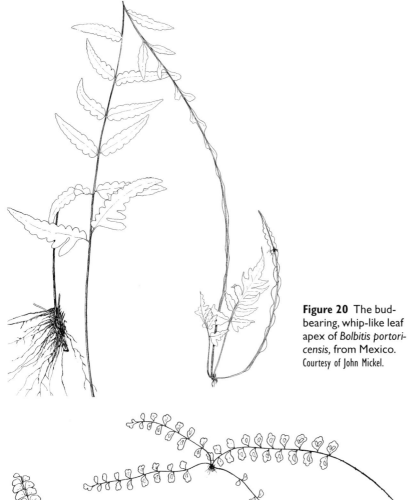

Figure 20 The bud-bearing, whip-like leaf apex of *Bolbitis portoricensis,* from Mexico. Courtesy of John Mickel.

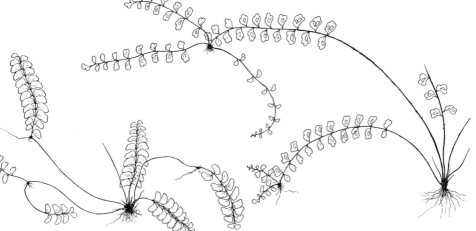

Figure 21 Reproduction by buds in two Mexican species of spleenworts. Left, *Asplenium stolonipes,* which produces buds at the top of an elongated petiole. Right, *A. soleirolioides,* which produces buds along the rachis, near the leaf apex. From Mickel and Beitel (1988).

develop immediately, without any resting stage, into long-creeping stems that bear leaves at wide intervals. The bud-produced stems remain attached via the petiole base to the original stem that gave rise to the leaf, thus becoming an integral part of the shoot system of the plant. Buds at the base of the petioles, or epipetiolar buds, can be seen in the hay-scented fern (*Dennstaedtia punctilobula*) of eastern North America. About one in every five of its leaves has them. Other ferns that commonly produce buds on the base of the petiole (sometimes as many as three or four) are *Histiopteris* (Figure 22), *Hypolepis*, and *Microlepia* (Troop and Mickel 1968). These plants spread readily by means of these buds, forming diffuse but extensive colonies.

Besides leaves, buds occur on stems. Some fir mosses (*Huperzia*) produce three-lobed buds, called gemmae, near the tops of their stems. The buds are themselves highly condensed stems, each bearing three leaves, and thus they appear trilobed. When struck by a falling raindrop, a bud summersaults away from the parent plant, lands on the soil, and sends forth a new shoot and roots. Near mature plants of fir mosses it is common to find new plantlets still attached to the buds.

Some species of whisk ferns (for example, *Psilotum*, Plate 20) and moonworts (*Botrychium* subgen. *Botrychium*) produce buds on the underground portions of their stems (Farrar and Johnson-Groh 1990). In greenhouses, whisk ferns sometimes appear unexpectedly in flowerpots or newly planted beds. This happens when their buds slough off in the soil and the soil is reused to pot other plants.

Sometimes buds are formed on greatly elongated stems called runners or stolons (Figure 23). These are well known to growers of sword

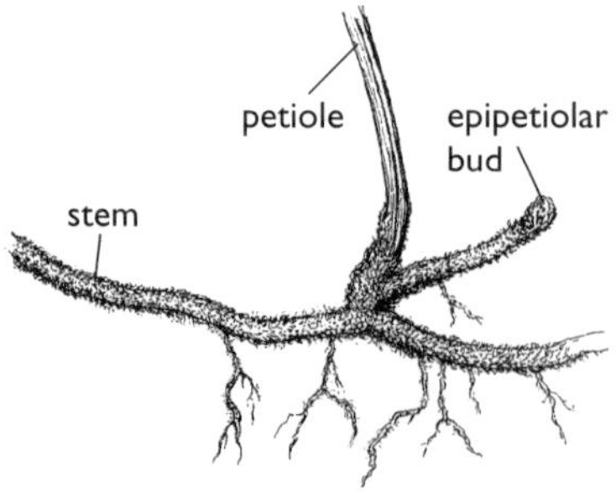

Figure 22 Epipetiolar bud in the bat-winged fern (*Histiopteris incisa*). From Mickel and Beitel (1988).

50

ferns and Boston ferns (*Nephrolepis*), usually cultivated in hanging wire baskets. The stolons are string-
like, and given enough time, hundreds will be produced and dangle out of the baskets, creating an
untidy appearance (Figure 24). Most growers cut
them off, but if allowed to grow
and touch the soil, the stolon will
form a bud that takes root. In nature, the terrestrial species of
sword ferns form extensive colonies—dense and hard to walk
through—by means of stolons.

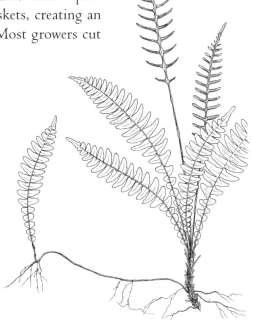

Figure 23 *Blechnum
stoloniferum*, repro-
ducing by stolons.
From Mickel and Beitel
(1988).

Figure 24 Left, hanging stolons of a sword fern (*Nephrolepis*). Right,
stolons with young plantlets produced from buds. Photographs by John Mickel.

51

Another fern reproducing by stolons is the ostrich fern (*Matteuccia struthiopteris*) of North America and Eurasia. Its stolons grow horizontally 1–2 inches (2.5–5 cm) below the soil surface, and after reaching some distance from the parent plant they turn upright and produce leaves. Usually an established plant will produce two or three new plantlets per year from separate stolons. By this method the ostrich fern can spread steadily through a garden bed, and if allowed to grow unchecked it will shade lower plants. Despite this aggressive tendency, it is one of the most popular ferns to plant in cool-temperate regions around the foundations of houses.

The erect sword fern (*Nephrolepis cordifolia*) is widely cultivated in the tropics because its many close, stiffly erect leaves make a good hedge or border. It produces stolons, like all members of its genus, but unlike them its stolons have starch-filled tubers resembling small potatoes about 1 inch (2.5 cm) in diameter. If the parent plant dies, or if the tubers are detached from the parent plant, the tubers can send up new leaves, thus acting like a kind of bud although their main function is food storage.

Buds also occur on the roots of ferns, especially in tropical epiphytes. The roots thread their way through mats of moss and humus that cover the trunks and branches of trees. Every so often the roots proliferate, sending up new buds with leaves—leaves seemingly popping up at random through the moss mat. Some common fern epiphytes that festoon tropical trees by their ability to spread from root buds are shoestring ferns (Vittariaceae), grammitids or dwarf polypodies (Grammitidaceae), spleenworts (*Asplenium*), and comb ferns (*Pecluma*).

Staghorn ferns (*Platycerium*) are another group of epiphytes that bear root buds. These ferns are widely cultivated in homes and greenhouses, usually in hanging wire baskets or tied to boards. Where their roots poke through the soil or around the base of the plant, the root tips transform directly into buds that give rise to plantlets consisting of circular leaves (shield leaves) tightly appressed to the soil. These plantlets, called pups, are cut off by growers and replanted (Figure 25). This method of propagation accounts for nearly all the commercially grown staghorn ferns worldwide; rarely are these plants raised from spores.

(Propagating staghorn ferns from pups is explained and illustrated by Hoshizaki and Moran 2001.)

Although root buds are most commonly found in epiphytes, a few terrestrial species produce them. Adder's-tongues (*Ophioglossum*) form extensive but sparse colonies from buds borne on elongated roots running 1–3 inches (2.5–7.5 cm) beneath the soil (Figure 123). The winged beech fern (*Phegopteris decursive-pinnata*), an Asian species that thrives when planted in gardens in the eastern United States, spreads readily by root buds and can soon fill a flower bed or border. The vegetable fern (*Diplazium esculentum*), whose fiddleheads are eaten in eastern Asia, also spreads by root buds—one reason it is easy to cultivate for food.

Whatever the organ on which buds are produced—root, stem, or leaf—one outcome is that plants in the wild are often clumped. They appear congenial, forming colonies or clusters of individuals. Sometimes the cluster might be only a patch about a square yard or meter, as in the strawberry fern (*Hemionitis palmata*), for example; at other times it might cover an area the size of a football field, as with certain species of sword ferns (*Nephrolepis*). Whatever the size of the colony, buds provide

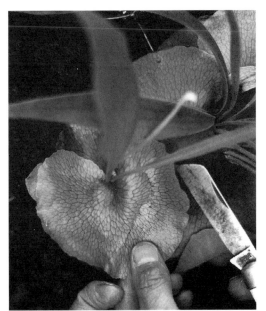

Figure 25 Pup of a staghorn fern (*Platycerium*) being removed by a grower. Note the two kinds of leaves: circular, appressed shield leaves, and elongate, arching to erect foliage leaves. Photograph by John Mickel.

a means besides sexual reproduction to rapidly colonize an area. They preserve favorable gene combinations of the parent plant—combinations that would likely be broken up by the indiscriminate shuffling that occurs during meiosis, the type of cell division leading to the formation of spores. If the parent plant is well adapted to a given environment, so will its bud-produced offspring, which will have exactly the same genetic constitution.

Buds are also important for sterile hybrids. Such plants cannot reproduce sexually because their spores are aborted. If they produce buds, however, they have a means to persist and even spread beyond the site where the hybrids first formed. For instance in eastern North America, hybrids between two species of fir mosses (*Huperzia lucidula* and *H. porophila*) persist by buds, and the hybrids can be found at some sites even after one or both of the parents no longer occur there. Throughout much of the New World tropics, certain *Blechnum* hybrids persist and have even become locally abundant by means of buds produced along their stolons.

Worldwide, an estimated 5% of fern species form buds. That is a modest contribution but suggests that asexual reproduction by buds provides an advantage in the highly competitive plant world. No fern species reproduces entirely by buds; all use buds in combination with sexual reproduction by spores and gametophytes. But when the risky business of sexual reproduction fails, buds can serve as a backup.

THE LIFE CYCLE OF FERNS

6

Hybridization and Polyploidy

When the second volume of *Flora of North America* was published in 1993, something new appeared within its pages, something never before seen in identification books. This volume, which describes the 420 different kinds of ferns and lycophytes that grow in the United States and Canada, displayed some rather curious-looking net-like diagrams depicting the relationships between species and their hybrids. Such diagrams, because of the network of relationships they portray, are called reticulograms (Figure 26).

Reticulograms are not evolutionary trees. They do not show the recentness of common ancestry between species, the kind of relationship created when species split from an ancestor as a result of natural selection acting upon a population of many individuals. Instead, reticulograms show which species have *come together* to form hybrids. They also indicate whether the hybrids are sterile (with aborted spores) or fertile (with viable spores). Nearly all hybrids are sterile when first formed, but if they double their chromosome number by a process called polyploidy, they automatically become fertile, producing viable spores.

Reticulograms were included in *Flora of North America* because the processes they show—hybridization and polyploidy—are important evolutionary mechanisms driving the formation of new species of ferns and lycophytes. Of the species treated in the flora, nearly 20% (about 100 species) are of hybrid origin *and* have become fertile through the process of polyploidy.

Polyploidy is perhaps best explained by example. Related species of ferns often have chromosome numbers that are multiples of a basic set. For instance, some species of wood ferns (*Dryopteris*) have 41 pairs of chromosomes in their somatic cells, other species have 82, and still others 164. All are multiples of 41, the lowest chromosome number in the genus. Similarly, most species of spleenworts (*Asplenium*) have 36 pairs of chromosomes in their somatic cells, others have 72, and a few have as many as 144 or 288. All these numbers are multiples of 36, and because 36 is the lowest number in the genus, it is called the base number. Those species with the lowest number in a series are called diploids (with two sets of the lowest number) whereas those with higher multiples are called polyploids. Depending on the number of chromosome sets involved, a plant can be either tetraploid (four sets), hexaploid (six sets),

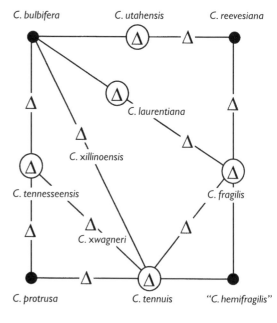

Figure 26 Reticulogram for North American bladder ferns (*Cystopteris*). Solid circles represent diploid species, triangles represent sterile hybrids, and circled triangles represent hybrids that doubled their chromosome number and are therefore fertile. "*Cystopteris hemifragilis*" is a hypothetical ancestor. Adapted from Flora of North America Editorial Committee (1993).

56

octaploid (eight sets), or so on. Maindenhair spleenwort (*A. trichomanes*, Plate 5) is an example of a species that consists of two races: diploid and tetraploid.

Polyploid formation typically starts with an abnormality in meiosis that gives rise to "unreduced spores" with two sets of chromosomes instead of the normal single set. These spores germinate and grow into gametophytes that produce the egg and sperm, and if the sperm fertilizes an egg on the same gametophyte—that is, if a self-fertilization occurs—the resulting zygote will contain four sets of chromosomes, two from the egg and two from the sperm. In other words, the zygote will be tetraploid, and so will be the sporophyte that develops from it. This new polyploid fern forms instantaneously at the moment of fertilization; no long, slow process of natural selection is involved.

Polyploidy is often associated with hybridization. Hybrids are formed when the sperm from one species swims to and fertilizes the egg of another. The hybrid zygote grows into a plant with normal roots, stems, and leaves, but this plant will be sterile. Its spores will be misshapen, blackened, and aborted. Spore abortion occurs because during meiosis the parents' chromosomes pair improperly, if at all, for physiological or structural reasons. Improper pairing results in the chromosomes being distributed unequally to the daughter cells—the cells that mature into spores—so that each cell (each spore) receives more than, or less than, the normal complement of chromosomes. This genetic imbalance causes spore abortion, and hybrid sterility. (In humans, the effects of having just one extra or one less chromosome can be seen in Down's syndrome, where there is an extra 21st chromosome, or in Turner's syndrome, where the Y (male) chromosome is missing. Mental retardation and sterility result, as well as other problems. During the irregular meiosis seen in fern hybrids, far more than just one chromosome is distributed unequally, so the end result is extremely severe: total abortion of the spores.)

Then polyploidy enters the picture. By doubling a hybrid's chromosome number, each chromosome will have a partner—its duplicate or homologue—to pair with during meiosis. Normal pairing can take place, and the chromosomes will be distributed equally to the daughter cells during meiosis. This results in viable spores, and the hybrid is now fertile (Figure 27). Thus the importance of polyploidy is that it confers automatic fertility to otherwise sterile hybrids, allowing them to reproduce sexually.

Once fertile, a hybrid can reproduce independently of its parents. It can spread by spores and establish its own range—a range that might extend far beyond those of the parents. The new populations of the fertile hybrid can be acted upon by natural selection and evolve new characteristics not found in either parent. In short, a hybrid stabilized by polyploidy gains reproductive and evolutionary independence.

Both hybrids and polyploids can arise more than once, independently. For example, Scott's spleenwort (*Asplenium* ×*ebenoides*), the hybrid between the North American walking fern (*A. rhizophyllum*, Plate 4) and the ebony spleenwort (*A. platyneuron*), could arise anywhere the two parents mingle, in eastern Pennsylvania, central Tennessee, or southern Missouri, for example. Fertile hybrids of the same parental species can have multiple origins, as has been well established by genetic studies. Scott's spleenwort, however, which is one of the most common spleenwort hybrids in eastern North America, has doubled its chromosomes and become fertile at only one site, in Georgia. Why it has not done so at other sites, and why other sterile fern hybrids have never become fertile, remain a mystery.

How do botanists detect polyploids and hybrids? Polyploids are usu-

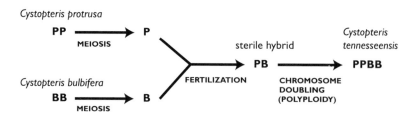

Figure 27 The origin of *Cystopteris tennesseensis* by hybridization and polyploidy. P represents one chromosome set of the *C. protrusa* parent; B, that of the *C. bulbifera* parent. Meiosis halves the chromosome number. Crossing between the two species results in a sterile hybrid. Polyploidy confers fertility to the hybrid by creating an extra set of chromosomes that can pair with the original set of chromosomes during spore formation.

ally discovered two ways. The surest is to count the plant's chromosomes, but this is tedious and time-consuming. The other is to infer polyploidy by measuring the lengths of cells. This method works because polyploids usually have larger cells than related diploids. An advantage to working with ferns and lycophytes is that single cells, in the form of spores, are easy to examine with a light microscope. Spores can be mounted in a drop of water on a slide and their lengths measured with a small scale mounted in the microscope's eyepiece (an ocular micrometer). Guard cells of the stomata can also be measured, but to examine them the leaf tissue must be made translucent by immersion in a solution of caustic chemicals—more laborious than putting spores in a drop of water. So spores are most commonly used to infer polyploidy. If the measurements show differences in spore diameter between suspected polyploids and known diploids, then polyploidy is probably present.

Detecting hybrids is easier than detecting polyploids because hybrids can usually be spotted with the naked eye. Hybrids appear intermediate between their parents but vary. They are not precisely in the morphological middle between their parents; they exhibit a range of variation between the two parental extremes. This variability results because the genetic instructions of both parents interact during the hybrid's development, creating a developmental tug-of-war, generating irregularities in characteristics such as leaf cutting, venation, and internode length. For example, a hybrid between a parent with simple leaves and another parent with singly pinnate leaves will exhibit a range of leaf cutting between shallow lobing and nearly single pinnation (Figure 28). This variability, often irregularly expressed, is what often allows an experienced botanist to detect hybrids.

Once a hybrid is suspected on the basis of morphological intermediacy, its spores are examined for abortion under a microscope. The presence of aborted spores provides further evidence that the plant is a sterile hybrid. Sometimes aborted spores appear so blackened and misshapen that they resemble soil particles, and one suspects that the slide preparation has been contaminated by dirt.

The parentage of a hybrid—which two species are involved in its formation—is usually determined on the bases of morphology and geography. But botanists nowadays have a powerful tool: enzyme electrophoresis, a technique that shows, in different individuals, the presence of slightly different protein enzymes (isozymes or allozymes) of the same type. Leaf-tissue extracts from the hybrid and its suspected parents are placed in slots cut into a slab of starch or acrylamide gel, and a high voltage is applied across the gel for a period of time. The molecules migrate through the gel at different rates, depending on their size, shape,

Tectaria incisa

T. panamensis

HYBRIDS

Adiantum latifolium

HYBRIDS
(A. xvariopinnatum)

A. petiolatum

Figure 28 Silhouettes of two fern hybrids and their parents, both examples from Costa Rica. The hybrids exhibit a range of variation between their parents.

and charge, and separate into distinct bands. The gels are then stained for a particular type of enzyme, making the bands visible. Often the two parents have different banding patterns, and the hybrid combines those of the parents. This technique is remarkably accurate; it can detect hybrids that are scarcely distinguishable from their parents on morphological grounds, as has been especially the case in bladder ferns (*Cystopteris*).

Once a hybrid has been found and its parentage established, it is named so that botanists can discuss it. The name can be either a formula or binomial. Formulas consist of the two parents' names with a multiplication sign × placed between them, such as *Adiantum latifolium* × *A. petiolatum*, *Psilotum complanatum* × *P. nudum*, and *Tectaria incisa* × *T. panamensis*. In contrast, hybrid binomials resemble normal scientific names but with the × placed before the specific epithet, as in *Adiantum* ×*variopinnatum* (*A. latifolium* × *A. petiolatum*), *Asplenium* ×*ebenoides* (*A. platyneuron* × *A. rhizophyllum*), and *Lygodium* ×*lancetillanum* (*L. heterodoxum* × *L. venustum*). It seems best to name hybrids with binomials instead of formulas. Binomials are stable whereas formulas are subject to change. A formula name can change if one or both of the parents' names change. This can happen when an older name is found (the rules of botanical nomenclature require that the oldest legitimate name be used), when a name is later considered a synonym of another (when two species are "lumped" together), or when parentage is proved different from the combination originally proposed. These changes do not affect a binomial, which stays the same no matter what happens to the names of the parents.

Hybridization and polyploidy have been well studied in North America, Europe, and Japan but have received little attention in the tropics, where most fern and lycophyte species occur. Research will almost certainly show that these two phenomena are just as common there as in the temperate zones. They are evolutionary mechanisms in action today, driving the formation of new species and generating new and more wondrous forms of ferns and lycophytes for the future.

CLASSIFICATION OF FERNS

7
The Falsely Famed Fern Allies

What do the fern allies—lycophytes, horsetails, and whisk ferns—have in common with the Irish elk, Panama hats, and Danish pastries? All are misnamed. The Irish elk was neither exclusively Irish, nor an elk. It was a deer, the largest that ever lived. A genuine Panama hat is crafted in Ecuador, not Panama. During the 1800s the hats were shipped from Ecuador to the Isthmus of Panama for sale or further distribution. Danish pastries originally came from Austria. They became associated with Denmark when Viennese bakers were brought to Copenhagen to mitigate the effects of a baker's strike. Similarly, the so-called fern allies are *not* a separate group of plants most closely related, or allied, to ferns. They either *are* ferns, as has been shown for the horsetails (*Equisetum*) and whisk ferns (*Psilotum* and *Tmesipteris*), or they are less closely related to ferns than are the seed plants, as is the case for the lycophytes (*Isoetes, Selaginella, Lycopodium, Lycopodiella,* and *Huperzia*). It is worth examining the evidence for these relationships—which make the old term "fern ally" obsolete—because it tells a story not only about the evolution of land plants but also about a revolution that has occurred in biological classification beginning in the 1990s.

Superficially, the fern allies (Figure 29) appear quite distinct from ferns, and for this reason some of them have sometimes been classified with groups other than ferns. In the middle 1700s Linnaeus classified the spike mosses (*Selaginella*), club mosses (Lycopodiaceae), and whisk ferns (Psilotaceae) with the mosses, which they resemble to a degree. He classified the horsetails and quillworts (*Isoetes*) with ferns but placed them at the beginning and end, respectively, of his treatment to emphasize their distinctness from typical ferns. It was not until the early 1800s that botanists suspected that all the fern allies are related to ferns. Both groups were shown to be alike in dispersing by spores and possessing internal vascular tissue. Defined by these two characteristics, the ferns and fern allies seemed related, forming their own group, a group distinct from the bryophytes (mosses, hornworts, and liverworts) and seed plants (gymnosperms and flowering plants).

This alignment of fern allies with ferns gained further support when, in the 1850s, botanists worked out the general life cycle of land plants. The cycle was shown to consist of two unlike alternating phases—the gametophyte and sporophyte—which impart a double life to the plant (Chapter 1). In ferns and fern allies, the two phases were found to be separate and free-living, each physically and nutritionally independent from one another. This further distinguished ferns and fern allies from bryophytes and seed plants, each of which has the two phases attached to one another (although in bryophytes it is the gametophyte that is the main conspicuous phase, whereas in seed plants it is the sporophyte). The apparently strengthened relationship between ferns and fern allies was soon reflected in classification schemes. In most classifications, the ferns and fern allies were formally named Pteridophyta, apart from Bryophyta and Spermatophyta (seed plants). Within the Pteridophyta, the ferns and various fern allies were ranked equally: the ferns as the Polypodiopsida, lycophytes as Lycopodiopsida, horsetails as Equisetopsida, and whisk ferns as Psilotopsida. The suffix -opsida denotes the rank of class in the taxonomic hierarchy. Sometimes botanists used different ranks for these groups, and therefore slightly different names, but the main groups were accepted by just about everyone. This classification best reflected the facts known at the time and held sway for nearly a century.

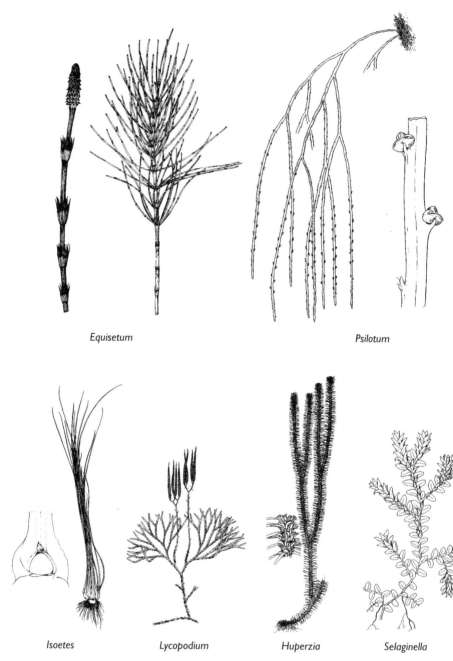

Equisetum

Psilotum

Isoetes

Lycopodium

Huperzia

Selaginella

Figure 29 The so-called fern allies. Horsetails (*Equisetum*) and whisk ferns (Psilotaceae) have been shown to be ferns. Ferns are more closely related to seed plants than to lycophytes (bottom row). *Psilotum, Huperzia,* and *Lycopodium* from Mickel and Beitel (1988); *Isoetes* and *Selaginella* courtesy of John Mickel.

Doubt was first cast upon this prevailing classification in the first decade of the 1900s. Edward C. Jeffrey, a plant anatomist from Harvard University, pointed out that ferns and seed plants both have large, complex leaves and a peculiar anatomical similarity known as a leaf gap, a gap in the vascular tissue where the leaf departs from the stem (the gap is actually filled by undifferentiated tissue, or parenchyma). Also, both groups bear sporangia on the lower surface of the leaves. In contrast, lycophytes have simple, entire, single-veined leaves that lack a leaf gap, and when these leaves bear sporangia, they do so on the upper surface or in the axil between leaf and stem. And as for horsetails, which have leaves unlike those of any other plant group (Figure 65), it was pointed out by the French paleobotanist Elie Antoine Octave Lignier that some early fossil relatives had broad laminate leaves, and therefore the leaves of horsetails probably had evolved by reduction. These characteristics suggested that ferns, horsetails, and seed plants might be more closely related to each other than they were to the lycophytes.

Since the 1930s many fossil discoveries have revealed what some of the earliest vascular land plants looked like. These plants arose during the early Silurian about 430 million years ago, a time when the oceans teemed with life—giant cephalopods, armored fish, trilobites, and eurypterids—but the land was largely uninhabited and empty, mostly bare rock dotted with low-growing algae and bryophytes. Along the wet coastal margins and muddy flats of this world appeared the first vascular plants, looking more like the beginning of an idea for a plant than an actual plant itself. They lacked roots and leaves, consisting entirely of Y-forked green axes branched in three dimensions. (We cannot call these axes "stems" because, by definition, a stem gives rise to leaves—organs these plants lacked). The plants stood stiffly upright, unlike their green algal ancestors, and were generally less than 12 inches (30 cm) tall. In the center of the each axis ran a strand of vascular tissue that conducted water and mineral nutrients. The surface of the axes was covered with cutin, a fatty substance that prevented drying, and at the tip of each axis sat a single sporangium, containing all the spores (Figure 30). The outer walls of these spores were thick and coated with sporopollenin, a substance that prevented drying while the spores were being blown about by air currents. These pioneer plants spread to all corners of the globe and turned the land green. They formed the first soils, increased oxygen in the atmosphere, and prepared the way for animal life.

Some of these early vascular plants gave rise to a group called the zosterophylls, which are now extinct. These plants differed from their predecessors by bearing several to many sporangia on the sides of the axes, not singly at the tip, and the sporangia were short-stalked and kidney-shaped, not sessile and ovoid (Figure 31). The axes branched unequally in many members of the group, with one fork becoming thicker so that the whole branching system had a distinct main stem with subordinate lateral ones. From the surface of these branches projected soft spines of tissue that increased the surface area for photosynthesis. These projections cannot be termed leaves because they lacked veins; instead, they are called enations. From these unequally branched, enation-studded plants with lateral sporangia, the lycophytes evolved.

The lycophytes have two distinguishing characteristics. The first is the single sporangium on the upper surface of the microphyll or in its axil, the angle formed between the stem and the leaf's upper surface (Figure 29). This position differs fundamentally from that of ferns, whose sporangia are borne on the lower surface of the leaf.

The second hallmark of lycophytes is a unique type of leaf called a microphyll, which is characterized by being simple (not divided), entire, and single-veined (Plate 11). Microphylls are sessile—never stalked like the leaves of most ferns and dicotyledonous seed plants. Although microphyll means "small leaf," it is a slightly misleading term. Most microphylls are small—usually less than about 3/4 inch (2 cm) long—but those of some quillworts (*Isoetes*) may be as long as 3 feet (1 m). Similar lengths were attained by the microphylls of tree lycophytes (lepidodendrids) that dominated the coal-forming swamps of the Carboniferous (Chapter 11).

No one is sure how microphylls evolved. One theory—the enation theory—claims that the microphyll is a vascularized enation, that is, an enation that became supplied with a vein (Figure 32). Another theory is that microphylls represent the transformed lateral sporangia of some zosterophyll-like ancestor. However they evolved, microphylls characterize lycophytes and are completely different from the type of leaf that

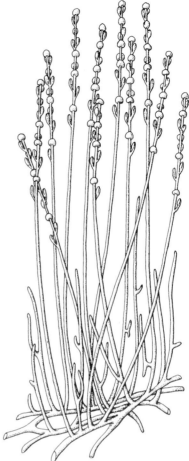

Figure 30 Two early land plants from the lower Devonian: *Cooksonia caledonica* (left) and *Aglaophyton major* (right), with spore cases at the branch tips. After Edwards (1986).

Figure 31 *Zosterophyllum myretonianum,* from the early Devonian. The diagnostic features of zosterophylls are clam-shaped sporangia borne laterally, not terminally, on the upright axes. After Kenrick and Crane (1997).

Figure 32 Evolution of microphylls, characteristic of lycophytes, according to the enation theory. Left to right, naked axis of an early vascular plant; an enation forms; a vein extends from the central vascular bundle to the base of the enation; the vein extends into the enation, forming a microphyll.

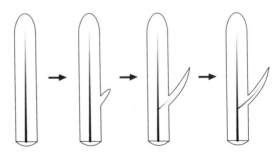

characterizes ferns and seed plants, a type of leaf called a megaphyll or euphyll. Megaphylls evolved from the three-dimensional, photosynthetic branching systems of early vascular plants by a three-step process (Figure 33). First, the branching system became flattened into one plane. Second, a green laminar tissue developed between the flattened branching system, filling in the space between the branches and forming a weblike lamina. Finally, some of the branches elongated more than other branches, overtopping them and producing a prominent central branch with subordinate lateral ones. The result was a broad leaf with many veins. The sequence of flattening, webbing, and overtopping can be seen in the fossil record in a series of intermediates. In fact, some fossils are so intermediate that it is difficult to determine whether they represent stem or leaf. Botanists debate whether megaphylls evolved only once in the common ancestor of ferns and seed plants or evolved several times independently in those groups. No one is sure what prompted the evolution of megaphylls; for the first 40 million years of their existence, land plants did quite well without them. Megaphylls first appeared during the Devonian some 410 million to 363 million years ago, a time when the concentration of carbon dioxide in the atmosphere dropped by about 90%. Some botanists believe that this drop fostered the evolution of megaphylls because they have a large surface area capable of absorbing carbon dioxide more efficiently (Kenrick 2001).

Evidence from the fossil record and morphology reveal that since nearly the beginning of vascular plant evolution, the zosterophyll–lycophyte lineage has been distinct from all other vascular plants. This dis-

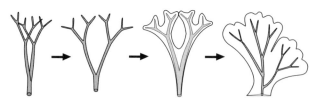

Figure 33 Evolution of megaphylls, characteristic of ferns and seed plants. Left to right, three-dimensional branching system of an early vascular plant; flattening of the branching system into a single plane; webbing between the branches; overtopping to produce central vein and subordinate lateral ones.

tinctness is further supported by DNA evidence. The base-pair sequences of six genes differ in the lycophytes as compared to ferns, horsetails, whisk ferns, and seed plants. Also, the chloroplast DNA of lycophytes contains a major structural difference: a 30,000-base-pair region is inverted relative to that in ferns and seed plants. Because the orientation of this region in lycophytes is the same as in bryophytes and green algae —evolutionarily earlier groups—evolutionists infer that lycophytes have retained the ancestral, noninverted condition whereas ferns and seed plants have inherited the inverted condition from a more recent common ancestor—an ancestor *not* shared with the lycophytes. In other words, ferns and seed plants are more closely related than either is to the lycophytes (Figure 34).

What does this imply for designating lycophytes as fern allies? It means that "fern allies," as applied to *Isoetes, Selaginella, Lycopodium, Lycopodiella,* and *Huperzia* is downright misleading. The true fern allies are the seed plants, with which ferns share a more recent common ancestor.

What about the other fern allies—the whisk ferns and horsetails? It turns out that they also have the 30,000-base-pair inversion in their chloroplast DNA, a trait linking them with ferns and seed plants. More specifically, studies of their DNA sequences indicate that they are nested among the ferns on the tree of life. The whisk ferns (*Psilotum* and *Tmesipteris*) share a branch with the adder's-tongue family (Ophioglossaceae), and the horsetails (*Equisetum*) share one with the Marattiaceae (Figure 34). Nowadays neither whisk ferns nor horsetails should be called fern allies—they *are* ferns.

Uncovering these relationships has forced botanists to change their classifications. The main goal in classification—and one that systematic botanists strive mightily to obtain—is to reflect the recentness of common ancestry because that best explains why organisms share certain traits. Nearly all botanists nowadays would reject classifying the lycophytes and ferns in a formal taxonomic group called the Pteridophyta. This grouping is not acceptable because ferns are most closely related to seed plants than to lycophytes. Although the lycophytes, ferns, and seed plants share a common ancestor far back in time, a group called the Pteridophyta does not include all the descendents of that ancestor be-

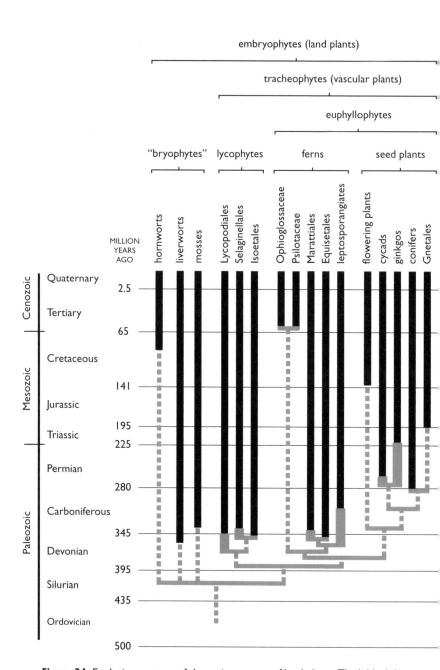

Figure 34 Evolutionary tree of the major groups of land plants. Thick black lines indicate a fossil record; gray lines, a fossil record for close relatives of extant lineages; gray dashed lines, a lack of fossil evidence. After Schneider et al. (2002).

cause it omits the seed plants. A group that does not contain all the descendents of a common ancestor is termed paraphyletic. The problem is that paraphyletic groups will always include at least one member more closely related to something *outside* the group. Botanists now wish to define groups that include *all* the descendents of a common ancestor—a monophyletic group. Lycophytes are monophyletic and can be called the Lycophytina. Ferns and seed plants form another monophyletic group, christened the Euphyllophytina.

These names are used in classifications quite unlike the ones developed in the 1800s. The current classification arose because new evidence from comparative morphology, fossils, and DNA demanded it, but it also reflects a shift in how botanists evaluate characteristics adduced as evidence of evolutionary relationships. Earlier botanists did not always distinguish between two basic types of characteristics: ancestral and derived. An ancestral characteristic is one that was present in an ancestor of a particular group. For instance, among vascular plants, the pteridophyte life cycle (Chapter 1) is ancestral because it was present in the first vascular land plants. In contrast, a derived characteristic is one that was not present in the ancestor of a group but evolved later. Examples of derived characteristics are microphylls in lycophytes and megaphylls in ferns and seed plants—the ancestors of both groups were originally leafless. When determining evolutionary relationships, it is essential to distinguish whether a characteristic is ancestral or derived because only derived characteristics indicate relationships; ancestral ones do not.

The dismemberment of the fern allies illustrates a revolution that has occurred in biological systematics since the 1990s. New sources of data (DNA and fossils), better methods (computer algorithms to analyze large data sets and generate evolutionary trees), and advances in theory (only derived characteristics should be used to determine lineages) have combined to yield spectacular progress in inferring evolutionary relationships. These relationships, expressed as evolutionary trees, serve as a framework for asking questions about biogeography, change in morphology and other characteristics, and the evolutionary process itself. Given all these advances and their implications for classifications, there has never been a more exciting time to be a systematist.

CLASSIFICATION OF FERNS

8

The Fern Fraternity

Although most people can recognize a fern, if pressed for a definition they have a hard time explaining exactly what one is. Most think of ferns as plants with large, finely dissected leaves, but there are many exceptions; in fact, one of the largest fern genera in the world, the paddle ferns (*Elaphoglossum*), has mainly undivided leaves (Figure 16 and Plate 10). I wish I could point to a single, obvious characteristic and say, "If the plant has this, then it's a fern," but I cannot. The best one can do is state what works most of the time. Nearly all ferns have young leaves spirally coiled in bud (fiddleheads; Figures 100 and 101), but a few ferns lack this characteristic, and the leaves of two cycad genera are spirally coiled in bud. Many ferns have light-colored projections or lines of aerating tissue (aerophores or pneumatophores) running along both sides of the petiole (Davies 1991). These lines are absent or hard to see in some ferns, but if you see them (Figure 45), you can be sure you are looking at a fern because no other plants have them.

If no single morphological characteristic defines all ferns, how do we know that ferns form a natural, or monophyletic, group—one that should be recognized in a formal classification? We know that ferns *do* form a natural group because of similarities in their DNA sequences

(Chapter 7) compared to other plants. Ultimately, it is these sequences that allow us to say whether a plant should be called a fern. This is not as satisfying as having a morphological characteristic to point to, but it is comforting to know that DNA studies have largely supported the traditional notions of which plants constitute ferns.

The results of DNA studies are usually presented in the form of an evolutionary tree, or cladogram—a diagram showing the branching patterns of evolution, the recentness of common ancestry, what is related to what. Cladograms serve as an excellent framework to explain the main groups of ferns, of which there are 10 (Figure 35). These groups are recognized here for convenience as orders in the taxonomic hierarchy, a rank indicated by the suffix -ales: Ophioglossales, Marattiales, Equisetales, Osmundales, Hymenophyllales, Gleicheniales, Schizaeales, Salviniales, Cyatheales, and Polypodiales. Unlike ferns as a whole, most of these groups have morphological characteristics that make them relatively easy to identify.

The first split at the base of the fern evolutionary tree gives rise to one branch leading to the Ophioglossales and the other leading to the rest of the ferns (in technical terms, evolutionists say the Ophioglossales is the sister group to the rest of the ferns, and vice versa). The Ophioglossales comprise two families, that of the adder's-tongues (Ophioglossaceae) and the whisk ferns (Psilotaceae). Both have subterranean, nongreen, mycorrhizal gametophytes (nearly all other ferns have surface-growing, green, nonmycorrhizal gametophytes). They also have reduced root systems, with roots that do not branch and lack root hairs, and in the whisk ferns, roots are altogether absent. Otherwise, these two families look quite different from each other and from other ferns, which makes them easy to distinguish.

The adder's-tongue family is distinctive because its leaves are divided into two parts: a sterile blade and a fertile, spore-bearing spike (Figure 36). No other fern has similarly divided leaves. Belonging to this family are the moonworts and grape ferns (*Botrychium*), and the hand ferns and adder's-tongues (*Ophioglossum*). Adders-tongues get their name from the supposed resemblance of the fertile spike to a snake's tongue.

The adder's-tongue family is the sister group to the Psilotaceae,

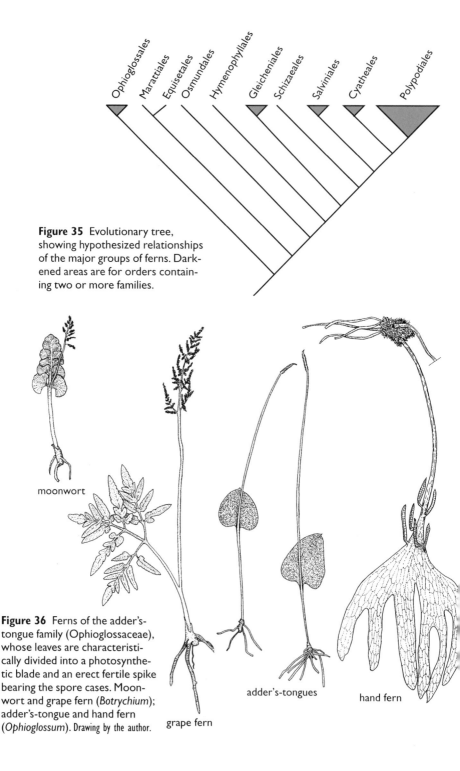

Figure 35 Evolutionary tree, showing hypothesized relationships of the major groups of ferns. Darkened areas are for orders containing two or more families.

Ophioglossales
Marattiales
Equisetales
Osmundales
Hymenophyllales
Gleicheniales
Schizaeales
Salviniales
Cyatheales
Polypodiales

moonwort

Figure 36 Ferns of the adder's-tongue family (Ophioglossaceae), whose leaves are characteristically divided into a photosynthetic blade and an erect fertile spike bearing the spore cases. Moonwort and grape fern (*Botrychium*); adder's-tongue and hand fern (*Ophioglossum*). Drawing by the author.

grape fern

adder's-tongues

hand fern

which comprises *Psilotum* and *Tmesipteris*. These plants lack roots and leaves. Their spore cases are divided into compartments—three in *Psilotum* (Figure 29), two in *Tmesipteris*—something seen elsewhere in ferns only in Marattiales. *Psilotum* (Plate 20) is common throughout the tropics and subtropics, usually growing on the root mantles of tree ferns or in the old, humus-filled axils of palm leaves, although it sometimes grows stiffly erect straight out of barren soil. *Tmesipteris* grows only in Australia, New Zealand, and certain islands of the southwestern Pacific, primarily as an epiphyte on the fibrous mantle of roots that invest the trunks of tree ferns. Because they do not look like most ferns, Psilotaceae were long considered apart from ferns, though related because they disperse by spores and have free-living gametophyte and sporophyte generations. DNA evidence, however, places the Psilotaceae squarely among the ferns and sister group to the adder's-tongue family.

Next on the evolutionary tree is the Marattiales, a group that boasts the longest fossil pedigree of any fern. (As suggested by Figure 35, the Ophioglossales is an older lineage, but paradoxically the whisk fern and adder's-tongue families do not appear in the fossil record until relatively recently, in the early Tertiary.) The ancestors of Marattiales first appeared at the beginning of the Carboniferous about 340 million years ago, a time when the first vertebrates were making the transition from life in the sea to life on land. When these animals crawled ashore, the marattialean tree fern *Psaronius* was there to greet them.

The Marattiales are easy to recognize. They have paired, fleshy, ear-like appendages called stipules, where the leaf stalk joins the stem (Figure 37). No other ferns have stipules, and no one knows what they do, if anything. Cuttings of stipules can be placed in soil and used to propagate the plants. An article on how to do this was once written by John Mickel (1981), my colleague at the New York Botanical Garden, and titled "*Marattia* propagation stipulated."

Another distinctive characteristic of the Marattiales is a cylindrical swelling on the leaf. These swellings occur at the base of the leaf stalk, along the leaf stalk (in some species), or along the midrib where the pinnae are attached. No other fern has these unusual swellings, which are called pulvini, but they are not the true pulvini characteristic of legumes

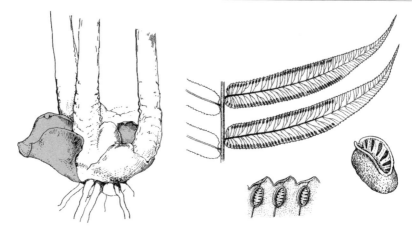

Figure 37 Characteristics of the Marattiaceae, as shown by *Marattia*. Left, stipules (a pair shaded) on either side of the petiole bases. Right, pinnae, with a close-up of sori, and a single synangium. Each slit is at the top of a single sporangium, and the sporangia have fused to form a compound sorus, or a synangium. From Mickel and Beitel (1988).

because they lack the reversible flexing action, which raises and lowers the leaf or leaflets (the sensitive plant, *Mimosa pudica*, whose leaflets fold when touched and slowly reopen if left undisturbed, is perhaps the most widely known example). Also distinctive of the Marattiales are their spore cases, which are large and (with one exception) fused laterally into a kind of compound sorus. This structure opens by a series of terminal pores or slits, each of which is centered over a single (but fused) spore case (Figure 37). Spores are released from the spore cases through the pores or slits.

A more recent and remarkable finding—again based on DNA evidence—is that the horsetails (*Equisetum*) nest among the ferns on the tree of life, related to the Marattiaceae or Osmundaceae (Pryer et al. 2001). In other words, horsetails are a kind of fern. No one had ever suspected this because the horsetails look utterly unlike ferns—or anything else, for that matter! They have jointed, green, photosynthetic stems, highly reduced leaves, whorled branches, and terminal cones (Figure 50 and Chapter 12).

On the fern evolutionary tree, all groups branching off above the Marattiales and Equisetales are often referred to as leptosporangiate ferns. They are characterized by one-cell-thick spore cases—a thinness alluded to by the prefix lepto-, Greek for thin. This distinguishes them from the previous fern families—and all lycophytes and seed plants—which have spore cases several cell layers thick. Developmentally, a leptosporangium originates from a single cell on the leaf surface, whereas a thick-walled eusporangium originates from several cells just beneath the surface.

The first group of leptosporangiates is the Osmundales, which contain widely known species such as the royal fern (*Osmunda regalis*), cinnamon fern (*O. cinnamomea*), and interrupted fern (*O. claytoniana*, Figure 38). The group dates back to the early Mesozoic, about 210 million years ago, when the first dinosaurs roamed the earth. A specialty of these ferns is stem armor formed by hard, rigid, overlapping leaf bases running down the stem. Together, the leaf bases and stem form a kind of thick composite trunk (Figure 84). During the Mesozoic, sturdy trunks of this type enabled many species to stand upright and become trees (Plate 16). The stem armor may also have protected the stem from herbivory; probably few dinosaurs cared to risk cracking a tooth on such tough stems.

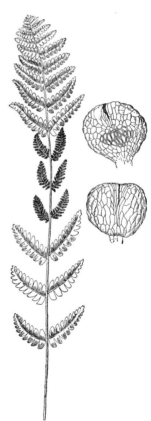

Besides armored trunks, Osmundales have distinctive spore cases. These are globose and open by a slit across the top (Figure 38). The splitting is accomplished by a patch of thickened cells, the annulus, located on one side of the spore case. The cells of the annulus contract as they dry, putting tension on

Figure 38 The interrupted fern (*Osmunda claytoniana*), from eastern North America, a species that has a longer fossil record than any other fern, extending back 200 million years to the late Triassic. At right are two views of the sporangium, the top one showing the annulus, a thickened patch of cells. From Clute (1901) and (the sporangium) Campbell (1928).

the top of the spore case, which eventually splits and ejects the spores within. The spores are green, unlike the brown or blackish spores of most ferns. Green spores can be seen in present-day species of *Osmunda*, whose spore cases appear green until after the spores are shed, and then appear dull brown.

The next group on the evolutionary tree is the Hymenophyllales, the filmy ferns, about 600 species strong. They also have green spores, but their most distinctive characteristic is the leaf blade. Between the veins, the blade tissue is only one cell thick. This thinness imparts a translucent, filmy appearance to the plants. Most filmies, as they are called, are small to medium-sized epiphytes in tropical forests. They reach their greatest abundance in cloud forests, where their thin leaves rarely dry out. In some cloud forests, they cover the trunks of trees so densely that they completely hide the bark beneath.

Another distinctive aspect of filmy ferns is their sorus. Most ferns bear sori on the lower surface of the leaf, but the filmies have them on the edge, at the tips of veins. Each sorus is protected by an indusium of modified leaf tissue, and the shape of this indusium characterizes the two main genera of the family, *Hymenophyllum* and *Trichomanes*. In *Hymenophyllum* the indusium consists of two lobes of tissue (Figure 39), whereas in *Trichomanes* the indusium is tubular or trumpet-shaped (Figure 40). Besides shape, *Trichomanes* has a long, bristle-like receptacle (the structure to which the spore cases attach) that protrudes beyond the mouth of the indusium. For this reason species of *Trichomanes* are often called bristle ferns. In contrast, *Hymenophyllum* has short, stubby receptacles hidden within the indusia.

Next is the Gleicheniales, a primarily tropical group. It contains four families (Cheiropleuriaceae, Dipteridaceae, Gleicheniaceae, and Matoniaceae) but only the Gleicheniaceae are widespread. The species of Gleicheniaceae typically form dense colonies on steep road banks and open areas. They are easy to recognize—even while racing by them in a car—because their pinnae fork repeatedly, giving rise to their common name, forked ferns (Figure 41).

Besides forked pinnae, the leaves grow in an unusual manner adapted to coping with dense vegetation (Figure 42). When a new leaf emerges

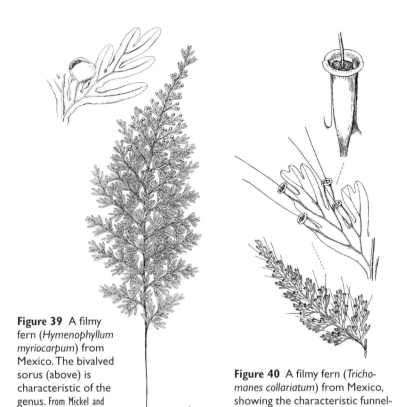

Figure 39 A filmy fern (*Hymenophyllum myriocarpum*) from Mexico. The bivalved sorus (above) is characteristic of the genus. From Mickel and Beitel (1988).

Figure 40 A filmy fern (*Trichomanes collariatum*) from Mexico, showing the characteristic funnel-shaped sorus with protruding receptacle. From Mickel and Beitel (1988).

Figure 41 A forked fern (*Sticherus*, Gleicheniaceae) from Honduras.

Figure 42 Characteristic leaf growth of forked ferns (Gleicheniaceae). A fiddlehead arises from a creeping rhizome (A); a resting bud forms at the apex while two pinnae develop beneath it (B); the pinnae unfurl (C); the bud resumes growth (D); the bud rests and another pair of pinnae develop beneath it (E); the pinnae unfurl (F); the process repeats itself (G). By this intermittent growth, the leaves of some forked ferns can reach 65 feet (20 m) in length, supporting their weight by reclining on the surrounding vegetation.

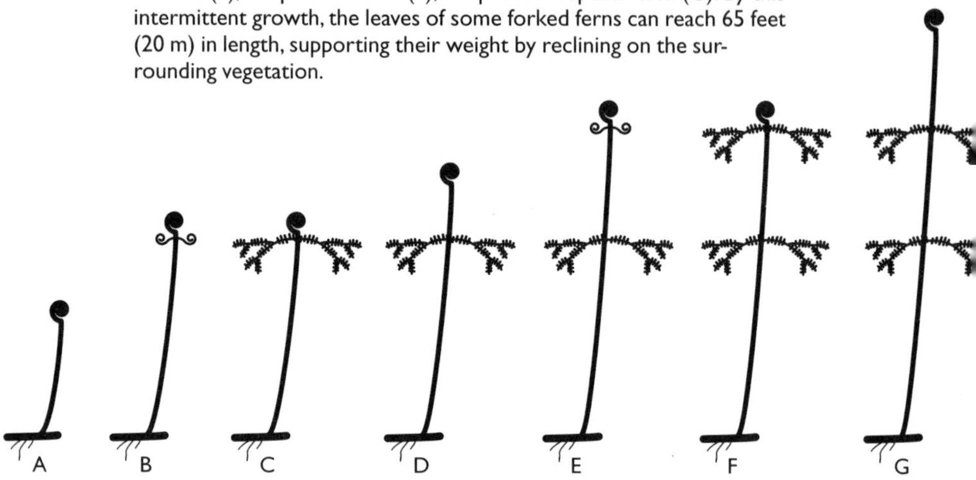

from the stem, it grows straight up for a while, then stops and forms a resting bud. Immediately beneath this bud a pair of lateral pinnae develop, and these unfurl and come to rest on the surrounding vegetation, which supports the weight of the leaf. After the pinnae have unfurled, the resting bud resumes growth. It continues to grow straight up, pencil-like, through the surrounding vegetation before stopping to produce another pair of pinnae. This mode of intermittent growth allows the leaf to poke up through dense vegetation unencumbered by lateral pinnae that would snag on twigs and leaves. Because the rest–growth cycle repeats itself many times, the leaves of some species can reach more than 65 feet (20 m) long, among the longest in ferndom.

Next is the Schizaeales, a diverse group vegetatively but one consistently characterized by spore cases completely encircled near the tip by the annulus (Figure 43). No other ferns have this kind of annulus. Two genera of Schizaeales merit mention. The first is *Lygodium*, a climbing fern usually found in open vegetation or along forest borders. Its stem, which is rooted in the soil, puts up leaves whose midribs twine around twigs and branches, elevating the leaf where it can receive more light

(Figure 44). The only other fern that climbs by means of a twining leaf midrib is *Salpichlaena*, a tropical American genus in the Blechnaceae, in the Polypodiales. By this twining habit, ferns have outdone flowering plants, none of which has a climbing leaf. A second genus of Schizaeales, *Anemia*, usually grows on the ground or rocks in seasonally dry habitats. Its leaves are divided like those of most ferns, but at the base they bear two tall, erect, fertile pinnae that have little or no green tissue (Figure 43). No other fern has this arrangement of the fertile pinnae.

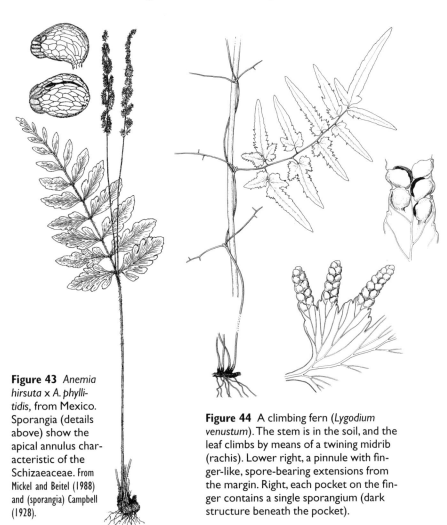

Figure 43 *Anemia hirsuta* x *A. phyllitidis*, from Mexico. Sporangia (details above) show the apical annulus characteristic of the Schizaeaceae. From Mickel and Beitel (1988) and (sporangia) Campbell (1928).

Figure 44 A climbing fern (*Lygodium venustum*). The stem is in the soil, and the leaf climbs by means of a twining midrib (rachis). Lower right, a pinnule with finger-like, spore-bearing extensions from the margin. Right, each pocket on the finger contains a single sporangium (dark structure beneath the pocket).

The next group, the Salviniales, consists of aquatic ferns that produce two types of spores: small male and much larger female ones, a condition called heterospory (Chapter 3). The Salviniales comprise five genera, two of which (*Azolla* and *Salvinia*) float, and the other three (*Marsilea, Pilularia,* and *Regnellidium*) grow in mud, typically around the shores of ponds or rivers. As a group, they are a diverse lot, difficult to characterize vegetatively by any obvious feature yet each distinct. *Azolla*, the mosquito fern, is the world's smallest fern, with leaves only as long as 1/32 inch (1 mm; Figure 128). Despite its small size, it is the world's most important fern economically because it is used as an organic fertilizer in the rice paddies of southeastern Asia (Chapter 30). Closely related to *Azolla* are water spangles, *Salvinia*, which has two rounded, floating green leaves and a third that is root-like, submerged, and whitish (Figure 124). One species, *S. molesta* (Plates 21–23), the molesting *Salvinia*, is infamous as an aggressive weed in waterways of the Old World and southern United States. A lot of money has been spent on its control (Chapter 29). The three remaining genera of Salviniales, which are classified in the Marsileaceae, typically grow in habitats that are at least seasonally muddy or inundated with shallow water. They are characterized by hard, bean-like reproductive structures called sporocarps along the petiole base (Figure 132). These represent folded, hardened pinnae that bear the sporangia within (Figures 134 and 135). The genera of Marsileaceae are easy to distinguish by the number of leaflets: *Marsilea* has four and resembles a four-leaf clover, *Regnellidium* has two, and *Pilularia* has none, its leaf consisting solely of a thread-like stalk.

The next group on the evolutionary tree, the Cyatheales, is informally called the tree fern clade. It contains the two main families of tree ferns (Cyatheaceae and Dicksoniaceae) and several lesser-known tropical families (Plagiogyriaceae, Hymenophyllopsidaceae, Lophosoriaceae, and Metaxyaceae). Although the close relationship of these groups is well supported by DNA evidence, the only morphological characteristics defining them have to do with minute details of their gametophytes and stem anatomy.

Most tree ferns fall easily into either the Cyatheaceae or Dicksoniaceae. Cyatheaceae are distinguished by bearing sori on the lower surface of the blades and having scales on the trunk and leaves (Figure 45). Dicksoniaceae bear sori on the edge of the blade and have wooly hairs instead of wide, flattened scales (Figure 46).

Finally, the Polypodiales is the last group—the most diverse and most frequently encountered in the world's vegetation. Nearly 80% of the world's ferns belong to this order, representing about 12,000 species in approximately 250 genera. The group is cosmopolitan and occurs on

Figure 45 Characteristics of the tree fern family Cyatheaceae: flat scales on the petiole base (left) and sori on the lower surface of the leaf (right).

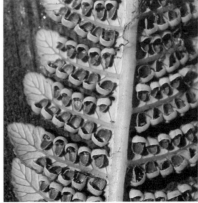

Figure 46 Characteristics of the tree fern family Dicksoniaceae: soft wooly hairs on the leaves (left) and sori along the margin of the leaflets (right). The indusium consists of two valves, imparting a clam-like appearance to the sorus.

83

every continent (except, of course, Antarctica, where only two species of vascular plants grow, neither of which is a fern). Polypodiales are distinguished by the annulus, which partially encircles the spore case and stops at the stalk (Figures 2, 5, and 12). Because the annulus does not completely encircle the spore case, it is said to be incomplete, or interrupted at the stalk. This contrasts with the condition in the other orders of leptosporangiate ferns, in which the annulus usually encircles the spore case obliquely, bypassing the stalk and forming a complete ring. In spite of their unconventional sporangial plan, the polypodialean ferns are a diverse lot. It is tempting here to discuss the major families and oddballs of the order, but that would be beyond the scope of this chapter, which is only intended to be a survey of the major groups of ferns.

CLASSIFICATION OF FERNS

9

Genres of Genera

Learning the meanings of the names of fern genera opens a little window that looks out onto pteridology, the study of ferns. Through it you can glimpse people who developed the science, the voyages that brought back to Europe many previously unknown and marvelous species, and the ancient cultures and what they believed about plants. Most of all, the view is dominated by the ferns themselves—their habits and habitats, spores and sporangia, leaves and life cycles.

Before opening this window, a bit of background about how genus names came into use. In Europe from the 1400s through the middle 1700s, herbalists and "natural philosophers" named plants with a phrase, usually short, sometimes long. This name, or polynomial, was written in Latin, the *lingua franca* of most written and spoken scientific communication until the 1840s. The bird's-nest fern, for example, was dubbed *Asplenium frondibus simplicibus lanceolatis integerrimis glabris*, "*Asplenium* with simple, lance-shaped, entire, nonhairy leaves." Polynomials served two purposes: they were handles for reference *and* short descriptions for distinguishing a species from related ones.

Polynomials worked well in northern Europe where there were relatively few plant species, but by the early 1700s serious problems arose.

Voyages of discovery had brought to Europe tens of thousands of previously unknown plant species, especially from the tropics. To distinguish these new species, polynomials had to be lengthened because more characters were needed to distinguish the increasing number of species. As polynomials grew longer, it became a nightmare to cross-reference species in different books because the names had changed. Also, the longer the polynomial, the harder it was to remember and the more unwieldy it was to pronounce. It seemed as if natural history was about to collapse under the sheer weight of its subject matter.

Finally, in 1753, Carl Linnaeus ushered in a system of naming that promoted stability and order. In *Species Plantarum* (species of plants), a book cataloging all the then-known species of plants, he gave each species a polynomial as his predecessors had done, but in the margin beside each polynomial was printed a single word, the *nomen trivialum*, as a kind of shorthand to refer to that species. These trivial names caught on. The entire botanical community soon adopted them in combination with the name of the genus to produce a new, two-word name, or binomial. Instead of saying *Asplenium frondibus simplicibus lanceolatis integerrimis glabris,* people uttered *Asplenium nidus* (Plate 3), the word *nidus* being Linnaeus's trivial name. This binomial system is still used today, but we refer to the trivial name as the specific epithet. Together, the name of the genus and the specific epithet form the name of the species. (Please note—and this is picky, I admit—that the specific epithet alone is *not* the name of the species; the species name consists of *both* words in tandem.)

Thus genus names came into use with the advent of the binomial system. Since 1753 more than 1000 names for genera have been proposed for ferns and lycophytes, but nowadays only about 350 of these are widely accepted. These names, whether accepted or not, display various aspects of pteridology.

Some fern names are so old that their origins are lost or only faintly discernible through the mists of history. For example, *Osmunda* might be derived from the Latin *os,* bone, and *munda,* cure, because the roots of this fern were used as a cure for rickets. Or it might be derived from the Latin *mundae,* to clean, since it was used medically to clean bones. Yet another possibility is that it comes from Osmunder, the Saxon god of war, or from the story of Osmund, of Loch Tyne, who hid his wife and child in a thicket of this fern, Moses-like, when the Danes invaded Scotland. No one knows which of these derivations, if any, is correct.

Several names were handed down to us from the ancient Greeks, which allows us to assign name origins with more confidence. The Greek word for ferns in general was *pteris*, from *pteron*, wing or feather, probably alluding to the feathery appearance of some ferns. *Pteris* is used today for a mostly tropical genus of about 250 species. (Incidentally, the *p* in *Pteris* is silent, although it can be heard in *Cystopteris, Dryopteris,* and *Haplopteris*.) Another name of ancient Greek origin is *Adiantum*, the genus of maidenhair ferns. It is derived from *adiantos*, unwettable, and refers to the water-repellent leaves. When water falls on a leaf, it beads up into silvery droplets that quickly roll off. Some early Greeks reasoned that because animals have separate sexes, so should plants. Thus they used *Thelypteris*, from *thelys*, female, and *pteris*, fern, for a fern with a more delicately cut blade—therefore more feminine—than the coarsely cut male fern (now called *Dryopteris filix-mas*). The Greeks also believed that a species of spleenwort—we are not sure which—was useful for treating diseases of the spleen. Accordingly, *Asplenium* is derived from the Greek *splen*, spleen. (Within *Asplenium* is a group of species sometimes distinguished as a separate genus, *Ceterach*, from *sjetrak*, an old name applied to these plants by Persian physicians.)

Gods and heroes from Greek mythology have lent their names to fern genera, although these names were adopted in modern times and not used by the ancient Greeks themselves. *Aglaomorpha* is derived from Aglaia (*aglaios*, splendid) one of the graces in Greek mythology, and *morphe*, shape. Presumably this Greek goddess, like the plant, had a splendid shape. Besides artists, poets, and musicians, the muses have inspired botanists. *Melpomene*, the muse of tragedy, has lent her name to indirectly memorialize U.S. pteridologist Earl L. Bishop (1943–1991), who researched this group of ferns but died of AIDS before publishing his results. *Terpsichore*, the muse of dance, celebrates a genus whose leaves dangle from the branches and trunks of tropical trees and appear to dance when blown by the wind (Figure 47).

Mortals have also found eternal memorial among the names of fern

genera. Some were travelers or collectors who sent specimens to botanists in the world's leading herbaria and were rewarded by having a genus
named after them. So honored was Edmond Davall (1763–1798), a Swiss
collector for whom *Davallia*, the genus of rabbit's-foot ferns, is named.
Llavea (Figure 48) is named after Pablo de la Llave (1773–1833), a traveler
in Mexico. *Jamesonia* (Plate 14), a distinctive genus of the Andean páramos, celebrates William Jameson (1796–1873), a Scottish physician who
collected plants around Quito, Ecuador.

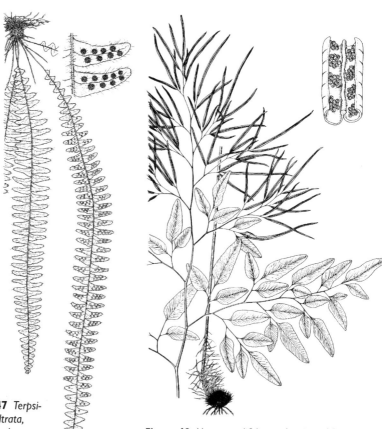

Figure 47 *Terpsi-
chore cultrata,*
from Mexico,
the genus named
after the muse of
dance. Its pendent
leaves dance when blown by
the wind. From Mickel and Beitel (1988).

Figure 48 *Llavea cordifolia,* endemic to Mexico
and Guatemala, the genus named after Pablo de
la Llave, a traveler in Mexico. The narrow segments bear the sporangia, the close-up (above
right) showing the sporangia in an enrolled segment. From Mickel and Beitel (1988).

Of course, pteridologists are memorialized in the names of fern genera. *Chingia* is named after Ren Chang Ching (1898–1986), famous not only for of his work on ferns but also for being the first Chinese scientist to work outside China with Westerners. He studied in London with preeminent British pteridologist Richard E. Holttum (1895–1990), who is commemorated by *Holttumia* (a fungus), *Holttumiella* (a fern), and *Holttumara* (an orchid). Ching also studied in Copenhagen with the great Danish pteridologist Carl Christensen (1872–1942), who is honored by *Christensenia*. Other Europeans memorialized are the French pteridologist Marie-Laure Tardieu-Blot (b. 1902), by *Blotiella*, and Swiss pteridologist Hermann Christ (1833–1933), by *Christella* and *Christiopteris*. In the United States, commemorated pteridologists include Rolla M. Tryon (1916–2001) of *Tryonella*, Warren H. Wagner, Jr. (1920–2000) of *Wagneriopteris*, and David B. Lellinger (b. 1937) of *Lellingeria*.

Sometimes people who were not fern experts—or even botanists—are honored among the names of fern genera. *Marsilea*, the water clover, is named after Count Luigi Ferdinando Marsigli (1656–1730), Italian botanist at Bologna, although he never worked on ferns. A closely related genus, *Salvinia*, the water spangle, is named after Antonio Maria Salvini (1633–1729), an Italian professor of Greek who helped botanists with their research. *Dennstaedtia* is named after August Wilhelm Dennstaedt (1776–1826), a German botanist who, as far as I know, never published on ferns. *Woodwardia* is named after Thomas J. Woodward (1745–1820), a British student of the algae. *Matteuccia*, the genus of ostrich ferns, honors Carlo Matteucci (1811–1863), an Italian electrophysiologist and politician. *Rumohra*, the "florist's fern" commonly seen in bouquets and flower arrangements, is named after Karl F. von Rumohr (1785–1843), an art student from Dresden.

Some names indicate the locality where the genus was first discovered. Thus we have *Afropteris, Costaricia,* and *Japanobotrychium*. One genus is named after Fuji, and when the mountain's name is Latinized (as required by the *International Code of Botanical Nomenclature*) to Fuzi and has *filix* (Latin for fern) tacked on its end, the result is *Fuziifilix*—a delightful name!

Habitats are also singled out. *Antrophyum* (Greek *antron*, cave, and *phyein*, to grow) alludes to caves because the genus was first described based on a species that grew near a cave entrance. *Phegopteris* (Greek *phegos,* beech, and *pteris,* fern) refers to a fern growing under beech trees, *Dryopteris* (Greek *drys,* oak, and *pteris*) to a fern under oaks (the dryads of Greek mythology were nymphs who inhabited oaks), and *Alsophila* (Greek *alsos,* grove or woodland, and *philein,* to love) to a fern growing among trees.

The vegetative organs of ferns also serve as the etymological root of names, and *Solanopteris* (Plate 25), the potato fern, provides a prime example. The name comes from *Solanum,* the genus of potatoes, and *pteris,* fern. Its main stem is slender and long-creeping, typical of most ferns in the Polypodiaceae, but along its length are lateral branches that become enlarged and hollow, resembling small potatoes (Figures 77 and 78). Ants set up housekeeping in these potato-like stems, and if anything disturbs the fern—such as an insect munching its leaves or a botanist trying to collect the plant—the ants scurry out of the potatoes and attack (Chapter 16).

Polypodium means many-footed, from the Greek *poly,* many, and *podion,* foot. The stems of these ferns creep over the substrate and bear on their upper surface two rows of slightly elevated leaf bases known as phyllopodia. This imparts the appearance of an upside-down creeping caterpillar with its two rows of feet (the phyllopodia) sticking up in the air (Figure 49).

Other names that have sprung from vivid imaginations are *Equisetum* and *Lycopodium.* Someone thought the bushy, tail-like shoots of *Equisetum* resembled a horse's tail (Latin *equus,* horse, and *seta,* bristle; Figure 50). In *Lycopodium,* the resemblance is stretched a bit: the type species, *L. clavatum,* one of the most widespread lycophytes in the world, has bristle-tipped leaves that impart a fury appearance to the branch tips. This furriness suggests a wolf's paw (Greek *lycos,* wolf, and *pous,* foot). When the di-

Figure 49 Stem of *Polypodium* (Greek *poly,* many, and *podion,* foot) with its many slightly elevated leaf bases above, the phyllopodia, sticking up. One leaf stalk is shown attached to its phyllopodium.

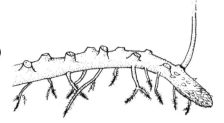

minutive Latin suffix -ella is tacked on the end of *Lycopodium,* the result is *Lycopodiella,* "tiny wolf's paw." The same suffix also makes an appearance in *Selaginella,* "like a small selago," selago being the old name for the club mosses now classified in the genus *Huperzia* (Plate 11).

Usually the leaves—not the stems—are the dominant organs of ferns, and one of the most frequently noted characteristics is leaf shape. Drooping, ribbon-like leaves give rise to the name of the shoestring fern genus, *Vittaria* (Latin *vitta,* ribbon or stripe, and *aris,* resembling; Plate 26). The flattened, antler-like leaves of staghorn ferns were evoked in the coining of *Platycerium* (Greek *platys,* flat, and *keras,* horn). The blades of *Schizaea* are split into narrow lobes (Greek *skizein,* to split), and the narrow fertile segments of *Ctenitis* are perpendicular to the midrib of the pinna and therefore resemble the teeth of a comb (Greek *kteis,* comb). A resemblance to oak (*Quercus*) leaves gave rise to the names *Quercifilix* and *Drynaria* (Greek *dryinos,* of oaks, and perhaps *aris,* like, or *aria,* just an

Figure 50 Horse-tails were named *Equisetum* (Latin *equus,* horse, and *seta,* bristle) because of their resemblance to a horse's tail. After Tippo and Stern (1977), by Alice R. Tangerini.

91

ending). *Dipteris* is so named because its blades are divided into two equal fan-shaped halves (Greek *di*, two, and *pteris*, fern; Figure 72).

Besides shape, the color and texture of leaves is used. Dull, bluish gray leaves are the namesake of *Pellaea* (Greek *pellos*, dusky), and a white to yellow powder on the lower surface of the leaves gives rise to the name *Pityrogramma* (Greek *pityron*, scurf, and *gramme*, line, the latter referring to the black lines of spore cases along the veins). Dull reddish hairs on the lower surface of the leaves are responsible for the name of *Pyrrosia* (Greek *pyr*, fire), a commonly cultivated genus (look at these hairs with a hand lens—each is exquisitely star-shaped). Similarly, *Niphidium* comes from the Greek *nipha*, snow, and *eidos*, like, alluding to the snow white covering of hairs on the lower surface of the blades in the type species. As an example of texture, *Hymenophyllum*, a genus of filmy ferns, takes its name from the membranous leaves only one cell thick between the veins (Greek *hymen*, membrane, and *phyllon*, leaf).

The midrib of the leaf, or rachis, is the namesake of the climbing fern, *Lygodium*, Its midribs twine around twigs and branches, supporting the leaf as it grows upward (Figure 44). To twine, the midrib must be pliant or flexible, which is the meaning of the Greek *lygodes*.

Venation is often used in fern classification and has served as a source of names. In *Campyloneurum* the secondary veins are arched between the primary lateral veins (Greek *kampylos*, arched, and *neuron*, vein), forming a distinctive pattern (Figure 51). In the small Asian genus *Dictyodroma* (Greek *dictyo*, net, and *droma*, running) the veins anastomose to form polygonal nets elongated, or running, toward the margin.

Some fern genera are named for their strikingly different spore-producing (fertile) leaves. Such leaves are called dimorphic and often lack green tissue, consisting mostly of narrow, skeletonized segments that bear the spore cases. These leaves tend to have longer petioles, bringing the spore cases up into the wind currents where their spores stand a better chance of being dispersed. After the spores are shed, the leaf wilts, in contrast to the green, photosynthetic leaves that remain. Adder's-tongues (*Ophioglossum* from the Greek *ophis*, snake, and *glossa*, tongue) bear spore cases thought to resemble a snake's tongue atop a long stalk. Closely related to *Ophioglossum* is *Botrychium*, comprising the grape ferns, moonworts, and rattlesnake ferns. Their fertile spikes are branched at the tip, and the branches bear clusters of round spore cases (Figure 36). The whole structure resembles a bunch of grapes, thus *Botrychium* (Greek *botrys*, bunch or cluster). The name of the sensitive fern, *Onoclea* (Greek *onos*, vessel, and *kleiein*, to close), refers to the segments of the fertile frond that roll up into hard, bead-like structures enclosing the sori (Figure 52).

Early taxonomists emphasized the shape of the sorus in their classifications and often used this characteristic for naming fern genera. Walk-

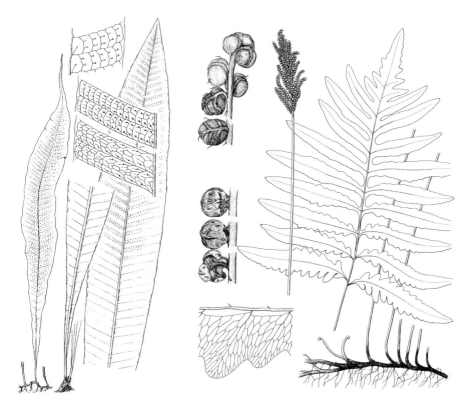

Figure 51 *Campyloneurum* (Greek *kampylos*, arched, and *neuron*, vein) has minor veins arching between the main lateral ones. Left, *C. repens*; right, *C. phyllitidis*—both from Mexico. From Mickel and Beitel (1988).

Figure 52 Sensitive fern (*Onoclea sensibilis*). The spore-producing leaf (center) differs greatly from the expanded, green photosynthetic leaf (right). Upper left, the hardened, modified pinnules enclosing the spore cases (Greek *onos*, vessel, and *kleiein*, to close). Lower left, the net-like veins.

93

ing ferns (*Camptosorus* from the Greek *kamptos*, curved, and *soros*) were named for the bent or crooked sori, a shape that results from the sori following the angles formed by netted veins (Figure 2). In the type species of *Microgramma* the sori are slightly elongated (Greek *mikros*, small, and *gramme*, line), and in *Microsorum* (Greek *mikros*, small, and *soros*) they are very small. As an example of the importance attached to soral characteristics, early taxonomists included in *Polypodium* any fern that had round sori without indusia (Figure 1), and in *Asplenium* any fern with elongate sori with an indusium. Nowadays, however, we know that such classifications are unnatural; similar soral characteristics may have evolved many times, independently. As my colleague John Mickel once pointed out, "Unfortunately for science, upon the sorus there's no reliance."

Early taxonomists also used the position of the sorus as a source of names. This is evident in *Cheilanthes* (Greek *cheilos*, lip, and *anthos*, flower) whose sori are located near the leaf margin and protected by an enrolled, lip-like leaf margin, a "false indusium" (Figure 53). Similarly, *Cryptogramma* (Greek *kryptos*, hidden, and *gramme*, line) has sori in short lines near the leaf margin, and these lines are hidden by a false indusium. Soral position is highlighted in *Acrostichum* (Greek *akros*, summit, and *stichos*, row), in which sori are borne toward the summit of the leaf; *Polystichum* (Greek *poly*, many, and *stichos*, row), in which sori are arranged in several regular rows; and *Anogramma* (Greek *ano*, upward, and *gramme*, line), in which the soral line that runs toward the segment tip.

Many ferns have sori protected by an indusium, and this structure has

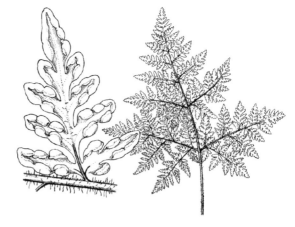

Figure 53 Sori of *Cheilanthes kaulfussii*, from Mexico, are protected by enrolled leaf margins (Greek *cheilos*, lip, and *anthos*, flower). From Mickel and Beitel (1988).

been another source of names. It is roof-like in many species of *Tectaria* (Latin *tectum*, roof, and *aria*, just a suffix) but absent in *Gymnocarpium*, which therefore has naked sori (Greek *gymnos*, naked, and *karpos*, fruit). The cup-like shape of the indusium (Figure 54) is emphasized in the name of the principal genus of tree ferns, *Cyathea* (Greek *kyathos*, wine cup; Plate 17). *Cystopteris* alludes to the inflated or bladder-like indusium (Greek *kystos*, bladder, and *pteris*, fern). In the genus of Boston ferns, *Nephrolepis*, the indusium is kidney-shaped and scale-like (Greek *nephros*, kidney, and *lepis*, scale; Figure 55). The large and diverse tropical genus *Diplazium* (Greek *diplazios*, double) has a double indusium, that is, two elongate indusia run back-to-back along the same vein (Figure 56). In *Hypolepis* (Greek *hypo*, below, and *lepis*, scale), a scale-like flap modified from the leaf margin is turned under to protect the sorus.

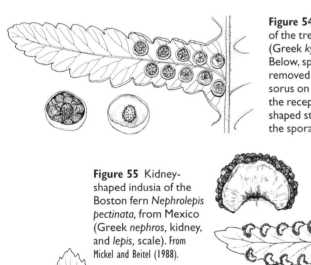

Figure 54 Cup-like indusia of the tree fern *Cyathea* (Greek *kyathos*, wine cup). Below, sporangia have been removed from the enlarged sorus on the right to show the receptacle, the knob-shaped structure to which the sporangia are attached.

Figure 55 Kidney-shaped indusia of the Boston fern *Nephrolepis pectinata*, from Mexico (Greek *nephros*, kidney, and *lepis*, scale). From Mickel and Beitel (1988).

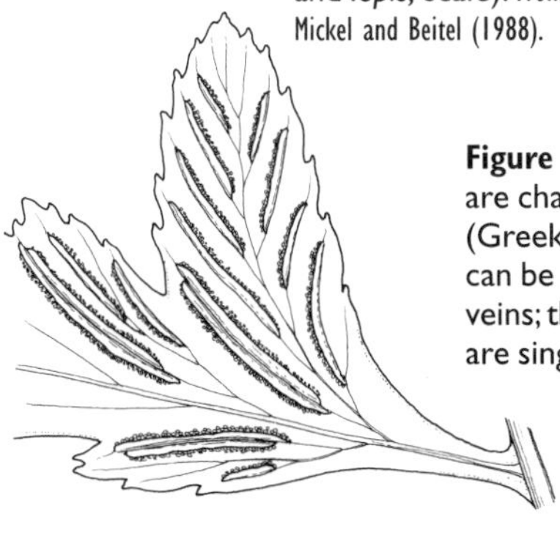

Figure 56 Back-to-back sori are characteristic of *Diplazium* (Greek *diplazios*, double) and can be seen here on the basal veins; those on the distal veins are single, not back-to-back.

Sometimes the sori bear protective structures among the spore cases. In *Pleopeltis* these structures are shield-shaped scales (Greek *pleos*, full or abundant, and *pelte*, shield), and in *Eriosorus* they are wooly hairs (Greek *erion*, wool, and *soros*, heap or mound). In the filmy fern genus *Trichomanes* (Greek *thrix*, hair, and *manes*, cup), a hair-like structure to which the spore cases are attached (the receptacle) protrudes from a cup- or funnel-shaped sorus (Figure 40).

Instead of calling attention to a diagnostic part of the plant, some names are purely whimsical, such as *Stylites* and *Ibyka*. *Stylites* is closely related to the quillworts (*Isoetes*, Plate 13) and is named after Saint Simeon Stylites (d. 459?), a Syrian hermit who lived 35 years on a small platform on top of a high pillar (Greek *stylos*, pillar or column). Similarly, the leaves are perched at the top an elongate, column-like stem. *Ibyka* means "pecked by cranes" and is the name of a genus of fossils related to modern-day horsetails (*Equisetum*). The original fossils were found in a quarry where the rocks were pecked, or hammered, by cranes—the mechanical kind, that is.

Finally, consider *Anapausia*, a name now treated as a synonym of the fern genus *Tectaria*. It comes from the Greek *anapausis*, rest, and presumably that is what the author did after he finished describing it. You too can rest now.

CLASSIFICATION OF FERNS

10
At the Movies

Describing a new species of fern was an integral part of the comedy *A New Leaf*, released in 1971. In the movie, Henrietta Lowell (played by Elaine May, who also directed the film) is a dowdy, kind-hearted botany teacher who is heiress to a fortune. She meets a scheming, middle-aged playboy, Henry Graham (Walter Matthau), who has squandered all his wealth and now plans to marry her for her money. On their first date he asks,

"Tell me about yourself, Miss Lowell. Your work, your hopes, your dreams."

"Well, I work as a teacher, and I also do field work and write monographs. On my last field trip I identified and classified all the varieties of fern on Jollybogo. It was one of the longest monographs I've ever written."

"I'd love to read it sometime," says Henry, rolling his eyes with boredom.

"My hope is to discover a new variety of fern that has never been described or classified."

"What happens if you find a new species that has never been described or classified?"

"Nothing terribly much, except that you are listed as its discoverer, and the entire species is named after you."

"Ohh . . . like Parkinson's disease being named after James Parkinson."
"That's right. Or the Bougainvillea being named after Louis de
Bougainville."
"Or like Brussels sprouts?" asks Henry.

They marry a week later and go off on their honeymoon (apparently to
Hawaii); however, Henrietta's social ineptness, bumbling, and general
naïveté incites nothing but contempt in suave, sophisticated Henry. So
while Henrietta is collecting tree ferns—she finds an unusual *Alsophila*
with a "vestigial indusium"—Henry is busy studying a toxicology textbook, planning to poison her at some convenient time with a commonly
used gardening chemical and inherit her fortune after she dies.

But shortly after returning from their honeymoon, Henrietta's dream
comes true. She blurts out the news to Henry:

"It's been accepted! My *Alsophila grahamii!* They've accepted it!"
"Try to speak calmly, my dear. What is it they've accepted?"
"It's a tropical tree fern, and I discovered it on our honeymoon, and
when I couldn't classify it, I thought it might be a true species. But I
couldn't believe it, so I sent it to Wagner at the University of Michigan, and Henry—it is! It's a true species! I've discovered a true species!"
"Well, that's nice. Very nice," says Henry, trying to conceal his
indifference. "Well, well. Now you'll be able to name a whole species,
won't you? Just like—What's his name?—Louis de Bougainville?"

But Henry is flabbergasted when Henrietta tells him that she plans to
name the new fern for *him*. He tries to dissuade her, but she insists. It is
only his love, she explains, that gives her the confidence to announce her
discovery to the botanical world, and the plant was found, after all, on
their honeymoon. As a token of her affection, she gives him a locket
containing a pinnule of the fern. Henry is momentarily moved but continues, coldheartedly, scheming to poison her.

The movie aside for a moment, how would Henrietta—or anyone else
for that matter—go about naming and describing a newly discovered
fern? Naming a plant involves assigning it a genus name and specific
epithet, followed by the author's name. For example, the scientific name

of the royal fern is *Osmunda regalis* Linnaeus. The first two words are italicized because they are in Latin—just as any foreign words would be italicized in an otherwise English text. *Osmunda* is the genus, and like other genus names, the first letter is capitalized. The second word, *regalis*, is the specific epithet (not the species name, or binomial, which is the genus name *plus* the specific epithet). It is spelled in lowercase, though some botanists preferred to capitalize the first letter when the word is derived from a person's surname or the name of another plant genus. Last comes the name of the person or persons who first named and described the species—in this example, Carl Linnaeus. Author names are often abbreviated to save space. For instance, Linnaeus is usually shortened to L. Sometimes two author names are given with the first enclosed in parentheses, as for the ostrich fern, *Matteuccia struthiopteris* (Linnaeus) Todaro. In this case, Linnaeus first classified the species in the genus *Osmunda;* later, Agostino Todaro transferred it to *Matteuccia.* There are other reasons that give rise to two authors following a binomial, but this is the most common one.

To many people, using Latin names seems pointless. Who can pronounce them, remember them, or know what they mean? Why not use common names that are easier to use and understand? One problem with common names is that they vary from region to region and from language to language. Even within a given locale or language, a species may have more than one common name, or the same common name might apply to different species. There is no guarantee of consistency. For example, some common names for one of the common club mosses in eastern North America, *Lycopodium digitatum*, are crowfoot club moss, flat-branched club moss, ground cedar, princess pine, or southern running-pine. In Quebec it is called *lycopode en éventail,* "fan-shaped lycopodium." The same common names have also been used for related but different species.

The advantage of using a Latin binomial is that it provides a single correct name. Also, the rules for giving these names are agreed on internationally. To dub a new plant with a proud new Latin name, you have to comply with five requirements prescribed by the *International Code of Botanical Nomenclature.* The *Code,* as it is called, has evolved over the years from the efforts of botanists who debate and revise it every 6 years at an International Botanical Congress. This meeting is held each time in a different city around the world.

The *Code*'s first requirement is that the rank of the new plant must be clearly indicated: species, subspecies, or variety, for example. Second, the plant must be given a name not used previously. For instance, if Henrietta wanted to call her new tree fern *Alsophila grahamii*, and if there already was an *Alsophila* with the specific epithet *grahamii*, then she must choose another epithet. She could select any word she desired as long as it is Latinized: *henryi, henrygrahamii, lowellii* (the *-i* or *-ii* indicates possession; in Latin, *Alsophila henryi* means "Henry's *Alsophila*"). Because botanical nomenclature starts with the publication of Linnaeus's *Species Plantarum* in 1753, any name published since then cannot be duplicated or reused. Checking the names for ferns published in the thousands of journals and books published since 1753 would be a daunting and time-consuming task were it not for a series of reference books called *Index Filicum*. The *Index* lists all fern names published since 1753. (*Index Kewensis* does the same for plant names generally.)

The *Code*'s third requirement is that a Latin description of the plant be published with the name. This is an anachronism from the days before the middle 1800s when Latin served as the international language of science and scholarship. In theory, all present-day plant taxonomists should read and write Latin, but in reality, few do. Most immediately turn their eyes to the (usually) English description following the Latin one. It is ridiculous to require a Latin description but not an illustration —an illustration could be readily interpreted by speakers of *any* language. Wisely, however, most botanists nowadays provide illustrations with their descriptions.

The *Code*'s fourth requirement is that a type specimen be designated and deposited in a herbarium. In effect, a type specimen says, "Here is what the author meant by the name." Usually the first type specimen, the holotype, is deposited in the herbarium where the author worked, and any duplicates (other plants or parts thereof from the same collection) in other herbaria are called isotypes.

Type specimens are essential to the practice of taxonomy. Examining them is often the *only* way of knowing how to apply a scientific name. This is especially true for names published during the 1700s and 1800s, when botanists had little idea about the mind-boggling diversity of the tropics and thus tended to record too few characteristics when describing new plants. In some cases, their descriptions are so inadequate that it is impossible to determine which genus—much less the species—the plant would be classified in nowadays.

Finally, the *Code* mandates that all the above information—rank, name, Latin description, and designation of type specimens—be published in a manner generally available to botanists throughout the world. In practice, this usually means publishing in scientific journals. The name of a new plant is not considered effectively published if only orally presented at a scientific meeting, or if the information about it is photocopied and sent to colleagues, or if it is published in a local periodical such as the *Ozark County Pantograph.*

In naming a new plant species there is no official person or committee who pronounces on the plant's validity and gives its imprimatur to publish. (When Henrietta refers to Wagner at Michigan—the late, famous pteridologist Warren H. Wagner, Jr.—we may assume that she means her paper was accepted for publication after it was "peer reviewed" by Wagner as well as other expert reviewers selected by the editor, a process followed in most scientific journal publication.) Moreover, there is no rule that says you need a Ph.D. in botany or membership in a scientific society to name a new species. Anyone can do it—provided, that is, they present evidence that the plant differs from any previously described and follow the rules. The evidence is scrutinized by a journal's editor and two or three referees chosen as peer reviewers. These folks are typically a surly lot who do not hesitate to reject a manuscript if it makes an unconvincing case. But if the manuscript is accepted, there is one last hurdle: the author must pay to have it published. Most botanical journals charge $50–100 per printed page to subsidize the cost of printing and distributing the journal.

Describing new species is not an activity of the past; it continues today. Between 1991 and 1995, about 620 new kinds of ferns—about 125 per year—were described worldwide, most from the species-rich tropics. In Mesoamerica (southern Mexico through Panama) 138 new ferns were described from 1985 to 1995—nearly 10% of the region's fern flora. Even in temperate regions, which are well known botanically, new species are still being found. For example, 29 new species of ferns were described from the United States and Canada between 1985 and 1993. Worldwide the number of new plants being discovered is increasing so rapidly that in 1991 the Missouri Botanical Garden created a new journal, *Novon*, devoted to handling the rising tide of new species descriptions submitted for publication. And *Brittonia*, a journal of taxonomic botany published at the New York Botanical Garden, dedicates many of its pages to descriptions of new species.

For many people, knowing the name of a plant imparts a certain feeling of power, as if they somehow control or better understand the plant. (This reminds me of many indigenous people in Amazonia who refuse to reveal their given names because, they believe, that surrenders a degree of spiritual control over them.) But, of course, the name itself usually tells us nothing about the plant. Where does it occur? What limits it range? What eats it? How does it grow? How is it affected by different climates? At what time of the year does it produce fertile leaves? Does it have any medicinal use? But names *are* important. We need them to attach information about the plants. "Without names, the knowledge of things is lost," wrote ancient Greek philosopher Isodorus.

But back to *A New Leaf*. In the last scene, Henry and Henrietta are canoeing in the Adirondacks, and their canoe capsizes in a rapids. Henry swims ashore without rescuing Henrietta, who he knows cannot swim. But dragging himself up from the riverbank, he finds a plant—*Alsophila grahamii!* (Yes, tree ferns do not grow in the Adirondacks, but it is a movie.) He frantically searches his pockets for the locket that Henrietta gave him to confirm his identification, but he cannot find it. At that moment he has a change of heart. He rescues Henrietta, and as the movie ends, they sit together on a log near the water's edge. Henry has turned over a new leaf.

FERN FOSSILS

II
Giants of the Carboniferous

Once, as a botany professor at the University of Arkansas at Little Rock, I received a phone call from a local farmer who had seen something strange in the woods. He was hunting when he came across some unusual markings on a wide, exposed sandstone ledge. "They looked like tire tracks in the rocks," he said, "but I know there weren't any cars around when those rocks were made, so what did I see?"

What he had seen—I am sure—was the fossilized trunks of giant lepidodendrids. Fossils of these trees are common in the sandstones and shales of Arkansas (Figure 57). They represent extinct plants related to modern-day quillworts (*Isoetes*, Plate 13), spike mosses (*Selaginella*), and club mosses (Lycopodiaceae), but unlike the low-growing plants of today, the lepidodendrids had pole-like trunks as tall as many a tree in today's tropical rain forests. Some reached 165 feet (55 m) and were 6 feet (2 m) wide at the base. For nearly 40 million years they dominated the swamps of the late Carboniferous, then spiraled into extinction about 225 million years ago at the end of the Permian (Figure 58).

Many people, such as the man who called me, become curious about lepidodendrids after seeing the patterns made by their trunks—patterns that resemble an alligator skin or, one might say, tire tracks. The patterns are so distinctive that the name *Lepidodendron* (Greek *lepido,* scale, and *dendron,* tree) refers to them. Each scale in the pattern is a "leaf cushion," either diamond-shaped or hexagonal, tightly arranged in spiral or vertical rows. The shape of the cushion and kind of row depends on the species. The patterns created by these leaf cushions are so pleasing that they have been used in architectural design. The Natural History Museum in London, which surely ranks among the handsomest buildings in that city, displays on its façade and in its main entrance hall many pilasters representing stylized lepidodendrid trunks (Figure 59).

Although united to the trunk, the leaf cushion was actually part of the leaf. Each cushion represents the slightly elevated former point of

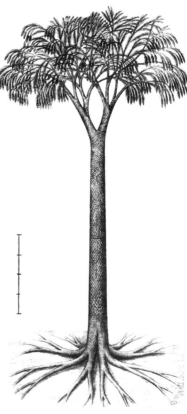

Figure 57 Bark of a fossil lepidodendrid tree resembles a tire track in the rock. Each unit in the pattern represents a slightly elevated leaf base, called a leaf cushion.

Figure 58 Reconstruction of a giant lepidodendrid. Scale, 4 m (about 13 feet). From Hirmer (1927).

104

attachment of a fallen leaf blade, one that was long, straight, narrow, and single-veined (Figure 60). Near the center of the cushion is a dot-like marking that indicates where the vein passed from the stem into the blade. One is tempted to interpret the cushions as a kind of dead, corky layer like the leaf scars on twigs of today's trees, but that would not be entirely correct. Unlike leaf scars on today's trees, leaf cushions were composed of living, green, photosynthetic tissue. How can we conclude that from fossils?

Two lines of fossil evidence lead to the conclusion. First, the outer surfaces of the cushions were covered by a cuticle, a thin, wax-like layer that prevents water loss. In today's land plants, cuticles cover living tis-

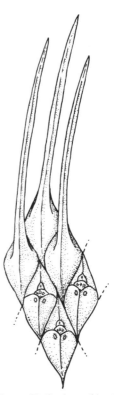

Figure 60 Surface of *Lepido-dendron* branch with attached leaves and leaf cushions where leaves have been shed. After Stewart and Rothwell (1993).

Figure 59 Stylized lepidodendrid pilasters in the Natural History Museum, London.

sues exposed to air; therefore, it seems reasonable to infer that cuticles also covered living tissue in lepidodendrids. Second, the surfaces of the cushions were dotted with stomata, microscopic pores through which carbon dioxide from the air diffuses into the plant. Stomata evolved for photosynthesis, a chemical process that occurs only in living cells. The presence of a cuticle and the possession of stomata indicate that leaf cushions were alive *and* photosynthetic (Thomas 1966, 1981).

If leaf cushions were photosynthetic, then they must have been green, the color of chlorophyll. The trunks of lepidodendrids, which were covered by leaf cushions, must have been green. This is quite unlike nearly all trees of today, which invest their trunks with a dead, non-photosynthetic bark layer, one that is usually some shade of drab brown or gray.

When it came to reproduction, lepidodendrids further differed from the trees of today by lacking seeds. Instead, they reproduced by liberating spores from cone-like strobili borne on the upper branches of their crown. Some lepidodendrids produced strobili only once toward the end of their life, then died. They were monocarpic, similar to the present-day century plants (*Agave*), puyas (*Puya*), and certain bamboos, which grow for many years, then flower, fruit, and die. Other lepidodendrids produced strobili many times throughout their lives.

The strobilus of lepidodendrids had a characteristic structure. It consisted of a central axis bearing spirally arranged rows of highly modified, spore-producing leaves called sporophylls. On the upper surface of each sporophyll sat a single spore case that produced either male or female spores. The male spores, or microspores, were typically 10–20 times smaller in diameter than the female spores. Because of their small size, microspores could be produced by the hundreds within a single spore case. The female spores, or megaspores, were larger because they were packed with food to nourish a future embryo. Typically, 16 or 8 megaspores were produced per spore case, and in some species, only one. Although male and female spores were produced in separate spore cases, they could, depending on the species, be borne in either the same strobilus (a bisporangiate strobilus) or separate strobili (monosporangiate strobili). These spores were the only way by which lepidodendrids reproduced; they had no means of vegetative reproduction such as buds or root proliferations (Chapter 5).

One genus of lepidodendrids dispersed its spores while intact strobili were attached high in the tree, but in all other genera the spores were shed as the strobili disintegrated. One by one, sporophylls dropped from the strobilus and fluttered into the swamp. On the water, they floated like little boats, conveying their cargo of spores away from the parent plant. Sporophylls that carried female spores are called aquacarps (Figure 61). Eventually, both male and female spores germinated and developed into male and female gametophytes, which in turn produced sperm and egg. Fertilization of the egg took place *on the water* while the female gametophyte was still attached to its floating sporophyll. Nothing like this occurs in today's trees, where fertilization almost always takes place above ground.

After the egg was fertilized, it formed an embryo whose early development took an unusual twist: its root aborted, and the first dichotomy of its *shoot* produced both the aerial stem and downward-growing rooting organ. The latter, although root-like, was not a true root in a developmental sense. It had the anchoring and nutrient-absorbing functions of a root, but the development, general form, and anatomy of a stem. This hybrid, root-like shoot system is called a rhizomorph.

The stem-like nature of the rhizomorph is revealed most clearly by the way it mirrored the branching pattern of crown (Figure 62). Both consisted of branches that forked equally in a Y-shaped fashion, and with each fork the branches narrowed until, finally, the apical growing point was exhausted and further growth was impossible. This predetermined growth limited the size and number of branches that the rhizomorph and aerial shoot could produce. It also imparted remarkable similarity to both the above- and underground portions of the plant

Figure 61 Aquacarps, the floating sporophylls of lepidodendrids (left, *Achlamydocarpon*; right, *Flemingites*). The shaded structure is the sporangium. After Phillips (1979).

and a relatively uniform appearance to individuals of the same species. If a lepidodendrid had been uprooted and stuck in the soil upside-down, it would have had much the same general architecture.

The rhizomorph grew precociously, outpacing the growth of the aerial shoot, and in some species extended 36 feet (12 m) across when fully developed. This stabilized the base of the tree before the aerial shoot bolted upward and produced a heavy crown of branches and leaves. The main branches of the rhizomorphs (the fossils of which are called *Stigmaria*) bristled with rootlets 4–12 inches (10–30 cm) long, quite unlike those of today's ferns and seed plants. They were arranged spirally in a regular and precise pattern around the main root, that is, they exhibited a rhizotaxy, analogous to phyllotaxy, the arrangement of leaves on a stem (Figure 62). Rootlets of today's ferns and seed plants are pro-

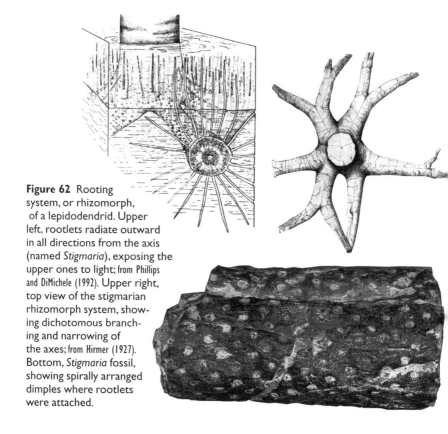

Figure 62 Rooting system, or rhizomorph, of a lepidodendrid. Upper left, rootlets radiate outward in all directions from the axis (named *Stigmaria*), exposing the upper ones to light; from Phillips and DiMichele (1992). Upper right, top view of the stigmarian rhizomorph system, showing dichotomous branching and narrowing of the axes; from Hirmer (1927). Bottom, *Stigmaria* fossil, showing spirally arranged dimples where rootlets were attached.

duced irregularly along the main root; they do not exhibit regular place-
ment like those of the leaves of ferns, lycopods, and seed plants. (The
only living plant exhibiting rhizotaxy is *Isoetes*, which also has a rhizomorph and is believed closely related to the lepidodendrids.) The
regular arrangement of lepidodendrid rootlets suggests the rootlets
were homologues of the leaves.

Other characteristics of the rootlets betray their homology with
leaves, and by extension the origin of the rhizomorph from embryonic
shoot tissue. The rootlets could abscise, or drop off, cleanly at a sepa-
ration layer at their base. This helped the plant as the main root elongated through the muck of the swamp—rootlets could shear off, allowing easier extension of the main root. Just as the leaves abscised,
leaving alligator-skin patterns on the trunks, so too did the rootlets
leave rows of shallow dimples in spirals on the main root. The dimples
are easily seen (Figure 62). They have the developmentally equivalent
origin of, or are homologous to, the leaf scars on the aerial shoot. Unlike the roots of most plants today, lepidodendrid rootlets lacked a root
cap to protect the growing tip from abrasion as it is pushed through the
soil. They also lacked root hairs to absorb water and mineral nutrients.
The regular arrangement of rootlets on the main root, their ability to
abscise, their lack of a root cap and root hairs—all these show that the
rootlets are developmentally modified leaves.

Rhizomorph rootlets also differ internally from the roots of today's
ferns and seed plants. Each rootlet contained a central air canal with a
vascular bundle along its edge, the same anatomy found in the rootlets
of present-day selaginellas and *Isoetes*. This raises the question of
whether the rootlets of lepidodendrids could absorb carbon dioxide
from the watery sediments in which they grew—a characteristic of present-day rootlets of quillworts, one that is related to their anatomy
(Chapter 20). One observation suggests they did have this ability. About
one-third of the mass of lepidodendrids consisted of the rhizomorph
axes and its rootlets, much more than other plants. This implies that the
rootlets did more than just anchor the plant and absorb water and nutrients. Some paleobotanists speculate that the rootlets, at least those exposed to light, photosynthesized, absorbing carbon dioxide (or carbon

dissolved in water as bicarbonate ion) from the sediments (Phillips and DiMichele 1992). This is supported by the lack of continuity between the phloem in the stem and roots, suggesting that sugars produced by the leaves could not be transported from the main stem to the roots. Presumably the roots manufactured their own sugars by photosynthesis.

Lepidodendrids also differed from today's trees by how they became arborescent. Temperate-zone trees grow wider every year by adding concentric layers of wood to the trunk, resulting in the annual rings. Without widening to support the weight of the new branches and leaves, the trunk would buckle. Lepidodendrids, however, produced little or no wood; instead, they became tree-like by widening their bark. This remained around the trunk as an extremely rigid layer, one that did not flake off or exfoliate like that of most modern trees and in which the leaf cushions expanded to accommodate the increasing width of the trunk (Chapter 17).

Lepidodendrids dominated the swamps of the Carboniferous in North America and Europe for about 40 million years, and along with their close relatives they account for more than half of the fossil species known from that period. They persisted in China for 40 million years more until the end of the Permian. They were a well-adapted and highly successful group. What caused their demise?

Apparently several factors conspired in their downfall. One was continental glaciation. The Carboniferous–Permian transition—the time when lepidodendrids were extirpated from North America and Europe—was marked by intense glaciation, especially in the southern continent of Gondwana. The amount of fresh water locked up in the glaciers lowered sea levels and increased salinity of ocean waters worldwide. This doomed many coastal swamps where lepidodendrids flourished. Another factor was drying caused by continental drift. By the late Permian, about the time lepidodendrids went extinct worldwide, the earth's landmasses had converged to form the supercontinent of Pangaea. Many coal swamps became locked deep within the interior of this vast supercontinent, far from the moisture-laden air of the oceans. They received less rain and, as a result, dried up. In some regions the drying was exacerbated by mountain building caused by continental margins crunching together during the formation of Pangaea. Newly elevated mountain ranges, such as the Appalachians, not only intercepted moisture-laden air heading inland but also provided sediments to fill the swamps. Thus the extensive swamps of the era dried, and the lepidodendrids wizened.

Lepidodendrids have passed into history, but their compressed, carbonized remains constitute one of the chief constituents of coal, which powers much of modern society. Brightly burning cannel coal—consisting almost entirely of lepidodendrid spores—testifies to how abundant these trees must have been. As I write, most of the energy flowing through my computer comes indirectly from lepidodendrids, whose leaves and trunks (and rhizomorph rootlets?) trapped the energy of sunlight hundreds of millions of years ago and converted it into the chemical energy of carbon–carbon bonds, in which form it has been stored ever since. Their remains fire not only our industry and commerce, but also our curiosity and imagination.

FERN FOSSILS

12
A Horsetail's Tale?

"I have never seen anything which so much astonished me," wrote Richard Spruce, perhaps the greatest botanical explorer of the 19th century. Spruce (1908), who had seen a lot while botanizing in Amazonia for 15 years, was writing about a stand of giant horsetails (*Equisetum*) near the village of Canelos, Ecuador, in the early 1860s:

> the most remarkable plant in the forest of Canelos is a gigantic *Equisetum*, 20 feet [6 m] high, and the stem nearly as thick as the wrist! ... It extends for a distance of a mile [1.6 km] on a plain bordering the Pastasa [Pastaza River] but elevated some 200 feet [60 m] above it, where at every few steps one sinks over the knees in black, white, and red mud. A wood of young larches may give you an idea of its appearance. ... I could also fancy myself in some primeval forest of Calamites, and if some gigantic Saurian had suddenly appeared, crushing its way among the succulent stems, my surprise could hardly have been increased.

The horsetails Spruce was familiar with in his native Yorkshire grew less than 3 feet (1 m) tall. Now he was reminded of the calamites (Calamitaceae), extinct cousins of the horsetails (Equisetaceae) that flourished in the swamps of the Carboniferous 345 million to 280 million years ago (Figure 63). Calamites soared to 60 feet (20 m) tall. Spruce's comment about "some gigantic Saurian" refers to amphibians, the dominant land animals of the Carboniferous, which no doubt thrashed their way through dense thickets of these plants. Is it possible that Spruce *did* find a calamite, thought to have gone extinct about 250 million years ago?

The only other person who claims to have seen a truly gigantic *Equisetum* was Édouard André, a French botanist and explorer. He also traveled to Ecuador, in the 1870s, and reported seeing huge plants near the town of Corazón on the western slopes of the Andes. His book about the trip illustrates the plants as several times taller than a man on horseback, much larger than any *Equisetum* known today (Figure 64). Although the illustration is delightful, André did not collect a voucher specimen to document it, and his claim is taken by professional botanists as it should be—*cum grano salis.* The cynic might even suspect that André intentionally exaggerated the size of the plants to sell more copies of his book and impress readers.

Spruce, however, must be taken seriously. He was a careful and painstaking observer, a first-rate botanist. Unfortunately, we will never know exactly what he saw because he also did not collect a specimen. But it is possible to guess what he saw by considering a few facts about horsetails and calamites.

(Unlike André, Spruce can be excused for not having collected a specimen to support his claim. Spruce was a tireless collector who sold dried, pressed plants to herbaria in Europe as his main source of income. He probably did not collect the giant horsetail at Canelos because he was on an urgent mission—at Her Majesty's behest—to reach the western slopes of the Andes. There he collected seeds of wild quinine trees (*Cinchona*) and smuggled them out of Ecuador aboard a British ship headed for India. The seeds were the starting stock for the extensive quinine plantations developed in India, Sri Lanka, and elsewhere, yielding medicine to fight what was, and still is, one of the world's most widespread and debilitating diseases: malaria. Even today, malaria afflicts about 100 million people around the world, and each year in Africa alone it kills about 1 million children. The best general account of Spruce's collecting activities and his contribution to botany is by von Hagen 1949.)

Horsetails and calamites differ from other plants by their round, hollow, jointed stems. The joints are where the stems can be easily pulled apart into separate, cylindrical segments—an activity that children and immature adults find terribly amusing. In addition, the stems are green, carrying out nearly all the plant's photosynthesis, and they grow in an unusual manner. Like other plants, their growth in length or height comes from the activity of an apical meristem, a group of actively dividing cells at the stem tip. Unlike other plants, this apical meristem gets smaller each time a new stem segment is produced, resulting in narrower and narrower segments, until the apical meristem is used up, and growth ceases. This mode of growth is referred to as apoxogenesis, and horsetails are the only modern-day plants that have it.

Figure 63 A calamite of the Carboniferous. From Hirmer (1927).   **Figure 64** The giant horsetails of Corazón. From André (1883).

The horsetails and calamites are also characterized by un-leaf-like leaves. These are borne in whorls at the stem joints, not spaced individually along the stem. The leaves of each whorl fuse laterally to form a sheath surrounding the base of the stem segment above (Figure 65). The sheath resembles the main stem, but its leaf-like origin is revealed by the presence of leaf tips that appear as teeth along the top edge of the sheath (in some species, such as the winter scouring rush, *Equisetum hyemale*, these tips fall away early and are therefore absent).

Besides their distinctive stems and leaves, horsetails and calamites bear spores in cones produced at the tips of the stems or branches. Each cone is composed of many tightly fitting, polygonal scales attached to a central axis (Figure 66). On the inner surface of the scale are several oblong yellowish sporangia filled with green, photosynthetic spores. When the spores are ripe, the central axis of the cone elongates, separating the scales and exposing the sporangia to the air. Upon drying, the sporangia split lengthwise and release the spores, allowing them to be carried away by air currents. The spores are helped on their journey by four strap-like structures called elaters that catch the wind. The elaters coil and uncoil in response to changes in humidity. When the air is dry they extend outward and create wind resistance so that the spores float (Figure 67). When the air is humid the elaters coil around the spore so that buoyancy decreases and the spore drops—with luck onto moist soil where it can germinate. Elaters occur only in horsetails and calamites and are evidence of the close relationship between these plants.

Although *Equisetum* and calamites share many distinctive characteristics, they differ in two respects. First, calamites bore modified leaves, called bracts, within their cones. Such bracts are absent in *Equisetum*.

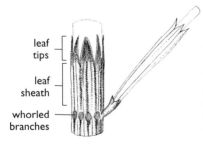

leaf tips

leaf sheath

whorled branches

Figure 65 Portion of stem of *Equisetum*, showing a joint or node, the point at which the whorled branches and leaf sheaths are produced. The stems can be easily pulled apart into separate segments at these joints.

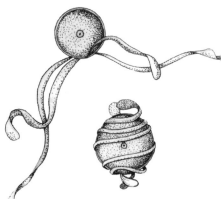

Figure 66 Cone of a scouring rush (*Equisetum hyemale*). The central axis of the cone has elongated, separating the scales (sporangiophores) that bear the sporangia (the small whitish structures attached to the scales).

Figure 67 Spores of *Equisetum* have strap-like appendages (elaters) that spread when the air is dry and coil around the spore when the air is humid.

Second, calamites became tree-like by widening their stems through secondary growth. *Equisetum* lacks this ability, which is why its species remain relatively small; basically, *Equisetum* is like the primary plant body of a calamite. Despite these differences, the two are much alike. It is possible that calamites still exist in a genetic sense, latent within *Equisetum*. Do genes for cambial activity lie dormant and unexpressed in modern-day *Equisetum?* Perhaps with a little genetic engineering we could learn how to turn on these repressed genes to produce a calamite, to create a botanical Jurassic Park.

Species of *Equisetum* have common names based on whether they produce whorls of branches from the stem joints. Those with unbranched stems (Figure 68) are called scouring rushes, referring to their use in scrubbing pots and pans. The plants are perfect for this use because their stems are roughened with tiny bumps of silica. They also conveniently occur along streams and on riverbanks, where pots and pans were washed. Nowadays their stems are used to sand the reeds of woodwind instruments. Species with branched stems are called horsetails because of the bushy appearance imparted by the whorls of branches (Figure 50). It was a horsetail that Spruce saw near Canelos, as is evident from his comparison of the plants to larches (*Larix*), which also bear whorled branches.

It is hard to believe that Spruce found a calamite. The plants have not appeared in the fossil record for the last 250 million years—about half the time that plants have existed on earth. It is unlikely that calamites would have persisted all that time without a trace, especially because they grow in environments where fossils frequently form, such as swamps and marshes. What, then, did Spruce see? South America harbors three species of *Equisetum*, all of which occur in Ecuador. Two grow at middle to high elevations in the Andes and are therefore unlikely to have been seen by Spruce in lowland Amazonia. But the third, *E. giganteum*, occurs in Amazonia and grows to heights of 15 feet (5 m) and widths of ½ inch (13 mm). As the specific epithet implies, it is the largest species in the genus (Figure 69). Spruce's description of the plants'

Figure 68 Unbranched stems of a scouring rush (*Equisetum laevigatum*) with cones at their tips.

Figure 69 Danish botanist Axel Poulsen holding a giant horsetail (*Equisetum giganteum*) in Ecuador.

height (20 feet, about 6 m) is taller than that recorded for *E. giganteum* but within a reasonable margin of error, considering that he was giving only an eyeball estimate. His estimate of the stems being "thick as the wrist" is, however, much more than that recorded in the largest plants today. Although Spruce was not prone to exaggeration in his botanical work, in this case he was probably so impressed by the plants' height that he overestimated their dimensions.

It is most likely that what Spruce saw was a robust, healthy stand of *Equisetum giganteum*. Yet in my more romantic, irrational moments—usually while standing in a patch of horsetails, pulling apart their stems joint by joint—I like to imagine that he *did* find a population of calamites and that those magnificent plants are not extinct after all but hiding somewhere deep within Amazonia, awaiting detection by some intrepid botanical explorer. And why not? The Ecuadorian Amazon is poorly explored. Benjamin Øllgaard, my colleague at Aarhus University in Denmark, is the only pteridologist who has ever collected in the southern region of Ecuador near Canelos, and his trips there have been short and few. Who knows what undiscovered plants still lurk there?

FERN FOSSILS

13
Hangers-on from the Mesozoic

In 1928, Oene Posthumus, a Dutch pteridologist, made a startling discovery. While examining herbarium specimens at the botanical garden in Bogor on Java, he came across an unusual fern from New Guinea and realized that it represented a new species of *Dipteris*. But from his knowledge of paleobotany he also realized that the specimen was a dead-ringer for a Mesozoic fossil fern, one that had presumably been extinct for millions of years (Figure 70). As an expert in the taxonomy of living and fossil ferns, Posthumus must have been thrilled, for he had simultaneously found a new species *and* a living fossil.

Although Posthumus's discovery was remarkable, his chances of finding a living fossil among the Dipteridaceae were actually quite good, and they would have been equally good in the closely related Matoniaceae. These two families are represented by abundant fossils in rocks of the Mesozoic, an era more popularly known as the Age of Dinosaurs (their fossils have not been found in older rocks). The era lasted from 225 million to 65 million years ago, during which time the two fern families reached their zenith. They thrived in the vegetation as the dominant herbaceous, ground-layer plants. They diversified taxonomically, with the Dipteridaceae boasting six genera and at least 60 species, the Matoniaceae eight genera and 26 species (Figure 71). Geographically, they flourished worldwide, occurring on all continents and extending from Greenland and Spitsbergen in the north to Tierra del Fuego and Antarctica in the south (Figures 73 and 74). Where better to find a living fossil than among a group that was abundant, diverse, and widespread?

But if paleobotanists are around millions of years from now and searching for fossils of present-day Dipteridaceae and Matoniaceae, they will not be as lucky. Nowadays the two families are an impoverished lot, a vestige of their former Mesozoic vigor: the Dipteridaceae claims only six species in one genus (*Dipteris*, Figure 72), and the Matoniaceae only four species in two genera (*Matonia*, Figure 72; and *Phanerosorus*). That means that for every one living species there are about nine fossil

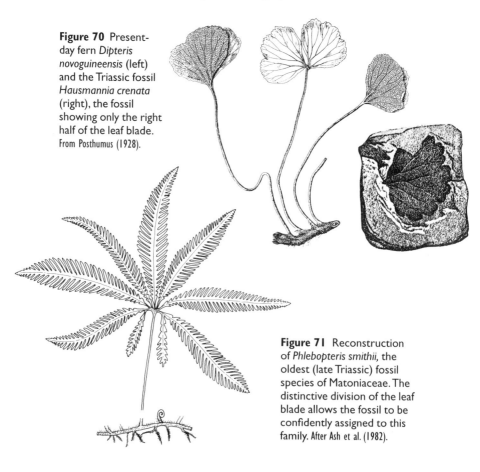

Figure 70 Present-day fern *Dipteris novoguineensis* (left) and the Triassic fossil *Hausmannia crenata* (right), the fossil showing only the right half of the leaf blade. From Posthumus (1928).

Figure 71 Reconstruction of *Phlebopteris smithii*, the oldest (late Triassic) fossil species of Matoniaceae. The distinctive division of the leaf blade allows the fossil to be confidently assigned to this family. After Ash et al. (1982).

ones. This is reflected by about 10 times more scientific papers having been published on the fossils than on living species. Besides being fewer, the living species are far less diverse morphologically than those seen in the fossils, especially in the form and dissection of the leaf blades.

The families are also more restricted geographically. They no longer occur worldwide but are confined to southeastern Asia (Figures 73 and 74). Even in that region the genera and their species tend to have narrow distributions. *Phanerosorus* is found only on Borneo and several small islands off the western coast of New Guinea; *Matonia* is limited to the Philippines, the Malay Peninsula, and Borneo. What caused this decline?

One explanation is ecological, suggested by the kinds of habitats in which the Dipteridaceae and Matoniaceae occur today. The present-day species grow in open or semiopen places. For instance, *Dipteris conjugata* and *Matonia pectinata* (Figure 72, and Plates 9 and 15), the two most widespread species, flourish on exposed mountain ridges and in forest edges and clearings. One place where these two species mingle—as did their ancestors during the Mesozoic—is Mount Ophir on the Malay Peninsula. This habitat was described by English naturalist Alfred Rus-

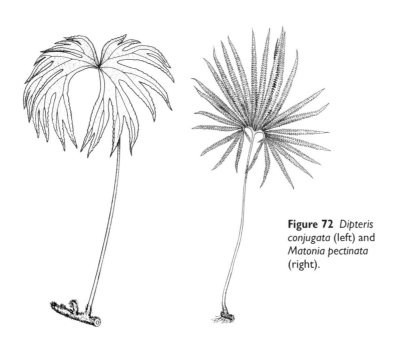

Figure 72 *Dipteris conjugata* (left) and *Matonia pectinata* (right).

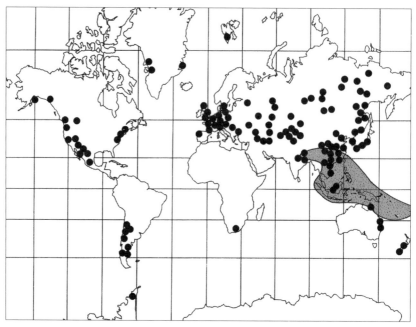

Figure 73 Mesozoic (dots) and present (shaded) distribution of the Dipteridaceae. After Corsin and Waterlot (1979).

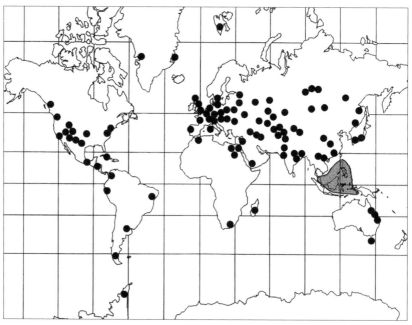

Figure 74 Mesozoic (dots) and present (shaded) distribution of the Matoniaceae. After Corsin and Waterlot (1979).

sel Wallace (codiscoverer with Charles Darwin of the theory of evolution by natural selection) in 1886:

> After passing a little tangled jungle and swampy thickets, we emerged into a fine lofty forest pretty clear of undergrowth, and in which we could walk freely. We ascended steadily up a moderate slope for several miles, having a deep ravine on the left. We then had a level plateau or shoulder to cross, after which the ascent was steeper and the forest denser till we came out upon the "Padang-Bata," or stone-field. . . . Parts of it were quite bare, but where it was cracked or fissured there grew a luxuriant vegetation, among which the Pitcher plants were most remarkable. . . . A few Coniferæ of the genus *Dacrydium* here first appeared, and in the thickets, just above the rocky surface, we walked through groves of those splendid ferns, *Dipteris Horsfieldii* [*D. conjugata*] and *Matonia pectinata*, which bear large spreading palmate fronds on slender stems [petioles], 6 or 8 feet [2 or 2.4 m] high.

Like the *Dipteris* and *Matonia* observed by Wallace, the two species of *Phanerosorus* (the other living genus of Matoniaceae) also grow in open habitats—usually limestone cliffs and often in full sun (Walker and Jermy 1982). In fact, nearly all species in the two families avoid shady habitats, instead growing in lightly shaded forests or sunny places.

Mesozoic species of the Dipteridaceae and Matoniaceae also grew in semiopen forests or open habitats. Early and middle Mesozoic forests were dominated by gymnosperms such as conifers, ginkgoes, Bennettitales, and cycads. Also present, but in fewer numbers, were tree ferns belonging to the Dicksoniaceae. All these plants had generally palm-like or spire-shaped crowns that cast a light shade; thus they tended to form open or semiopen forests where plenty of sunlight reached the ground. Dipteridaceae and Matoniaceae thrived in such forests and also in open habitats where they sometimes formed "fern prairies" along with other ferns (grasses and sedges, which abound in open vegetation today, had not yet evolved).

All this changed in the late Cretaceous, the last period of the Mesozoic. The prevailing gymnospermous trees were gradually replaced by newly evolved angiospermous ones. These new trees towered as tall as 120 feet (40 m) and bore broad crowns with layers of branches that caught much of the sunlight. Beneath these trees were layers of smaller trees and shrubs, as well as vines, epiphytes, and lianas, which intercepted what little light had managed to filter through the canopy. Together these plants cast a dense shade on the forest floor (in tropical rain forests today, the ground usually receives less than 1% of the light above the trees). Thus, as angiosperms replaced gymnosperms in the late Mesozoic, the open and semiopen forests gave way to deeply shaded ones. For the Dipteridaceae and Matoniaceae that had thrived for millions of years, the future looked dark. They were unable to adapt, and during the late Mesozoic their numbers and abundance plummeted. After that, they are virtually unknown in the fossil record.

This cannot be the entire explanation for the families' decline. It does not explain, for example, why they became restricted to southeastern Asia and not elsewhere.

But change in the late Mesozoic was not all bad for ferns. Some eventually adapted to the shady forests and diversified into the species-rich groups we see in today's tropical forests. This is especially true of the polypodiaceous ferns, those that have a sporangium with a vertical annulus interrupted at the stalk (Figure 1). Some of the most evolutionarily specialized members of this group of families, such as the rabbit's-foot ferns (Davalliaceae) and polypodies (Polypodiaceae), are almost entirely epiphytic, adapted to life on the trunks and branches of angiospermous trees. Their evolution was probably promoted by the rise to dominance of deep-shade flowering plant forests at the end of the Cretaceous.

If there was ever an example of the importance of fossils to understanding life on earth, it is the story of the Dipteridaceae and Matoniaceae. Without fossils, how would we know about the past richness and abundance of these ferns worldwide? How would we know about the decline of gymnosperms and rise of angiosperms at the close of the Mesozoic? Plant fossils from the Mesozoic give us reason to rejoice—just as they did for Oene Posthumus.

FERN FOSSILS

14
The Fern Spike

About 25 miles (40 km) south of Copenhagen lies Stevns Klint, a chalky limestone bluff overlooking the Baltic. The bluff is uninterrupted in its whiteness except for a horizontal band of grayish green clay ³⁄₈–4 inches (1–10 cm) thick. The Danes call this layer *fisk ler*, fish clay, because fish bones and scales are found in it. Geologists date its age at 65 million years and have designated it as the official boundary between two great periods of geological time: Cretaceous and Tertiary.

The clay layer marks not only geological time but also one of the most severe extinctions in the history of life on earth. This extinction occurred on land and in the air and sea, dooming 65–70% of the world's species. Its most famous victims were the dinosaurs, but hordes of lesser-known creatures were also wiped out. Particularly hard hit were single-celled organisms: 90% of all genera of protozoans and algae disappeared, and most marine plankton vanished with such dramatic suddenness that they form an abrupt boundary—easily seen in the rocks—referred to by geologists as the "plankton line."

What caused the extinction is hotly debated by scientists from many fields. The evidence with which they wrangle comes from disciplines as diverse as ballistics, climatology, volcanology, mineralogy, paleontology, and astronomy. Particularly thought-provoking has been evidence from palynology, the study of pollen and spores. This botanical sub-discipline has uncovered extraordinary evidence about the mass extinction—evidence largely derived from fossil fern spores.

Before examining this evidence, it is necessary to review the theory that most researchers accept as the best explanation of what caused the extinction. The impact theory claims that an asteroid slammed into the earth, pulverizing itself and nearby crustal rocks. Dust and smoke from the collision flew into the atmosphere and engulfed the entire planet for months or possibly years, blocking sunlight. According to computer simulations by scientists at the National Aeronautics and Space Administration, the earth was so dark that for months you would literally not see your hand in front of your face. Without sunlight, photosynthesis shut down and vegetation perished. Food chains collapsed, causing many animal species to become extinct. Upon settling, the dust cloud that enshrouded the planet formed the clay layer found at nearly all Cretaceous–Tertiary boundary sites around the world, such as the one at Stevns Klint.

In spite of the darkness, there was fire. Scientists postulate that some of the impact's ejecta was hurled above the earth's atmosphere and then reentered the atmosphere hot enough to glow. Heat from this material would have touched off wildfires worldwide. Such a scenario might sound like unsubstantiated gloom and doom, but geologists have found soot in the clay layer that if deposited in only 1–2 years could only have been produced by burning of vegetation equal to half of the world's present forests.

The impact theory is strongly supported by two kinds of evidence also found within the clay layer. The first is the abundance of iridium, a metal rare in the earth's crust but plentiful in asteroids. The second is the presence of shocked quartz grains—tiny quartz crystals with internal deformation bands caused by tremendous sudden pressure. Besides the boundary clay, such quartz grains are found only at meteorite craters and nuclear test sites.

Geologists believe that they have found the impact crater where the asteroid hit. The Chicxulub crater lies off Mexico's Yucatán Peninsula and is exactly the right age: 65 million years. It measures about 110 miles (175 km) wide, and to form a crater that big, scientists estimate that the asteroid must have been about 10 miles (16 km) in diameter. Upon impact, it would have released the energy of roughly 1000 times that of all the world's nuclear weapons exploded simultaneously. In short, according to the impact theory, the earth's vegetation at the close of the Cretaceous looked like the charred landscape of a forest-fire prevention poster.

Palynological studies of Cretaceous–Tertiary boundary rocks from around the world reveal a startling change. In the late Cretaceous, fossil fern spores account for 15–30% of the total pollen and spore microfossil record, with seed-plant pollen accounting for the rest. But immediately above the boundary, in the earliest Tertiary rocks, fern spores jump to as much as 99% of the total. Then, within the next 4–6 inches (10–15 cm) of overlying rock, the percentages drop to previous levels. Palynologists refer to this jump as the fern spike because of the sharp, upward-pointing V that results when the percentages are plotted on a graph (Figure 75). The first plants to revegetate early Tertiary landscapes were ferns. Later, the ferns were largely replaced by more slowly growing seed plants.

What could have caused such an explosion in the fern population? Ferns readily invade disturbed environments such as bare volcanic slopes

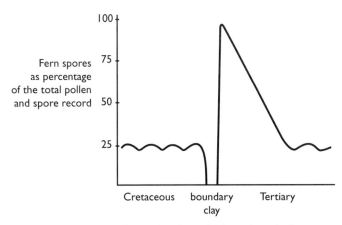

Figure 75 The fern spike, above the boundary clay layer.

or recently burned forests. They colonize quickly and in large numbers by producing billions of spores carried by the wind. It seems likely that when the land lay ravaged after the asteroid impact, ferns formed an advance guard for plant succession. They moved in, established a foothold, and prepared the landscape for other plants. For a while (scientists cannot say how long with certainty), ferns dominated the vegetation, turning the landscape green once again with the lush growth of their leaves. Their abundance in the postimpact vegetation accounts for the high percentage of spores in rocks of that age.

The fern spike gives scientists a rare view of the extinction. Most other biological evidence about the extinction is taxonomic—an accounting of the number of species, genera, and families that dropped out in the final stage of the Cretaceous. In contrast, the fern spike shows change at an ecological level. It tells of the reorganizations that occurred within plant communities and the fluctuations in the relative abundance of plants.

The end of the Cretaceous is commonly associated with the demise of the dinosaurs; hardly anyone thinks about plants. But what revegetated the toasted terrains of the early Tertiary tells a story just as crucial to understanding what happened 65 million years ago as the extinctions themselves. Critical evidence comes not only from organisms with box-office appeal such as the dinosaurs, but also from more modest beings such as ferns.

FERN FOSSILS

15

How Old Are Ferns?

It is often said that ferns are an old group, having evolved long before the gymnosperms and flowering plants that dominate landscapes today. This is only partly true, however, and in some ways downright misleading. Geologically speaking, the great bulk of today's fern families and genera are of recent origin, having evolved *after* the appearance of the first flowering plants. Understanding this sheds light on certain aspects of fern biogeography.

The oldest fern fossils date back to the early Carboniferous about 345 million years ago. This was a time when amphibians and reptiles first roamed the land and insects first took to the air; dinosaurs, birds, and mammals had not yet evolved. Fossil remains of these early ferns can be confidently identified as such because their sporangia resemble those of certain modern-day ferns, but these ancient ferns differed greatly from those of today. Most had stems that branched repeatedly and at odd places to form elaborate shoot systems, and the arrangement of their internal vascular tissues (xylem and phloem) was unlike anything found in ferns today. Because of these differences, they are classified in their own families apart from modern ferns—families with spellbinding names such as Anachoropteridaceae, Botryopteridaceae, and Psalixochlaenaceae. They went extinct by the end of the Carboniferous or early Permian roughly 290 million to 270 million years ago, but before doing so they or their relatives gave rise to lineages leading to present-day ferns.

By comparison, the oldest fossil gymnosperms, all of which belong to families now extinct, also date back to the early Carboniferous, roughly 340 million years ago. They are about as old as ferns. As for flowering plants, they first appeared during the early Cretaceous, about 140 million years ago, about 200 million years *after* the first ferns and gymnosperms.

If the ages of extinct fossil groups are omitted, and only the ages of present-day families of ferns and gymnosperms are considered, do the ferns turn out to be older? The present-day fern family with the longest fossil record is the Marattiaceae, which thrives in wet, shaded, tropical forests around the world. It arose in the lower Carboniferous, about 340 million years ago, and was represented by *Psaronius,* a genus of extinct tree ferns that flourished in the peat-forming swamps of the period. By comparison, the oldest extant gymnosperm families are the ginkgoes (Ginkgoaceae) and cycads (Cycadaceae, sometimes divided into three families), which first appeared in the late Permian, about 225 million years ago. Thus if present-day families are compared, ferns are about 70 million years older than gymnosperms.

The Marattiaceae, however, is a relatively small group of ferns, containing only about 100 species of the approximately 12,000 worldwide. What about the majority of fern species? How do their ages compare to that of the earliest angiosperms and gymnosperms?

About 80% of all ferns belong to families that are known collectively as the polypodiaceous, or "derived leptosporangiate," ferns. They are characterized by an annulus that encircles the sporangium for nearly three-quarters of its circumference and that stops at the stalk (Figure 1). These ferns also share major similarities in the sequence and structure of their DNA. Examples of common polypodiaceous ferns are the spleenworts (Aspleniaceae), chain ferns (Blechnaceae), wood ferns (Dryopteridaceae), and polypodies (Polypodiaceae). Undisputed polypodiaceous ferns first appear in the fossil record during the late Cretaceous, about 75 million years ago. This makes them *younger* than the first

130

flowering plants and gymnosperms, which appear in the fossil record about 140 million and 230 million years ago, respectively. So much for the notion that all ferns are older than flowering plants!

The nonpolypodiaceous, or "basal leptosporangiate," ferns include groups such as the tree ferns (Cyatheaceae and Dicksoniaceae), forked ferns (Gleicheniaceae), royal ferns (Osmundaceae), and filmy ferns (Hymenophyllaceae). The position of their annulus varies, but most are characterized by a complete, oblique annulus, that is, one tilted at an angle so that it bypasses the stalk and completely encircles the spore case (Figure 43). These ferns have a longer fossil record than the polypodiaceous ferns, dating back to the early Permian, about 270 million years ago.

But the relatively recent origin of the majority of ferns—the polypodiaceous ones—helps explain how certain species or groups of species came to be shared between different regions or continents. For example, the American tropics and Africa–Madagascar share 27 species of ferns and lycophytes that do not occur anywhere else in the world. The two regions also harbor 87 pairs of sister species or groups of closely related species, in which one member of the pair occurs in the American tropics and the other in Africa–Madagascar. How did two regions separated by the Atlantic Ocean come to share the same species or pairs of closely related ones?

There are two possible explanations. First, there is long-distance dispersal of spores. It might seem hard to believe that spores could travel all the way across the Atlantic Ocean, much less survive such a long trip, but fern spores can be carried long distances by the wind, and they have been found in the high atmosphere. Experiments have shown that they can tolerate the cold temperatures and the intense ultraviolet radiation present in the upper troposphere. Second, there is continental drift. This explanation claims that the same species, or pairs of closely related species (or the ancestors of such pairs), were present on the landmass formed by Africa–Madagascar and South America before the continents drifted apart.

How can one choose between these two explanations? This is where age of ferns comes in. According to geologists, South America and

Africa began separating in the south about 120 million years ago and were finally severed at their last point of connection (near the present-day Ivory Coast and the easternmost bulge of Brazil) about 95 million years ago. This is 20 million years *before* the polypodiaceous ferns evolved. Because such ferns did not exist when South America and Africa–Madagascar were joined, continental drift cannot explain the existence of the same species of polypodiaceous ferns on both continents (Moran and Smith 2001). Long-distance dispersal probably gave rise to the similarities. The same argument can be made for the fern species in common between New Zealand and Australia. For a long time it was believed that the occurrence of these species in both regions was a legacy of continental drift. But New Zealand and Australia were isolated by continental drift about 80 million years ago. This was long before most ferns, the polypodiaceous ferns, ever existed (or perhaps not; see Schneider et al. 2004); therefore, drift cannot account for joint New Zealand–Australian distributions (Brownsey 2001, Perrie et al. 2003). Continental drift could be invoked for geologically older fern families such as the tree ferns (Cyatheaceae and Dicksoniaceae), filmy ferns (Hymenophyllaceae), and anemias and climbing ferns (Schizaeaceae), but even for them the possibility of long-distance dispersal cannot be ruled out.

The fossil record reveals that some fern species can be extremely old, exhibiting little or no change throughout their long history. Evolutionary biologists call this lack of change stasis. The interrupted fern (*Osmunda claytoniana*), which grows nowadays only in eastern North America (Figure 38), has the longest duration of any living fern species, being known from fossils in Antarctica of late Triassic age, about 200 million years (Phipps et al. 1998). Another old species is the sensitive fern (*Onoclea sensibilis*) of eastern North America and eastern Asia (Figures 52 and 112). Its fossils have been found in early Tertiary rocks about 55 million years old in Greenland, the western United States, Canada, Japan, easternmost Russia, and the United Kingdom (Rothwell and Stockey 1991). How does the duration of the interrupted and sensitive ferns compare to species of flowering plants? The average span of a flowering plant species in the fossil record is about 3.5 million years (Niklas et al. 1983), so the interrupted and sensitive ferns have persisted for a long time. (Paleontologists have yet to calculate the average duration for fern species.)

Although some fern species are old, others can be quite young. The tropical American genus *Jamesonia* is a good example. It contains about 20 species, all of which have stiffly erect, linear leaves tipped by a fiddlehead that never completely uncoils (Figure 76 and Plate 14). Its pinnae are small, round, and crowded together, packed on top of one another like a stack of coins. *Jamesonia* grows only in páramo, a type of treeless, alpine vegetation generally above 9000 feet (3000 m), mostly in the Andes. Only within the past 2 million to 3 million years have the Andes been thrust high enough to allow páramo vegetation to form, suggesting that *Jameso-nia* is only 3 million years old or younger—recent by geological standards. (By comparison, our own genus, *Homo*, first appeared about 2 million years ago.) This same reasoning about recentness applies to about 60 species of *Huperzia* (Lycopodiaceae; Plate 11), also restricted to páramos.

Finally, some fern species might be much younger. This appears to be the case for the log fern (*Dryopteris celsa*), a species of eastern North America, which probably originated during the last glacial maximum, only 18,000 years ago. The log fern is a fertile species that arose by the processes of hybridization and polyploidy illustrated by the Tennessee bladder fern (Figure 27). Strangely, the ranges of its two parents do not overlap—something that would be

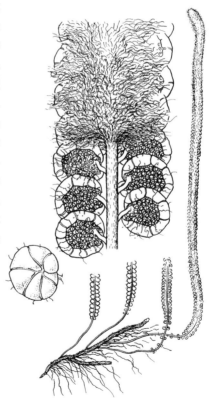

Figure 76 *Jamesonia*, a genus characteristic of páramos. In the close-up, the wooly hairs have been removed from the lower pinnae, revealing the enrolled pinna margins (false indusia) and sporangia. At the lower left is the upper surface of a pinna. From Mickel and Beitel (1988).

necessary for hybridization to occur. One parent, Goldie's wood fern (*D. goldiana*), is distributed from Maine to the southern Appalachians, to Minnesota, and the other parent, the southern wood fern (*D. ludoviciana*), is restricted primarily to the coastal plain of North Carolina to Louisiana. How did these two species get together and hybridize to form the log fern? It seems likely that during the last major glaciation, Goldie's wood fern was pushed south until it came into contact with the southern wood fern. The two species then hybridized. After the glaciers retreated, Goldie's wood fern advanced northward and gradually came to occupy the its more northern range. The southern wood fern remained in the southern coastal plain and Gulf States, and their the hybrid log fern came to occupy an intermediate range with slight overlap between both parents. If true—and it seems likely it is—then the log fern is of very recent origin, geologically speaking.

The problem with the notion that ferns are an old group is that it lumps together about 12,000 species of present-day ferns that originated at different times and places. Some of these species are old and have a long fossil history, but most (about 80%) are recent, belonging to families younger than the first flowering plants. Indeed, some fern species appear to have evolved only within the last 2 million to 3 million years, and some only since the last Ice Age. Ferns did not arise simultaneously as a single monolithic group, yet regardless of where and when they appeared, may they all live long and prosper!

ADAPTATIONS BY FERNS

16
The Potato Fern

Getting acquainted with the potato fern, the tropical American genus *Solanopteris,* can be a painful experience. In modified stems that resemble small potatoes (Figures 77 and 78, and Plate 25) it harbors fierce ants, especially those of the genera *Azteca* and *Camponotus.* If you poke the fern, even slightly, ants rush out of the stems and swarm over your fingers and run up your wrists until they find a tender place to clamp onto vengefully. They did that to me the first time I collected one of these ferns in Costa Rica. It felt like the hairs were being singed off my hands.

Do not worry about this if you visit a rain forest anywhere from Costa Rica to Peru, the range in which potato ferns occur (Figure 79). Chances are you will not see any of the five species because they thrive high in the forest canopy, usually on the outermost portions of branches and twigs. Like other epiphytes, they derive all their nutrients from rain, dust, and organic matter that falls from above; they are *not* parasites on the host tree. With luck you might spot a potato fern on a fallen branch or among the tree branches bordering sunny riverbanks, but there is little chance you will get bitten by ants unless you disturb the fern.

The so-called potatoes inhabited by the ants develop from short lateral branches. These are borne along slender, long-creeping stems typ-

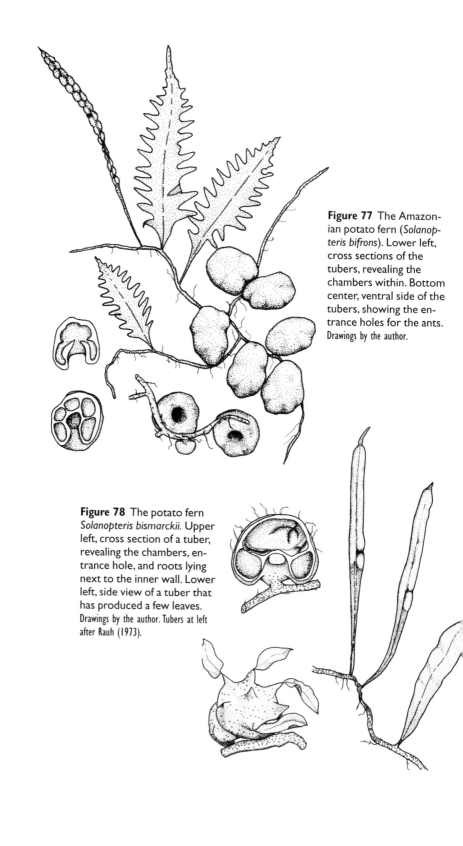

Figure 77 The Amazonian potato fern (*Solanopteris bifrons*). Lower left, cross sections of the tubers, revealing the chambers within. Bottom center, ventral side of the tubers, showing the entrance holes for the ants. Drawings by the author.

Figure 78 The potato fern *Solanopteris bismarckii*. Upper left, cross section of a tuber, revealing the chambers, entrance hole, and roots lying next to the inner wall. Lower left, side view of a tuber that has produced a few leaves. Drawings by the author. Tubers at left after Rauh (1973).

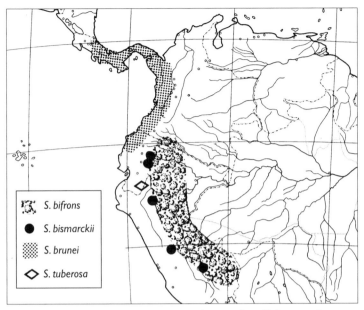

Figure 79 Distributions of four species of potato fern (*Solanopteris*).

ical of most species of Polypodiaceae. The short lateral stems swell and become about the size a golf ball (Hagemann 1969). Although they do not look like stems, their stem-like nature is revealed by the fact that they occasionally bear leaves (Figure 78). Potato-like stems develop on plants in cultivation even though ants are absent. Because the modified stems resemble potatoes, they are called tubers, the botanical name for this kind of structure. The potato-like appearance is alluded to in the name *Solanopteris* (from *Solanum*, the genus of potatoes, and *pteris*, fern).

Solanopteris differs from the closely related *Microgramma* only by the presence of tubers. It has been shown that *Solanopteris* is nested (Chapter 7) among the species of *Microgramma* on the fern evolutionary tree. For this reason, botanists now classify the species of *Solanopteris* in *Microgramma* (León and Beltrán 2002; see Chapter 7 for a discussion of the rationale of why this is done and the problems in recognizing paraphyletic groups taxonomically).

There is an entrance hole for the ants on the ventral surface of the tuber. Inside, the tubers contain hollow chambers with smooth inner walls. Roots sprout around the rim of the entrance hole and grow *into* the chambers instead of out into the surrounding substrate. Once inside, the roots flatten themselves against the walls of the chambers and bear a dense covering of absorbent brown hairs (Figure 78).

At first, botanists thought the tubers collected and stored rainwater trickling through the entrance hole. This idea was discarded when field observations showed that the tubers were held close to the surface of the branches and their entrance holes were oriented downward—not what you would expect if they collected rainwater. Later observations painstakingly established that ants were associated with the plants, and botanists came to realize that the tubers sheltered ants, providing them with a safe place to lay eggs and brood young. The ants also enjoy a free meal by munching on the soft, juicy, inner tissue of young tubers—an activity that widens the chambers for the ants' future use. In return, the plants received protection from their tiny boarders.

It turns out, however, that the early idea about tubers holding water was partly correct, but not because water trickles into the entrance hole. The ants bring organic debris into the tubers and leave behind dead pupae and frass, all of which decomposes to form rich organic humus. This accumulates within the tubers, leaving no room for ants. The ants abandon clogged-up tubers and set up housekeeping in fresh, unsullied ones. The deserted tubers undergo a change: they shrink slightly, compacting the humus within, and their outer walls degrade, becoming permeable to water. The humus within absorbs any water that permeates the tubers, and this water and any dissolved nutrients are imbibed by the roots plastered against the inner walls of the tuber. The abandoned, humus-filled tubers are like little sodden sponge balls sitting high up on the branches in the forest canopy (Gómez 1974, 1977, Wagner 1972).

These sponges provide a life-giving supply of water for the plants. Although potato ferns grow in rain forests where moisture generally abounds, the canopy can be a harsh, drought-prone environment, subject to withering sunlight, scorching temperatures, and parching winds. These factors are far more severe in the canopy than on the forest floor, and epiphytes, which cannot rely on a constant supply of moisture from the soil, are in danger of dehydration.

Solanopteris is the only tropical American genus of ferns to have evolved a symbiotic relationship with ants—it is the only myrmeco-phytic one in the New World. In the Old World tropics, there is also only one fern genus that has evolved ant-inhabited stems: *Lecanopteris.* It comprises about 13 species, all found in southeastern Asia, mostly in the archipelago from Sumatra to New Guinea. *Lecanopteris* also belongs to the Polypodiaceae but is not closely related to potato ferns. *Lecanopteris* differs from *Solanopteris* by having only one kind of stem, and this stem is greatly widened and flattened as if someone had stepped on it. Within this stem are extensive galleries where the ants live (Gay 1991, 1993).

Because of their relationship with ants, potato ferns have received more attention than most in the American tropics, yet much remains to be learned about them. The ant–fern relationship has been studied in the field primarily in one species from Costa Rica. Surely, exciting things are waiting to be found in the South American species—discoveries that could turn out to be more than just small potatoes.

ADAPTATIONS BY FERNS

17

How Ferns Become Trees

Answer this: a tree grows 6 inches (15 cm) taller per year. If you nail a sign to its trunk 4 feet (120 cm) above the ground and return 2 years later, how high will the sign be? Beguiled by the numbers involved, some people answer 5 feet (150 cm). But the correct response is 4 feet (120 cm). The sign stays at the same height because any segment of a mature tree trunk grows only in width, not in height.

Growth in width is vital to becoming a tree. Trees must be able to widen their stems to support the increasing weight of new branches and leaves above. Without this ability, the stems would buckle. The trees around us—mostly conifers and dicotyledonous flowering plants—widen their stems by producing wood from a thin layer of dividing cells, the vascular cambium, located just beneath the bark. This growth in girth produces the rings of wood seen on cut trunks. Growing wide and woody is so common that we tend to think of it as the only way to become a tree. Yet ferns lack the ability to produce wood and thereby widen their stems. How, then, do they become tree-like?

Tree ferns (Plate 7) have evolved two basic methods for arborescent growth. First, they strengthen their stems internally with hardened tissue called sclerenchyma (from the Greek *scleros*, hard). This tissue runs lengthwise along the stem, surrounding the conducting tissues (xylem and phloem) and around the periphery of the stem (Figures 80 and 81). This reinforces the stem like steel rods used in concrete pillars. (Botanically speaking, sclerenchyma cannot be called wood because it lacks conducting cells and is not produced by a vascular cambium.) Because sclerenchyma is strong and resists rot, tree fern trunks are choice material for construction in the backwoods of the tropics. In the American tropics, it is common to see tree fern trunks supporting foundations of thatch-roofed houses or roofs of open porches.

Also, it is comon to see tree ferns left standing, like lonely sentinels, after forests have been cleared for pastures. Farmers generally do not cut tree ferns because the sclerenchyma is so hard that it quickly dulls an ax or chain saw. In fact, it is downright dangerous to cut tree ferns with a chain saw. Shreds of sclerenchyma get caught between the chain and blade, snapping the chain and causing it to fly off. If a farmer manages to cut down a tree fern and leaves it lying in his pasture, there is another problem. The trunks may take 10–15 years to decompose, during which time cattle are prone to trip over them. So farmers usually leave tree ferns standing, and the result is scenic, tree-fern-studded pastures.

The second way that ferns become trees is by propping up their stems with an external layer of dense, wiry, interlocking roots. This layer, the root mantle, is usually two to five times wider than the diameter of the stem (Figure 82). Rigid and durable, it protects the stem like a coat of mail and, more important, effectively widens the stem, thereby enabling it to support the weight of the plant above. The root mantle is usually widest at the base of the trunk where it has had more time to develop.

Root mantles have been put to some unusual uses. They can be cut into blocks called tree fern fiber for use as a substrate for growing epiphytic orchids. Horticulturists treasure tree fern fiber because it is durable and orchids take to it readily. Tree fern fiber is now hard to find for sale in nurseries because it is illegal to import tree ferns, all species of which are protected under CITES, the convention regulating international trade in endangered species of plants and animals. Another use is carving into flowerpots or statues (Plate 8). In Mexico, such carv-

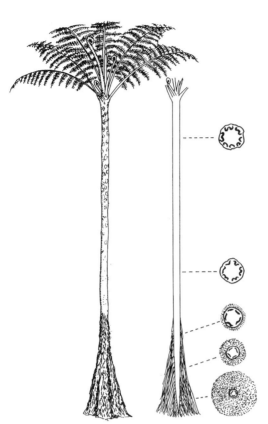

Figure 81 Cross section of a tree fern (*Cyathea*) trunk. Black tissue (sclerenchyma) surrounds conducting tissue (xylem and phloem) and runs up and down the trunk, lending structural support. Photograph by Benjamin Øllgaard.

Figure 80 Structure of a typical tree fern. Left, growth habit—note the widening root mantle at the base of the trunk. Middle, longitudinal section of the plant at left—note how the stem tapers toward the base. Right, cross sections at various levels of the trunk. Stippling represents the root mantle, and the black squiggly lines represent sclerenchyma that runs up and down the trunk for support.

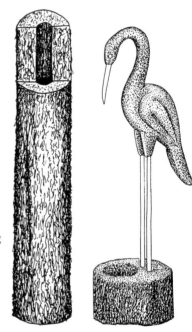

Figure 82 Left, tree fern trunk with the root mantle surrounding an empty cylinder formerly occupied by the stem. Right, example of *maquique* from Mexico, carved from a root mantle of a tree fern trunk; the hole in the base is where the stem was removed.

ing is called *maquique* (Figure 82). Both uses rely on the toughness of the root mantles, testifying to how well they serve in supporting the stem.

Perhaps the most unusual use of tree fern trunks is found in the islands of Vanuatu (formerly the New Hebrides), northeast of New Caledonia. People there carve the trunks into stylized images of faces or full figures and then coat them with a thin layer of clay or mud that, when dry, is painted with vegetable or mineral colors (Figure 83). These have two uses. The main one is for the series of rituals that accompany a man's elevation in religious and social rank. For each advance in grade, a skilled craftsman is hired to carve a tree fern figure that will be used in the ceremony, then left to slowly decay on the ceremonial ground.

Also in Vanuatu, tree fern trunks are carved to represent the heads of ancestors and are mounted over the doors of men's ceremonial houses as a finial projecting horizontally from the top of the roof. The ancestor's face looks downward upon anyone entering or leaving the lodge, sizing people up as to whether they have broken taboo and should not enter the building. If someone has done something they should not, then the ancestor can make them sick through supernatural punishment.

Root mantles were present in *Psaronius* (Marattiaceae), the oldest fossil

Figure 83 Ceremonial figures from Vanuatu (left, Ambrym Island; right, Banks Island) carved about 1900 from root mantles of tree fern trunks. The figure on the right shows traces of the light-colored plaster-like coating that was painted on it; headdresses of leaves or feathers would have been placed on top. In both sculptures the tree ferns are upside-down; tree ferns are widest toward the base, where the root mantle has had the most time to accumulate. Courtesy of Metropolitan Museum of Art, the Michael C. Rockefeller Memorial Collection, gift of Nelson A. Rockefeller, 1972.

fern known. It thrived alongside calamites and lepidodendrids in the coal swamps of the Carboniferous 345 million to 280 million years ago. Thanks to its root mantle, its trunks reached 9 feet (3 m) tall. The root mantles had a secondary, incidental function: they served as a substrate for many species of epiphytes. These plants threaded their roots and stems through the mantle, gaining a firm foothold on the side of the trunk (Rothwell and Roessler 2000). The same thing still happens on tree ferns (Cyatheaceae and Dicksoniaceae) in tropical forests today. In fact, some present-day species of fern epiphytes grow almost exclusively on tree fern root mantles, and others grow there in much greater frequency and abundance than on the trunks of seed plants, which lack a root mantle (Moran et al. 2003).

Another ancient tree fern that used roots for support is *Tempskya*, which thrived in North America, Europe, and Japan during the Cretaceous 141 million to 65 million years ago. Its trunks grew to 18 feet (6 m) tall and 1 1/2 feet (0.5 m) wide. *Tempskya* was unlike anything today, with a trunk formed by a matrix of dense roots that supported numerous, branched, pencil-thick stems (Figure 84). In some cross sections, as many as 180 stems can be counted, but these did little to support the trunk—that work was done by the matrix of roots. This support is especially evident at the base of trunks more than 10 inches (25 cm) wide, where the stems have usually rotted away completely, leaving only the roots to bear the weight of the trunk (Figure 83). *Tempskya* became a kind of self-supporting epiphyte.

The many-stemmed construction of a *Tempskya* trunk imparted a peculiar appearance to the tree (Figure 84). Unlike today's tree ferns, which bear their leaves at the top of the trunk, *Tempskya* bore its leaves along the length of the trunk. Nobody knows what fern family *Tempskya* belonged to, although many suspect the Schizaeaceae. For the sake of convenience it is usually placed in its own family, Tempskyaceae.

Another fern family that produced arborescent species in the past is Osmundaceae. Most species today, such as the cinnamon fern (*Osmunda cinnamomea*), interrupted fern (*O. claytoniana*), and royal fern (*O. regalis*), have short underground stems that might become massive but not treelike. But during the Mesozoic, the family gave rise to tree genera such as

Osmundicaulis, Palaeosmunda (Plate 16), *Thamnopteris*, and *Zalesskya.* They widened their stems by investing it with tightly overlapping, hardened leaf bases (petioles) and, to a lesser extent, roots that ran through and between these, binding them together (Plate 16).

I once got a lesson in how hard *Osmunda* leaf bases are and, by extension, how well they would have supported a central stem in a tree-like fossil species. I was taking a pteridology course at Mountain Lake Biological Station in western Virginia, a course offered by Warren H. (Herb) Wagner, Jr., one of my thesis advisors. One day he requested that I prepare a cross section of an *Osmunda* rootstock to show to the class. I dug up a plant and tried cutting through the leaf bases with a new razor blade; it barely nicked the surface. I had to resort to a carpenter's saw, eventually accomplishing the task. The result, however, was worth it. The sectioned rootstock revealed a narrow, white stem dwarfed in the center by the surrounding armor of many black leaf bases. Although narrower, this rootstock differed little in basic structure from the trunks of its Mesozoic relatives.

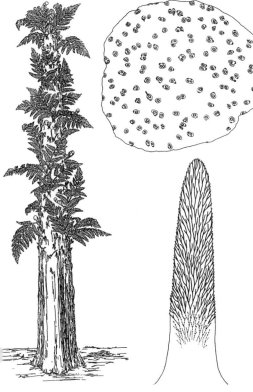

Figure 84 *Tempskya,* a fossil tree fern from the Cretaceous. Left, growth habit, showing leaves borne along the length of the trunk. Upper right, cross section of trunk, showing the numerous stems embedded in the root mantle. Lower right, longitudinal section through a trunk, showing stems branching as they grew upward; dotted lines toward the base represent decaying stems. From Andrews and Kerns (1947) with permission from the Missouri Botanical Garden.

Besides ferns, the tree habit evolved among the lycophytes. Although lycophytes lack arborescent species today, some of their relatives in the Carboniferous, the lepidodendrids, were trees of gigantic proportions (Chapter 11). They towered 30–165 feet (10–55 m) tall and had trunks as wide as 6 feet (2 m), which is large even in comparison to today's trees. But they became arborescent by increasing the outer bark layer (Figure 85); they did not produce wood. Lepidodendrids produced bark in such prodigious amounts that it forms one of the chief constituents of the coal in certain Illinois mines.

Growing alongside the lepidodendrids were the calamites (Calamitaceae; Chapter 11), the relatives of modern horsetails (Equisetaceae; Chapter 12). Their trunks soared to 90 feet (30 m) tall and 24 inches (60 cm) wide and were supported by widening layer of wood produced by a vascular cambium. In this respect they became arborescent in a manner similar to the arborescent species of flowering plants and conifers.

Ferns and lycophytes show that there is more than one way to achieve the same result. Not all plants must become arborescent by widening their stems with wood to support their increasing weight. Hardened tissues, root mantles, sheathing leaf bases, and enlarged outer bark work just as well. We must toss out the notion that all plants become trees the same way as pines and pecans. If we do not, we will be barking up the wrong tree.

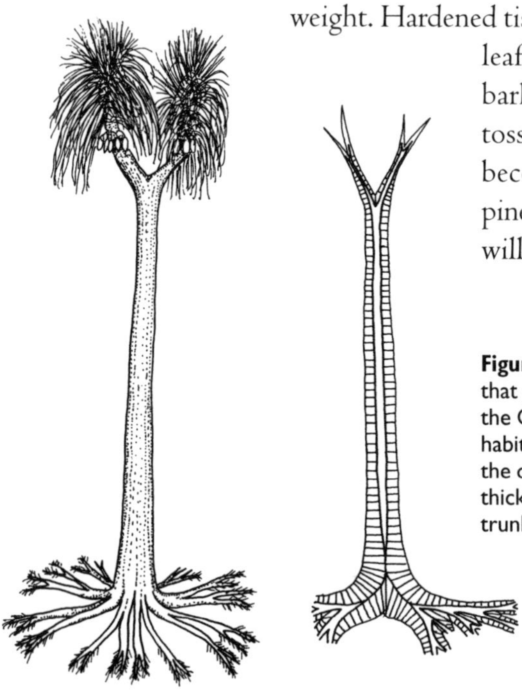

Figure 85 *Sigillaria,* a lycophyte that grew in the coal swamps of the Carboniferous. Left, growth habit. Right, longitudinal section; the outer bark layer (ruled) was thickened and supported the trunk.

ADAPTATIONS BY FERNS

18

Iridescent Ferns
and Their Shady Behavior

I first laid eyes on *Trichomanes elegans,* a terrestrial species of filmy fern (Figure 86), in February 1988 after arriving in a remote rain forest in Panama. The plant was growing along a dark trail and stood out because of its brilliant, metallic blue-green leaf. The color was so intense, and the blade so thick and shiny, that the plant looked like the plastic ferns occasionally seen in cemeteries, inexpensive restaurants, and outdoor floral displays. For a moment, I thought that it *was* a plastic fern put there by my waggish collecting partner.

I rubbed the leaf blade between my fingers—it was real, sure enough. But the metallic blue-green still seemed phony. As I viewed the blade from different angles, the color shimmered over the surface, but when the blade was viewed nearly edge-on, the color vanished and the leaf assumed the normal green of chlorophyll. Would anyone back home believe me about the colors? I decided to photograph the plant and uncased my camera loaded with high-speed film for the deep shade of the forest floor. I aimed, focused, and pushed the light-meter button. The meter's needle plunged to zero—too dark. A photograph would have to wait for another plant in a brighter spot.

After returning to the United States, I learned that this was my first encounter with an iridescent fern. Only a handful of fern species are iridescent, all of them tropical (Plate 10). They glisten metallic colors like the *Trichomanes*, but some are sky blue rather than blue-green. I wondered what strange alchemy produced iridescence, and how it benefited the plants, if at all. A trip to the library revealed that the answers to these questions had been sought for, not surprisingly, by several botanists.

The first to investigate iridescence was Ernst Stahl, a German morphologist working in Bogor on Java. In 1896 he examined an iridescent selaginella (*Selaginella willdenowii*, Plate 24) and speculated that its blue metallic sheen was caused by granules of a reflective pigment embedded in the cuticle—the thin, nonliving layer of fat or wax covering the outer walls of the plant's epidermis.

No further research was done on iridescence for 75 years, when Denis Fox and James Wells, researchers from the Cranbrook Institute of Science in Michigan, reexamined the same species studied by Stahl. They observed that when the plant's leaves were wetted with water or alcohol, or were allowed to wilt, the iridescence disappeared. Conversely, when wet leaves were allowed to dry, or when wilted leaves regained their turgidity, the iridescence reappeared. Fox and Wells (1971) concluded from these observations that iridescence must be caused by an optical effect rather than a pigment.

The next step forward was in the mid-1970s from David Lee, presently at Florida International University and one of the world's leading authorities on how leaves interact with light. He pointed out

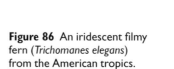

Figure 86 An iridescent filmy fern (*Trichomanes elegans*) from the American tropics.

148

that *Selaginella willdenowii* contains no iridescent pigments extractable with organic solvents and that any such pigments are unknown in plants and animals. Furthermore, studies with a light microscope did not reveal pigment granules embedded in the cuticle. These observations (Lee 1977, 1986, Lee and Lowry 1975), along with those of Fox and Wells, nailed the lid on the coffin of the pigment hypothesis.

But how is the iridescence produced? Lee pointed out that the behavior of the colors could be explained by an optical phenomenon called thin-film interference. This occurs when a thin layer or film is present between two substances with different light-refracting qualities, such as water and air. Depending on the thickness and refractive index of the film, certain wavelengths of light (colors) constructively or destructively interfere after they are reflected from the top and bottom layers of the thin film. If the crest of the wave reflected from the bottom layer coincides, after having traveled back up through the layer, with the crest of the wave reflected off the top of the layer, then the light waves reinforce each other, and the color intensifies. Such waves are said to constructively interfere (Figure 87). If the two waves do not coincide after reflection from the top and bottom surfaces of the thin layer—if they are out of synch, with the crest of one wave lining up with the trough of the other—the two waves cancel, or destructively interfere. In this situation, no color of a given wavelength is produced, and the apparently

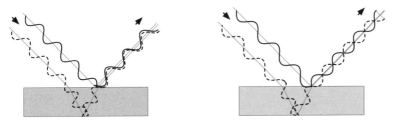

Figure 87 The principle of thin-film interference. The shaded rectangle represents a thin film, which has a refractive index different from that of the material above and below it. The difference causes light to be reflected from the top and bottom surfaces of the film. If the reflected waves align in unison (left), they reinforce each other (constructive interference) and produce iridescence. If the crest of one wave aligns with the trough of the other (right), the two waves cancel each other (destructive interference) and no color is produced.

paradoxical situation arises in which light plus light equals darkness. In *Selaginella* and *Trichomanes* the thin layers are just the right thickness so that blue light is intensified by constructive interference and nearly all other wavelengths cancel because of destructive interference.

Although this explanation of interference colors might seem strange or hard to understand, the phenomenon is familiar to everyone. It causes the rings of rainbow colors seen on puddles or wet asphalt covered by a film of oil. It produces the colors seen on coated lenses of cameras and binoculars, as well as the metallic colors on the wings of certain butterflies and beetles. It also gives rise to the colors seen on the surfaces of bubbles that form over coffee grinds on a filter after boiling water has been poured over them. The surfaces of the bubbles exhibit small patches of swirling colors spanning the entire spectrum, from red to green to blue. The particular color depends on the thickness of the bubble's thin film (the film tends to be thinnest toward the top of the bubble and thickest toward the base). The colors can be easily seen against the dark background of the coffee grinds; a lighter background would backscatter incident light, diluting the colors.

Lee suspected that iridescence in *Selaginella willdenowii* is caused by a thin layer in the upper epidermis. This layer would reflect more blue light and transmit more red; thus the leaf would appear blue. In 1978 he began a search for the predicted thin layer with Charles Hébant from the University of Montpellier, France. They started by calculating the exact thickness of a thin layer necessary to reflect blue light in a plant cell wall. That thickness turned out to be 71–80 nm (a nanometer, nm, being only a billionth of a meter). They prepared extremely thin cross sections of the leaves of two iridescent selaginellas, *S. willdenowii* and *S. uncinata*, and examined the sections with a transmission electron microscope. In the outer cell wall of the upper epidermis they found not one, but two thin layers parallel to one another—an arrangement known to intensify iridescent colors in animals and insects. The thin layers were absent in the noniridescent leaves that develop when normally iridescent plants are grown in full light. These findings firmly associated the thin layers with iridescence.

Besides selaginellas, thin layers have been found in iridescent ferns. So far only five species (*Danaea nodosa, Diplazium tomentosum, Lindsaea lucida, Teratophyllum rotundifoliatum,* and *Trichomanes elegans*) have been studied but that is enough to show that the location of the thin layers can vary from species to species. In *Danaea, Diplazium, Lindsaea,* and *Teratophyllum,* the layers are located in the outer cell wall of the upper epidermis and oriented parallel to one another—just as in the selaginellas (Figure 88). But the number of layers is 18–30 instead of just 2 as in the selaginellas (Gould and Lee 1996, Graham et al. 1993, Nasrulhaq-Boyce and Duckett 1991). In *Trichomanes* the layers are located in the chloroplasts, not the outer cell walls of the upper epidermis. The chloroplasts contain dark bodies called granae that are stacked to form layers of exactly the right thickness to reflect blue light. Because these thin layers are inside the cell instead of in the outer cell walls, they are not affected by wetting, which otherwise changes the refractive index of the thin layers, causing them to lose their blue reflectiveness. Thus the blade of *Trichomanes elegans* remains iridescent when wet.

Although they differ in the details of their thin layers, iridescent ferns and selaginellas have one thing in common: they tend to grow in deep shade. This suggests that iridescence is an adaptation to dark environments. A plant on the forest floor dwells in light levels that are typically less than 1% of the full sunlight above the forest, and light that

Figure 88 Multiple thin layers in a transverse section of the outer cell wall of the upper epidermis of an iridescent fern (*Lindsaea lucida*). Transmission electron micrograph by David Lee.

dim severely limits photosynthesis for most plants. (At the La Selva Biological Field Station in Costa Rica, David Lee found that the mean percentage of full sunlight for a spot on the forest floor harboring *Trichomanes elegans* was only 0.25%.) But low light is only half the problem. The light quality—the amount of different colors composing the light—is also poor. Red light is scarce because most of it has been absorbed by the overhead vegetation. In red-depleted light, plants languish because red is the color most efficiently used in photosynthesis. Thus, from a plant's point of view, the forest floor is a strenuous place because it is not only dark but also deficient in red light.

It is under these dark, stressful conditions that iridescent species are almost always found; therefore, the iridescence is presumably beneficial in this type of environment. Exactly how does it benefit? One idea is that iridescence allows more of the scarce red light to pass through the epidermal cell wall to the chloroplasts, where photosynthesis takes place. Increased transmission of red light might enhance photosynthesis and improve growth. It is also known that red light interconverts two plant hormones, phytochrome red and phytochrome far-red, whose relative amounts control certain physiological processes in the cell. But ideas about the adaptive significance of iridescence still need to be tested; no one knows for certain what the significance is, if any. It could be something we do not see, with the iridescence merely a beautiful by-product.

Iridescent ferns and selaginellas *do* have adaptations for life on the dark forest floor. Most plants have 20–200 chloroplasts per cell, each measuring only 4–6 µm (0.00016–0.00024 inch) in diameter. But iridescent ferns and selaginellas have 1–12 chloroplasts per cell, each measuring 10–27 µm (0.0004–0.0011 inch) in diameter. Having fewer but larger chloroplasts allows the formation of a nearly continuous layer for capturing light (Figure 89).

The light-capturing ability of these plants is further enhanced by the shape of the outer cell walls of the upper epidermis. In selaginellas and *Teratophyllum*, these walls are curved like a convex lens. When seen en masse under high magnification, they resemble plastic-bubble packing material (Figure 90). The lens-like shape focuses light on the chloroplasts at the back of the cell, and these orient themselves parallel to the

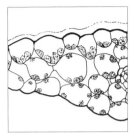  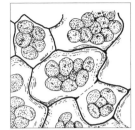

Figure 89 Sections of *Teratophyllum rotundifoliatum* leaves, showing the chloroplasts (shaded) situated at the bottom of the upper epidermis cells. Light is focused on the chloroplasts by the lens-shaped outer walls of the cells. Left and middle, cross sections. Right, a paradermal section, cut in nearly the same plane as the surface of the blade. After Nasrulhaq-Boyce and Duckett (1991).

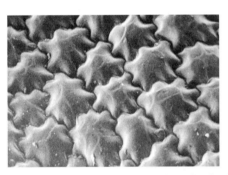 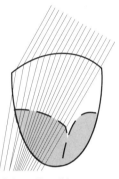

Figure 90 Left, convex upper epidermal cells of *Selaginella willdenowii*; scanning electron micrograph by David Lee. Right, ray-tracing diagram, showing how light rays are focused by the convex outer cell wall of the upper epidermis. This bending focuses more light on the chloroplasts (shaded); after Lee (1986).

leaf surface to present the greatest amount of surface area for capturing incoming light.

These light-capturing adaptations of iridescent ferns and selaginellas can be likened to the camera with which I tried to photograph *Trichomanes elegans* in Panama. The thin layers in the plant's upper epidermis act like the coating of the camera's lens, reflecting more of some colors and less of others. The convex outer cell wall corresponds to the lens, focusing light toward the back of the cell. And at the focal point sit the chloroplasts that, like a camera's film, absorb the incoming light and effect change. Of course, this analogy can be carried too far. Iridescent ferns and selaginellas work well on the dark forest floor—my camera does not.

ADAPTATIONS BY FERNS

19
Leaf Scales and Water Uptake

It is a typical hot July afternoon on a limestone hill prairie in southern Illinois. A botanist and his companion are trudging up the prairie toward a wooded ridgetop where they stop to rest in the shade of some junipers and blackjack oaks. While resting they notice a patch of the scaly polypody (*Pleopeltis polypodioides*) on a nearby rock ledge. The patch is completely dried out; its leaves are curled and twisted into rough C and J shapes, and the pinnae are rolled inward from the tips, exposing their lower surfaces, covered by hundreds of tiny whitish scales. Overall, the plant looks dead and contorted, as if gripped by rigor mortis (Plate 17).

The botanist tells his friend that this moribund condition is only temporary. Within hours after the next soaking rain, the plant will revive, its leaves will expand into vibrant green photosynthetic organs, and the whole patch will appear as if an expert gardener has cared for it all along (Figure 91 and Plate 18). But until it rains, asserts the botanist, the leaves' curled condition will protect their upper surfaces and prevent excessive moisture loss. Also, the scales on the underside of the leaf (Figure 92) prevent drying by covering some of the stomata, the tiny pores through which water evaporates out of the leaf.

Later in the day, however, the botanist reconsiders his explanations

about why the leaf curls. Why should curling protect the upper surface? Presumably, that side loses little moisture because it lacks stomata.
It would make more sense if the *lower* surface were protected by the
curling. After some thought, the botanist, a bit embarrassed, admits to
his friend that his previous explanation about leaf curling might not be
correct.

Similar thoughts occurred to Louis Pessin, a physiological plant ecologist, in the early 1920s. Pessin worked in Mississippi where the scaly
polypody grows on the trunks and branches of trees, especially live
oaks. He saw how the fern curled upon drying, and he knew that many
other ferns with densely scaly leaves did the same. Pessin wanted to
know why these ferns curled to expose their lower surface instead of
curling to hide it. To find an answer, he decided to experiment.

He tested his hunch that the lower surface of the leaf, which contains
the stomata, loses water more rapidly than the upper surface. To do this
he detached leaves of the scaly polypody from their stems and created
four test groups of four leaves each. In the first group, he coated both

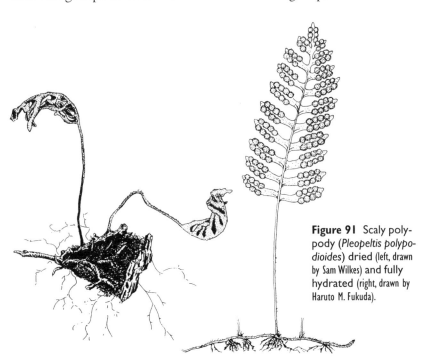

Figure 91 Scaly poly-
pody (*Pleopeltis polypo-
dioides*) dried (left, drawn
by Sam Wilkes) and fully
hydrated (right, drawn by
Haruto M. Fukuda).

Figure 92 Lower surface of a scaly polypody (*Pleopeltis polypodioides*) leaf, showing the scales that channel water into the middle of the leaf. Each scale is dark at its point of attachment. The three large darker dots near the upper margin of each pinna are sori. Photograph by Gordon Foster.

sides of the leaves with petroleum jelly, which prevents water from evaporating out of the leaf. In the second, he coated only the upper surface of the leaves and left the lower uncovered. In the third, only the lower surface was coated. The fourth was left completely uncoated. Pessin then weighed the leaves and then placed them in a desiccator, an airtight chamber with a moisture-absorbing chemical at the bottom. Every day for one week he removed the leaves and weighed them.

As expected, Pessin found that the completely sealed leaves lost the least amount of water, and the unsealed ones the most. More revealing was that the leaves sealed only on their upper surfaces lost nearly twice as much water as the leaves sealed only on their lower surfaces. This meant that curling did little to prevent the leaf from further drying.

The experiment also showed that leaves could lose nearly all their water and remain alive. Some lost as much as 76% of their normal moisture content, which is a staggering amount for plants, most of which would die after losing only 8–12%. (Botanists have since found that as much as 97% of the scaly polypody's water can be lost without harming the plant.) Scaly polypody can lose all the free water in its leaves, that is, water not hydrating organic molecules inside the cells. The fern then toughs it out and waits until the next rain comes. Leaf curling is not an adaptation to prevent moisture loss; the fern does not need such an adaptation because its tissues tolerate extreme drying. But why, upon drying, do the leaves curl to expose their *lower* surfaces?

Pessin speculated that the fern exposed its lower surface for the purpose of catching raindrops to rehydrate the leaf. He knew that the roots played an insignificant role in rehydration because they did not absorb water fast enough. He could demonstrate this by placing the roots of a dried plant in water. The plant will rehydrate, but only after a few days—far more slowly than if the leaves were wetted and placed in a humid chamber. To test his idea that the underside of the leaf absorbs water, Pessin repeated his previous experiment but in reverse; he rehydrated the leaves of his four test groups instead of drying them. He did this by suspending the dried leaves over distilled water in a humidity chamber. As before, he weighed the leaves before putting them in the chambers, and then each day for one week he reweighed them.

Pessin (1924, 1925) found that the leaves with an *un*coated lower surface absorbed water twice as fast as those with the same surface coated. This meant that rehydration occurred through the lower surface, not the upper. It now seemed that exposing the lower surface upon drying made sense after all: it helped rehydrate the leaf after a rain.

(Many ferns that shrivel and curl upon drying also expand rapidly upon rehydrating. I first experienced this during a collecting trip to a dry valley in Ecuador. I gathered several ferns that were completely shriveled and in poor condition for making herbarium specimens. They were left in a sealed plastic bag overnight, along with other plants. The next morning, the ferns had rehydrated and were gloriously lush and green— just right for the plant press!)

Pessin's experiments demonstrated three things about the scaly polypody: it lost moisture primarily from the lower surface of the leaf, it tolerated extreme drying, and its lower leaf surface absorbed water rapidly during rehydration. Only one question remained: How does water enter the leaf during rehydration? Like all land plants, the leaves of the scaly polypody are covered by a thin, water-impermeable layer called the cuticle. This layer keeps water inside the leaf from evaporating. But just as it retains water within, so too it prevents water outside the leaf from entering. Plant physiologists since Pessin showed that water bypasses the cuticle by moving into, and then through, scales on the underside of the leaf (Müller et al. 1981, Stuart 1968). Each scale consists of two parts: a flat, disk-like portion composed of many dead, empty cells, and a stalk composed of a single row of four to eight living cells (Figure 93). The lowermost cell of the stalk is in contact with the tissue of the middle part of the leaf, or mesophyll. When the leaf is wet, water is drawn by capillary action into the dead cells of the disk-like portion of the scale. The water is then taken up by the living stalk cells and funneled into the mesophyll where it is imbibed by thirsty cells. Experiments have shown that this path can be traveled by water in as little as 15 minutes. The net result is the reexpansion of the leaf.

Functionally, the scales of the scaly polypody resemble those of certain members of the pineapple family (Bromeliaceae), of which Spanish moss (*Tillandsia usneoides*) is an example. Spanish moss is actually a flowering plant, not a moss. It dangles from trees, especially live oaks, throughout the Gulf Coast plain, creating the quintessential landscape of the deep South. The whole plant is covered by a frosting of tiny silvery scales that hide the green of the leaf. The scales absorb moisture droplets from the air, supplying *all* the plant's water and mineral needs—roots are entirely lacking. By absorbing nutrients from the air, Spanish moss is able to festoon telephone lines, barbed wire, and cyclone fences. But Spanish moss differs in one important respect from the scaly polypody: its leaves are succulent and remain so during times of drought. They do not dry and curl or tolerate drying as do the leaves of scaly polypody.

The study of drought-tolerant ferns has given plant physiologists the opportunity to learn how delicate cell membranes, organelles, and

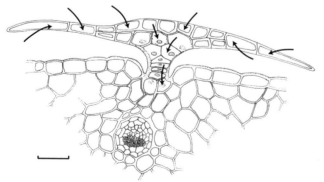

Figure 93 Movement of water (arrows) into the leaf scale (shown in longitudinal section) of scaly polypody (*Pleopeltis polypodioides*). The upper cells are dead and empty whereas those of the stalk are living. Scale bar, 50 μm (0.02 inch). After Müller et al. (1981).

the machinery of photosynthesis can survive extreme drying yet rehydrate rapidly without damage. Physiologists are interested in this because of its potential use in developing new strains of crop plants adapted to arid climates. The results of their studies have been published in the scientific journals of their trade—journals that often go unread by members of my tribe, the plant taxonomists. Yet how I wish I had known earlier about their research! It would have saved me from embarrassment one hot July day on a limestone hill prairie in southern Illinois.

ADAPTATIONS BY FERNS

20
Some Quirks of Quillworts

"I found it!" said Brian Sorrell, sounding enormously pleased.
"It's *Isoetes lacustris.*"
"Are you sure it's not one of those look-alike plants?" I asked.
"Take a look at the leaf cross section," he said, tossing me a plant.

Brian, a native New Zealander and lecturer in aquatic botany at Aarhus University, Denmark, and I were wearing chest-waders and standing waist deep in the chilly waters of Lake Kalgaard in central Jutland. We had come here in early June to collect *Isoetes* for Brian's research on gas movement in aquatic plants. I had just doubted his identification because many aquatic plants in the lake, especially *Littorella* and spike rushes, have leaves that appear confusingly similar to those of *Isoetes.*

I caught the plant that Brian had tossed and examined it. Unlike most plants, it had cylindrical leaves tapered to a point. They formed a lax rosette on top of a short, stubby stem, from which dangled whitish roots still clinging to globs of red mud. I pinched one of the leaves in half and examined the broken end; it had four air chambers. Brian's identification was correct: *Isoetes* is the only plant with four air chambers in its leaves (Figure 94).

As a morning mist lifted off the lake, Brian and I continued to search for *Isoetes*, all the time being followed by a curious pair of black-necked grebes. We waded easily over the sandy-gravelly lake bottom, virtually unimpeded by aquatic plants. We knew that the clear water, sandy sediment and sparse vegetation meant that Lake Kalgaard was an oligotrophic lake. This kind of lake has few nutrients in its bottom sediment, and its waters contain precious little carbon dioxide, one of the raw materials of photosynthesis. This explains why Lake Kalgaard harbors so few plants—the nutrients are so scarce that the plants cannot get enough to grow into dense populations. Nevertheless, *Isoetes* flourishes here and in other oligotrophic lakes, sometimes forming extensive underwater beds that look like blackish green shag carpets.

Why does *Isoetes* thrive in infertile lakes where many other plants cannot? The answer lies in the way it absorbs and conserves carbon dioxide. Brian pointed to the plant I was holding: "See those air chambers?" he said. "They allow carbon dioxide to move throughout the leaf. But the carbon dioxide is absorbed by the *roots*, not the leaves. It has a completely different way of acquiring carbon dioxide compared to other plants." I knew that terrestrial plants absorb carbon dioxide from the air through tiny pores, called stomata, in their leaves, and that submerged aquatic plants absorb it from the water (primarily as bicarbonate, HCO_3^-) directly through their leaves or stems. But how strange that *Isoetes* mines carbon dioxide from the sediment with its roots! Brian pointed out that this method provides 70–100% of the plant's carbon, and it is a good strategy: because of bacterial activity, the interstitial water in the lake sediment contains 5–100 times more carbon dioxide than the overlying water. By taking advantage of this reservoir of abundant carbon dioxide, *Isoetes* can successfully compete with other plants.

Brian and I stuffed a plastic sandwich bag full of *Isoetes* and sped back to the university. In the laboratory, we sliced the roots and leaves with a razor blade to make thin sections for examination under a microscope. These sections revealed the peculiar anatomy of the plant. The roots have a large central air chamber with a vascular strand attached to its periphery (Figure 95). This arrangement is identical to that of the lepidodendrid trees that dominated the coal-forming swamps of the Car-

Figure 94. A quillwort, *Isoetes lacustris*. Left, growth habit. Upper right: leaves detached, each showing a single sporangium at the base. Lower right, close-ups of the bases, showing air chambers and cross walls in longitudinal section at the left. At the right, the four air chambers can be seen in cross section at the top; at the bottom is a single sporangium, containing the spores, and above the sporangium is an ovate structure called the ligule, whose function is unknown. Drawing by the author.

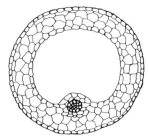

Figure 95 Root of *Isoetes lacustris* in cross section, showing the air chamber and the peripheral vascular bundle. This anatomy is identical to that of the lepidodendrid trees of the Carboniferous.

boniferous 345 million to 280 million years ago (Stewart 1947). It is one of several reasons *Isoetes* is believed related to these extinct plants.

The thin sections of the leaves also showed that the plants lack stomata. Stomata are found in nearly all other vascular plants, but they would, of course, be useless in *Isoetes* because it gets carbon dioxide from underwater sediment (stomata are present, however, in those species of *Isoetes* that grow in seasonally inundated habitats and can get carbon dioxide from the air at least part of the year). But by far the most conspicuous feature of the thin sections was four large air chambers that occupied 70–80% of the cross-sectional area of the leaf. The rest of the leaf was a matrix of solid, green photosynthetic tissue.

The air chambers in the roots and leaves serve as a conduit for carbon dioxide. This gas diffuses from the sediment across the root surface and up the central chamber of the root and into the leaves. Once in the leaves, the carbon dioxide traverses the air chambers until it is removed by the surrounding green photosynthetic tissue (Boston 1986, Madsen 1987, Wium-Andersen 1971).

The passage of carbon dioxide through the leaf chambers is interrupted by numerous septae, or cross walls. These can be seen on the leaf surface as whitish transverse streaks every 3/16–3/8 inch (5–10 mm; Figure 94). They serve to strengthen the leaf and prevent flooding should the chamber be punctured or torn. Brian examined a septum under the microscope and found it perforated by numerous pores. "The pores occur in the septae of other aquatic plants," said Brian, "so it's really not surprising to find them in *Isoetes*. Because of the pores, the septae offer almost no resistance to the movement of carbon dioxide."

But carbon dioxide is not the only gas to traverse the chambers; oxygen, a waste product from photosynthesis, does likewise. Oxygen, however, diffuses in the opposite direction from carbon dioxide, namely, from the leaves where it is produced to the roots and into the sediment. Once in the sediment, it combines with iron to form an oxidized zone of ocher around the roots (Tessenow and Baynes 1975, 1978). This was the red mud clinging to the roots of the plant that Brian had tossed me. Certain species of fungi and bacteria thrive in this oxidized zone, known as the rhizosphere, and depend upon it entirely for their existence. They cannot live elsewhere in the oxygenless sediment of the lake. Our examination of the thin sections showed how exquisitely adapted *Isoetes* is to its method of carbon uptake from the lake sediment. But one adaptation we could not see—a physiological one called crassulacean acid metabolism, more comfortably known as CAM—modifies the way carbon dioxide is processed in photosynthesis and is another secret to the success of *Isoetes* in oligotrophic lakes (Keeley 1981–1998).

CAM was first discovered in *Isoetes* in 1979 by Jon Keeley, an ecologist at Occidental College, Los Angeles. His colleagues were astonished because CAM had previously been known only in desert plants such as cacti and stonecrops (the latter belong to the Crassulaceae, the family in which the photosynthetic pathway was first found). In these plants, CAM is an adaptation to conserve water. But this explanation does not make sense for *Isoetes:* Why would an aquatic plant need a water-conserving adaptation? Keeley and his colleagues now believe they know the answer.

Normally, plants absorb carbon dioxide during the day when their stomata are open and photosynthesis is taking place. At night, when photosynthesis is shut down, their stomata close and carbon dioxide is not absorbed. The advantage of CAM is that it allows the uptake of carbon dioxide at night. This carbon dioxide, however, cannot be used immediately because no sunlight is available to drive the process. What CAM does is store carbon dioxide by attaching it to an organic molecule to form (primarily) malic acid, a substance that flavors apples (*Malus*) and citrus fruits. The malic acid is broken down during the day to release the carbon dioxide for use in photosynthesis.

This roundabout pathway benefits desert plants by allowing them to open their stomata at night when temperatures are lower and the evaporative power of the air is less, resulting in less moisture loss from the plant. The benefit for *Isoetes,* however, is different. CAM increases the time during which the plants can accumulate carbon dioxide—day *and* night, instead of only during the day as in non-CAM aquatic plants. Furthermore, CAM recycles carbon dioxide produced inside the plant by cellular respiration. Most of this would normally be lost, but CAM re-captures it, stores it, and makes it available again for photosynthesis.

Paradoxically, *Isoetes* can also grow in eutrophic lakes, that is, lakes rich in nutrients and abounding with carbon dioxide. In fact, when cultivated and supplied with abundant nutrients, *Isoetes* grows more luxuriantly than it does under nutrient-poor conditions that simulate oligotrophic lakes. Why, then, does *Isoetes* seem to prefer oligotrophic lakes over eutrophic ones? The main reason appears to be competition with other plants for light. In eutrophic lakes, *Isoetes* is usually shaded by larger, faster-growing plants such as pondweeds (*Potamogeton*), water lilies (*Nymphaea*), and coontails (*Ceratophyllum*). Smaller organisms also take their toll; plankton cloud the nutrient-rich water and intercept sunlight before it falls on the plant. More importantly, algae, sponges, and diatoms colonize the surface of the leaves of *Isoetes* and further rob the plants of light (Plate 13). The effect of all this competition is that *Isoetes* languishes and eventually dies, and for that reason it is rare or absent in eutrophic lakes (Sand-Jensen and Søndergaard 1981, Sand-Jensen and Borum 1984).

As Brian and I cleaned the lab after our day's work, I began to realize the complexity of factors that restricts *Isoetes* to oligotrophic lakes. To be sure, *Isoetes* has the unusual adaptations of CAM photosynthesis and carbon dioxide uptake from roots that allow it to thrive in oligotrophic lakes. But it would also flourish in eutrophic lakes were it not for competition for light with other aquatic plants.

ADAPTATIONS BY FERNS

21
Bracken, the Poisoner

On the grounds of the Missouri Botanical Garden in St. Louis, nestled in a grove of oaks and sassafras, rests the mausoleum of Henry Shaw, who founded the garden in 1859. The grove's ground cover consists mostly of liriope (*Liriope muscari*), ivy (*Hedera helix*), and creeping euonymus (*Euonymus fortunei*), but there also flourishes a colony of bracken fern (*Pteridium aquilinum* var. *latiusculum*, Figures 96 and 97). This colony was started from a single rhizome planted by horticulturalist George Pring in 1910 (Pring 1964). (In the past, bracken has been classified as a single species containing twelve varieties, following the taxonomy by Tryon 1941. Nowadays, most fern taxonomists, including myself, believe that many of the varieties recognized by Tryon should be elevated to the rank of species because they are morphologically distinct and, in some cases, cross with each other to form hybrids with aborted spores.) Since then the colony has spread like a malignant cancer so that now it covers nearly the entire western side of the grove. As it spreads, the colony's large, overlapping leaves rob the smaller ground-cover plants of sunlight, and these sun-starved plants eventually weaken, decline, and die. Occasionally, portions of the bracken patch are removed to allow the smaller ground covers some sunlight to recuperate. This is a laborious and tedious task because bracken's deep underground rhizomes are hard to eradicate. Here and elsewhere, bracken is such an aggressive weed that one wonders why it does not take over the world (Figure 98).

Fortunately, bracken's aggressiveness in nature is checked by enemies that devour it. Cattle, horses, and sheep readily graze it; they especially relish the tender young fiddleheads (Figure 99). Even people find its fiddleheads delicious; in Korea and Japan they are cooked as a vegetable and sometimes served in bars as a kind of salty snack food (Hodge 1973). In 1969 the demand for bracken fiddleheads in Japan was so great that they had to be imported from Siberia. In the United States, Korean families around Los Angeles gather bracken fiddleheads in the spring. The fiddleheads are prepared by soaking them overnight in cold water, boiling, soaking again, rinsing, and sautéing with onions, garlic, soy sauce, and sesame seed oil. On the plate they look like thin brown noodles and have a taste and texture similar to that of asparagus. In the nearby San Bernardino National Forest, gathering bracken fiddleheads has become so popular that in 1981 the U.S. Forest Service started to issue permits and had to restrict the activity to selected areas. Each year about 1500 people apply for permits and pick nearly 16,000 pounds (7200 kg) of fiddleheads. For people who do not want to pick their own, bracken fiddleheads can be bought in Asian grocery stores for about $6.00 per pound. They are often sold in clear plastic packages containing a brown sauce. Bracken can be tasty, but it has also been implicated in stomach cancer. One should not eat much of it for long periods.

Far more formidable than the mammals who devour it are insects. Bracken is chewed, sucked, mined, bored, and galled by more than 100 species of insects worldwide, most feeding exclusively on bracken. All parts of the plant are vulnerable. Why, then, with so many eating it, does bracken abound? The answer, in large part, is that it fights back with poisons. Its living tissues are filled with chemicals that kill or deter the organisms that eat it.

The most diabolical of bracken's poisons are ecdysones, a class of hormones that promote molting (or ecdysis) in insects. Bracken is loaded with these hormones and produces more kinds than any other species of plant—even its gametophytes have them. When ingested,

Figure 96 Bracken: *Pteridium aquilinum* var. *latiusculum,* from northern Wisconsin (above), and *P. caudatum,* from southern Florida.

Figure 97 Bracken (*Pteridium aquilinum* var. *latiusculum*) bears sori near the leaf margin, which is rolled inward, protecting them when young. As the sporangia mature, the leaf margin is pushed back. Photograph by Charles Neidorf.

Figure 99 Bracken fiddlehead, edible but possibly carcinogenic if much of it is eaten over a long time. Photograph by John Mickel.

Figure 98 Bracken (*Pteridium aquilinum* var. *latiusculum*) forms extensive colonies through its deep, long-creeping rhizomes. Photograph by John Mickel.

ecdysones discombobulate the insect's normal development, usually by overstimulating it to cause uncontrolled molting. The insect soon dies or continues to live but with little chance for survival.

A curious testimony to the ruthlessness of ecdysones comes from an archaeological site associated with Hadrian's Wall in England, built around A.D. 100. There, the Romans covered the floors of their stables with litter composed of bracken and lesser amounts of straw, tree branches, and bryophytes. One stable was strewn with bracken litter containing about 250,000 shells of pupae of the stable fly (*Stomoxys calcitrans*). When entomologists examined these puparia, they found that almost all showed arrested stages of development. The most likely explanation is that the insects had, as larvae, eaten the bracken litter, and as a result, their development was derailed. (Bracken is still used for bedding or litter and has several advantages over straw. It absorbs moisture, insulates well, and contains more nitrogen than traditional wheat or barley straw. When enriched with dung or urine, it decomposes rapidly—a great advantage if the litter is composted or spread over a field.)

Besides ecdysones, bracken produces thiaminase, an enzyme that breaks down thiamine, or vitamin B_1. Livestock often suffer from vitamin B_1 deficiency after grazing on bracken a long time. This usually occurs in the spring when cold weather delays the growth of pasture grasses but not that of bracken. Its young leaves develop and stand tall and erect above the pasture grasses, acting as a beacon for grazers. Unfortunately for livestock, the concentration of thiaminase is highest in young leaves (it falls sharply after the leaves unfold). In Britain, before the days of the automobile, bracken-induced thiamine deficiency was so common in horses that it received the name "bracken staggers." The most obvious symptom of poisoning is that the sick horse would stagger sideways for two or three steps, then stabilize itself by spreading its legs wide apart. Besides staggering, other symptoms included hemorrhaging, inflammation of the inner surface of the eyelids, fever, excessively strong heartbeat after mild exercise, and severe muscular tremors. If the debilitated animal continued to eat bracken, the coup de grâce was often a massive seizure. The British veterinarian James Herriot, who wrote *All Creatures Great and Small*, was occasionally called upon to treat cases of bracken staggers.

Another poison in bracken's arsenal is hydrogen cyanide (prussic acid). Unlike ecdysones and thiaminase, which are ready and waiting in the plant's tissues, hydrogen cyanide is produced on the spot in response to a munching insect. As the insect's mandibles tear into the plant, the damaged tissues release an enzyme that splits prunasin, a molecule also present in the plant's tissue; the split yields hydrogen cyanide, which kills or deters the attacking insect.

Plants that produce hydrogen cyanide are called cyanogenic. Bracken is facultatively cyanogenic, that is, it can switch on or off the production of prunasin (Cooper-Driver 1985, 1990, Cooper-Driver and Swain 1976). This switching correlates with the age of the plant and its environment. In general, young leaves are more cyanogenic than older ones, and plants growing in the shade are more cyanogenic than ones in the sun. No one knows, however, what role this switching plays in the fight against bracken-eating insects.

An example from entomology shows how effectively cyanogenic plants can kill insects. In the days before hydrogen cyanide could be bought from chemical supply companies, entomologists stuffed their killing jars with the crushed leaves of cherries. The leaves released hydrogen cyanide, which accumulated in the jars in concentrations high enough to dispatch insects in a matter of minutes. (Prunasin gets its name from *Prunus*, the genus of cherries. You can smell the hydrogen cyanide by crushing leaves or—even better—scraping the bark of cherry twigs. The odor resembles that of burnt almonds; it reminds me of the Good Humor Toasted Almond ice cream bars I used to eat as a kid.)

The most abundant poisons in bracken's arsenal are tannins, a group of compounds whose bitter taste discourages plant eaters. Besides tasting bad, tannins are toxic if ingested in large quantities. They bind to cellular enzymes that govern the energy-yielding chemical reactions of life. Because these enzymes are the same in most living organisms, tannins defend against a wide variety of enemies.

Fortunately for humans, cooking removes most of the tannins and destroys thiaminase. Nevertheless, eating too much bracken can be dangerous. Research has documented that people living in Britain and Japan, two areas where bracken fiddleheads are commonly eaten, develop stomach cancer more often than people who live elsewhere. Laboratory tests have confirmed that bracken is carcinogenic in animals. Rats, cows, Japanese quail, guinea pigs, and sheep all developed cancer when fed a diet high in bracken. Even feeding on the spores caused cancer in lab animals (Simán et al. 1999). These laboratory results prompted plant chemists to search for the active cancer-causing chemical. In 1986, Japanese researchers isolated a molecule they believed to be the culprit; they named it ptaquiloside. (Papers on various aspects of the biology of bracken can be found in Perring and Gardiner 1976, and Thompson and Smith 1990.)

Contemplating the bracken colony near Henry Shaw's mausoleum, I find it difficult to evoke images of ruthless poisoning. The grove seems so peaceful and idyllic. But bracken's success there and elsewhere is no accident; bracken is the Lucrezia Borgia of the fern world.

22
Spira Mirabilis

Marvel for a moment at a fern fiddlehead. It stands like a watch spring coiled and ready to unwind. Its smooth spiral shape contrasts strongly with the amorphous irregularity of its surroundings, and as it spirals inward upon itself, the midrib narrows gradually until it ends in a tender young growing tip tucked safely in the center of the spiral (Figure 100). If lateral pinnae are present, these too spiral inward on their own midribs, so that little fiddleheads may be present, fractal-like, on the main one (Figure 101). So elegant is this spiral, so exquisite is its shape, that the fiddlehead has become firmly associated with ferns in the minds of most people. What many do not realize, however, is that the fiddlehead has some unusual mathematical properties. It represents one of two kinds of spirals commonly found in nature, and this spiral results from a particular type of growth.

The first kind of spiral is the equable spiral, or spiral of Archimedes, named after the ancient Greek mathematician and philosopher who first fully described it. It can be illustrated by the way a sailor coils a rope upon a ship's deck. Because the rope is uniform in thickness, each whorl is the same breadth as the one that precedes or follows it. A mathematical property of this spiral is that a radius drawn from the center and meeting the curve will slowly change its angle with that curve as the number of whorls increases and become more nearly circular. With each turn, the angle changes more and more toward 90° (Figure 102).

The second type of spiral—the one found in fiddleheads—is the equiangular spiral. It was first described by the French philosopher and mathematician René Descartes in 1638. He envisioned a spiral with whorls that, instead of maintaining their same width as in the archimedean spiral, grew continuously in such a way that a radius drawn from the center would meet any point along the curve at a constant angle—thus, an equiangular spiral (Figure 103; Cook 1914, Thompson 1942). Spiraling outward, each whorl is wider than the one preceding it. A fern fiddlehead has this type of spiral because its midrib widens at a constant rate as it spirals toward the base of the stalk; the constant rate maintains the equal angle.

The equiangular spiral has several remarkable mathematical properties. It is often called the logarithmic spiral because the vector angles about the pole are proportional to the logarithms of the successive radii.

Figure 100 Fiddlehead of *Stigmatopteris ichthiosma,* from western Ecuador.

Figure 101 Fiddlehead of *Thelypteris decussata,* from Costa Rica, with smaller fiddleheads formed by the lateral pinnae. Photograph by Jens Bittner.

Another name is the geometrical spiral because radii at equal polar angles are in geometric progression. In the early 1700s the British astronomer and mathematician Edmund Halley, of comet fame, called it the proportional spiral because parts of a radius cut off by successive whorls are in continued proportion (Figure 103). This is perhaps the most visually striking aspect of the curve—its self-similarity, its unchanging shape as it grows. The larger spirals are just expanded versions of the smaller spirals within. These interrelated mathematical properties led the celebrated Swiss mathematician Jakob Bernoulli (1645–1705) to refer to the spiral as the *spira mirabilis*, or wonderful spiral.

The *spira mirabilis* crops up repeatedly in nature, sometimes in quite unexpected places. It can be found in the shells of *Nautilus*, ammonites, and foraminifera. It is present in plants that have their flowers arranged in a scorpioid cyme, a type of inflorescence that branches repeatedly to one side at a constant angle (such as in heliotropes, borages, and forget-me-nots). It can be seen in the spiral path taken by a flying insect drawn toward light; the insect does not fly directly to the light but orients itself at a constant angle to the light while flying toward it. Other instances of the spiral can be found by drawing out its axis of coiling in

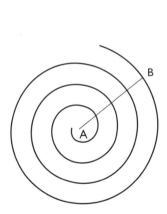

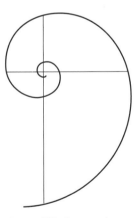

Figure 102 Archimedean or equable spiral; the radius AB bisects the spiral at an angle that varies, approaching 90°.

Figure 103 Equiangular spiral; the radii chop off same-shaped parts and always cross any point of the spiral at the same angle.

three dimensions, that is, a conical helix. In such instances it can be seen in the curvature of the ram's horn, gastropod shell, cat's claw, beaver's tooth, and plant tendril. These examples show that the *spira mirabilis* is not only widespread in nature but also indifferent as to the kind of tissue or material involved. What, then, causes it to form?

The key is unequal growth of the inner and outer surfaces. Whenever one surface grows more than the other, coiling occurs automatically. This differential growth occurs regardless of the material involved— shell, bone, hair, flesh, or plant tissue. In fern fiddleheads, unequal growth is caused by cells on the outer surface (the surface farthest from the axis of coiling) elongating more than those on the inner. The spiral shape of the fiddlehead persists as long as this unequal growth is maintained. The fiddlehead uncoils only when cells on its inner surface start to elongate, and it completely straightens out only when cells of the inner surface have elongated to the same length as those on the outer (and now lower) surface. Botanists have fancy words to describe this unequal growth; the term hyponastic curvature is used when the lower side elongates more, and epinastic curvature when the upper side elongates more.

Presumably a gene (or more likely, several genes) stimulates cells to elongate, and when this gene is turned on for one side but not for the other, curvature results. No gene(s) encode(s) for the final shape of the fiddlehead per se, only a difference in timing of cell elongation.

Other instances of coiling are provided by the fern world. The twining, helically coiled rachises of the two genera of climbing ferns—*Lygodium* and *Salpichlaena*—result from unequal growth on the inner and outer surfaces of the midribs of their compound leaves. These twine around twigs and branches for support so that the distal parts of the leaf can be elevated to a place in the sun. The tendrils of flowering plants coil by the same kind of unequal growth.

Other examples of coiling arise not from elongation but from shrinkage. The resurrection fern (*Pleopeltis polypodioides,* Plates 17 and 18), common on tree trunks in the southeastern United States and American tropics, has leaves that curl inward as they dry, assuming rough C or J shapes. Curling occurs because cells on the upper surface shrink more

upon drying than the cells on the lower surface. When the leaf is wetted, the cells on the upper surface reexpand and the leaf straightens out.
The same explanation applies to the resurrection plant (*Selaginella lepido-
phylla*), native to dry forests from Texas and New Mexico to southern
Mexico. This plant is popular in horticulture because of its ability to
curl into a ball when dry and uncurl into a flat rosette when watered.
The curling and uncurling is purely mechanical, dependent on dead cellulose cell walls losing and imbibing water. The plants will curl and uncurl long after they have died.

The principle of curvature from unequal expansion has a familiar
household example: the thermostat (Stevens 1974). The heart of this
device consists of two metal strips, one of brass and the other of iron,
both of equal length and joined together. When heated, the brass expands more than the iron, curling downward around the iron strip (Figure 104). This curling and (upon cooling) uncurling turns the furnace
off and on.

There is pleasure in discovering that all these examples of curvature
follow from the same simple principle of unequal growth. There is also
pleasure in seeing the *spira mirabilis* repeated over and over in nature in a
variety of living things, especially fern fiddleheads. It shows harmony
and structure in nature, a satisfying regularity. Reflecting on this order-
liness, the English botanist Nehemiah Grew concluded in his *Anatomy of
Plants* (1682), "Nature doth everywhere geometrize."

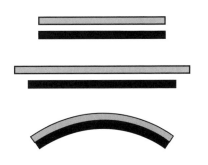

Figure 104 The principle of the
thermostat reveals how unequal
growth causes curvature. Strips of
brass and iron of the same length
(top) are heated (middle), and the
brass expands more than the iron.
If the strips are joined and heated,
the greater expansion of the brass
strip makes both curve (bottom).
Similarly, elongating plant cells make
their less elongated neighbors
curve, too.

23
Robinson Crusoe's Ferns

The year is 1704 in the Juan Fernández Islands, located about 360 miles (580 km) from the western coast of South America and 33° south of the equator (Figure 106). The *Cinque Ports*, a British privateer galley of 18 guns, lies anchored in a small bay off one of the islands named Más a Tierra. Having just been refitted and reprovisioned, she is now ready to prey on Spanish shipping along the coasts of Chile and Peru. The entire crew is eager to set sail except for a stubborn and combative sailor named Alexander Selkirk. He argues that the ship is unseaworthy and demands to be left behind in self-imposed exile on the unpopulated island. The next morning the *Cinque Ports* raises anchor and sails away—without Selkirk.

As it turned out, Selkirk's decision to stay on the island was a good one. The *Cinque Ports* soon foundered off a small island near the coast of Peru, and the crew was captured by the Spanish navy, tortured, and thrown into a dungeon in Lima. They probably suffered more hardships in prison than did Selkirk, who was completely alone and living in a cave. For food and clothing Selkirk hunted feral goats, the descendants of ones originally released by settlers during an ill-fated attempt at colonization in 1596. The goats thrived because they were free from

178

predators and had an ideal habitat: rugged, mountainous terrain with hardly any level land. El Yunque, the tallest peak in the archipelago, exemplifies the harshness of the terrain. Its knife-edge ridges connect its peak at 3002 feet (915 m) above sea level to other peaks. One ridge is incised by ravines so deep and precipitous that it is called the Cordón Salsipuedes, the "get-out-if-you-can mountains" in Spanish.

Four years and four months after being left on the island, Selkirk was rescued by fellow privateers. He then spent the next 2½ years with his rescuers, pirating in the Pacific. After docking in England, Selkirk recounted his adventures to the literati of London, who were eager to profit from the demand for exciting travel stories set in the New World. His accounts inspired Daniel Defoe to write *Robinson Crusoe.*

But Selkirk was not the first living being to find refuge on the islands. Ever since the islands were volcanically extruded above the waves about 4 million years ago, they have served as a home to hundreds of plant and animals, most of which were blown off course by winds or arrived by chance. Among these wayward immigrants were a disproportionately large number of ferns. Their story illustrates the importance of long-distance spore dispersal in the biology of ferns.

The Juan Fernández Islands currently harbor 54 species of ferns, and these grow in nearly every habitat from the highest peaks down to the seashore. Exposed rocky ridges present two species of forked ferns (*Sticherus pedalis* and *Sticherus quadripartitus*). Mossy rocks shelter a maidenhair fern (*Adiantum chilense*), fragile fern (*Cystopteris fragilis*), and filmy fern (*Hymenophyllum cruentum*, Figure 105). Dark caverns in peaty floors of cloud forests harbor a species of spleenwort (*Asplenium macrosorum*).

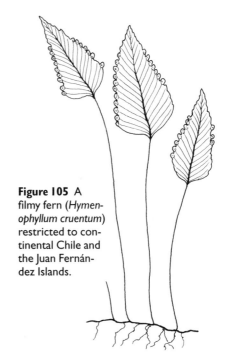

Figure 105 A filmy fern (*Hymenophyllum cruentum*) restricted to continental Chile and the Juan Fernández Islands.

Cocos

Galápagos

PERU

• Lima

CHILE

Juan
Fernández

Falkland

Figure 106 South America and some nearby islands.

Lowland habitats disturbed by people, such as clearings and old fields, support *Histiopteris incisa, Megalastrum inaequalifolia* var. *glabrior,* and *Rumohra berteroana.*

But the islands' greatest fern opulence lurks in the upper reaches of deep ravines. As moist sea air is forced up these ravines to elevations above 1500 feet (500 m), it cools and its moisture condenses, creating cloud forests ideal for many species of ferns. Here abound tree ferns such as *Dicksonia berteriana, Lophosoria quadripinnata,* and *Thyrsopteris elegans.*

The fibrous root mats investing their trunks often support filmy ferns such as *Hymenophyllum cuneatum, Trichomanes exsectum,* and *T. philippianum.* A remarkable fern of the cloud forests is *Blechnum schottii.* Its rhizome begins growth on the forest floor, where it produces only sterile leaves. Its tip meanders about until it finds a tree trunk; the rhizome then climbs, adhering to the trunk with rootlets emanating from its ventral surface. Eventually, the rhizome produces spore-bearing leaves that resemble skeletonized versions of the sterile leaves. It is an impressive sight, an entire plant hanging off the side of a tree trunk at heights up to 15 feet (5 m), with its skeletonized fertile leaves held erect near the apex.

Another island habitat dominated by ferns is open, rocky slopes. Here grow dense populations of a tree blechnum (*Blechnum cycadifolium*) that grows only in the Juan Fernández Islands. Its stout trunk, as tall as 6 feet (2 m), bears a rosette of stiff, singly pinnate leaves at the top. The plants resemble cycads and, when growing together in groves, are eerily reminiscent of a forest from the Age of Dinosaurs. Because they break the incessant winds that rush up the hillsides, the blechnum groves are often sought as protected tranquil spots. "They're great places to snuggle down and eat lunch while on field trips," says Tod Stuessy, a plant taxonomist and one of the leading experts on the flora of the islands.

The Juan Fernández Islands illustrate a common characteristic of oceanic island floras: they harbor a high percentage of fern and lycophyte species compared to the continents. In the wet tropical forests of Central and South America, ferns and lycophytes generally compose 7–10% of the vascular plant flora. For instance, at the Smithsonian Institution's research station on Barro Colorado Island in the Panama Canal, ferns and lycophytes compose about 8% of the vascular plant flora; at the La Selva Biological Field Station in Costa Rica, ferns are about 9%; and in the Venezuelan Guayana (the territory of Amazonas and the state of Bolívar in southern Venezuela), ferns are about 8%. In contrast, the ferns of the Juan Fernández Islands compose 15% of the vascular plant flora. The fern floras of other oceanic islands are similarly rich: Easter Island, Hawaii, and Guam have about 14% ferns; Fiji and the Galápagos Islands, 20%; Cocos Island, Costa Rica, 35%; St. Helena, 40%; Marquesas Islands, 34%; Kermadec Islands, 35%; and Tristan da

Cunha, 42%. High percentages of pteridophytes characterize most, if not all, oceanic island floras (Smith 1972, Tryon 1970).

Why are there relatively more fern species on islands than on the continents? The answer lies primarily in the size of propagules of ferns versus seed plants. In ferns, the units of dispersal are dust-like spores that can be easily picked up by the wind and carried hundreds or thousands of miles. On the other hand, most seed plants bear larger, heavier fruits and seeds that cannot be readily dispersed long distances. Ferns, therefore, disperse more often to oceanic islands; seed plants, less frequently. Because ferns arrive more readily, oceanic islands harbor relatively more fern species than seed plants.

The Juan Fernández archipelago provides some outstanding examples of truly long-distance spore dispersal. Some ferns originally came from faraway places such as Australia, Tasmania, New Zealand, and various islands in the southern Pacific. *Hymenophyllum ferrugineum* (Figure 107), a filmy fern that grows in shady, protected places on mountaintops, apparently came from New Zealand where it still grows today, 5500 miles (8900 km) away. Other fern species appear to have evolved from closely related ones that dispersed long ago to the islands. *Asplenium chondrophyllum*, an endemic that grows in seaside rock crevices and overhangs, is most closely related to *A. obtusatum*, which grows in Australia, New Zealand, and southern Chile. *Arthropteris altescandens* (Figure 108), another endemic, has its closest kin in Tahiti and Samoa.

An even more striking example of long-distance dispersal is *Grammitis poeppigiana* (Figure 108). Besides the Juan Fernández Islands, it grows in South Africa, the Kerguelen Islands, Amsterdam and St. Paul Islands, Australia, Tasmania, New Zealand, Chile, Argentina, the Falkland Islands, and Tristan da Cunha. Its distribution surrounds Antarctica more closely and completely than any other fern. Long-distance spore dispersal is the only way this species could have reached so many scattered, remote islands—islands that were never linked by land bridges in the geological past.

Besides long-distance dispersal, the life cycle of ferns (Chapter 1) lends itself to colonizing faraway places. A single spore can arrive on an island, germinate, and develop into a gametophyte that in most species of ferns is bisexual, bearing both male and female sex organs (antheridia and archegonia). Self-fertilization can occur and give rise to a new spore-bearing plant. Seed plants, on the other hand, face problems that ferns do not have to worry about. If the newly arrived individual of a seed plant is an entirely carpellate individual, it might be that staminate individuals are not present to provide pollen for fertilization. Or animals needed for pollination may not be present, either. The absence of insect pollinators is one of the reasons why orchid species, which require highly specific pollinators, are few on oceanic islands, even though they disperse by dust-like seeds scattered by winds just as readily as fern spores. (Hawaii, for example, has only three native species of orchids.)

A newly arrived fern spore may develop into a gametophyte that can

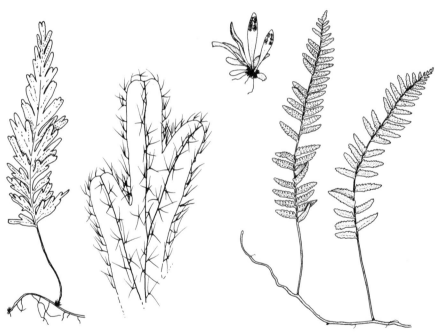

Figure 107 The filmy fern *Hymeno-phyllum ferrugineum*, from New Zealand. Left, whole plant; the leaves in nature are pendent. Right, pinna apex, showing stellate hairs. Drawing by the author.

Figure 108 Left, *Grammitis poeppigiana*, a fern distributed around the southern hemisphere, especially at high latitudes. Right, *Arthropteris altescandens*, an endemic of the Juan Fernández Islands whose closest kin are in Tahiti and Samoa. Drawing by the author.

self-fertilize and produce a new sporophyte, but the offspring are a long way from the source population and therefore unlikely to breed with any more individuals from there. This lack of interbreeding allows new characteristics to become fixed in island populations. New traits that arise can spread without being overwhelmed by alternative traits from the source population. If enough new characteristics accumulate, the result is a new subspecies or species. This is how many island endemics originate.

Evolution fostered by isolation probably gave rise to most of the Juan Fernández Islands' endemics, which constitute 25 of the 54 fern species (46%) on the islands. In some, however, the species became endemic by going extinct elsewhere in their range. For these, the islands serve as a refuge, a kind of retirement home instead of a cradle. An example is *Thyrsopteris elegans,* a tree fern belonging to the Dicksoniaceae and the only species in its genus (Figure 109). It is a vestige of a once-diverse

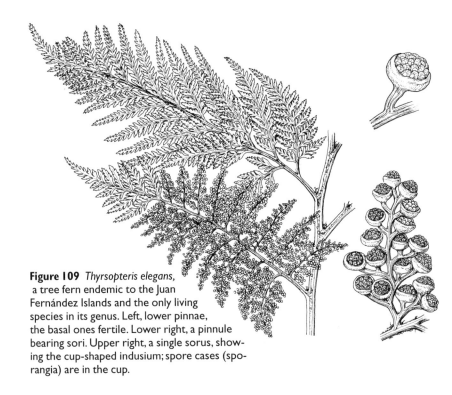

Figure 109 *Thyrsopteris elegans,* a tree fern endemic to the Juan Fernández Islands and the only living species in its genus. Left, lower pinnae, the basal ones fertile. Lower right, a pinnule bearing sori. Upper right, a single sorus, showing the cup-shaped indusium; spore cases (sporangia) are in the cup.

group that dominated the understory of Mesozoic forests 170 million to 80 million years ago (Harris 1961). Fossils of the group are known primarily from Spitsbergen, Greenland, and the United Kingdom. But fossils also reveal that *Thyrsopteris* grew on the mainland of Chile during the Cretaceous about 70 million years ago (Menéndez 1966). *Thyrsopteris* must have persisted on the continent until at least 4 million years ago, when the Juan Fernández Islands were first formed, after which it migrated to the islands and then became extinct on the mainland.

Nowadays, however, *Thyrsopteris* needs more than long-distance dispersal to survive. Nearly four centuries of habitation by people have left the islands a diminished place for ferns. Most of the forests at lower elevations have been cut, and overgrazing by cattle has caused widespread soil erosion. Goats have nibbled the vegetation to nubbins and prevented forest regeneration. An introduced species of bramble (*Rubus*) sprouts everywhere, forming dense, impenetrable thickets that also prevent forest regrowth. Forests and the ferns they harbor have dwindled.

But there is hope for the islands' ferns. Chileans increasingly support conservation efforts. Environmental educators are teaching the people who live on the islands about the archipelago's unique plants and animals. Chilean researchers are finding new ways to reforest land and are expanding their collaboration with foreign biologists. Perhaps with better management, the islands will continue to serve as a refuge for ferns, just as they did three centuries ago for Alexander Selkirk.

24

Sino-American Relations

Jonas Petrus Halenius, a student of the great Carl Linnaeus, probably suffered a nervous stomach on 22 December 1750. On that day he had to undergo the public ordeal of defending, in Latin, his doctoral dissertation in the Great Caroline Lecture Hall at the University of Uppsala. The dissertation was titled *Plantae Rariores Camschatcenses* (rare Kamchatkan plants), and it might have given him good cause for nervousness because he had neither researched it nor written it!

Nowadays, doctoral students are expected to research and write their own dissertations—and show some originality and critical thought to boot! But such was not the case in Halenius's day. Back then everyone knew that the dissertation represented the professor's effort, not the student's. The purpose of the oral examination was to test the student's fluency in Latin, knowledge of the rules of formal disputation, and ability to express thoughts coherently. The professor benefited because the student had to bear all costs of publishing the dissertation. These procedures for advanced academic degrees were accepted at Swedish universities until 1852 (Graham 1966, Stearn 1957).

Botanists today are interested in Halenius's (or I should say Linnaeus's) dissertation because it is the first mention of one of the most striking disjunctions in the distribution of plant life on earth: the similarities between the floras of the eastern temperate portions of North America and Asia. These two regions share more genera and species than any other two regions on earth (Boufford and Spongberg 1983, Kato 1993, Kato and Iwatsuki 1983, Li 1952). Given the great distance separating them, the two regions might be expected to have few or no species in common. The flora of eastern North America might be expected to be more similar to that of western North America or Mexico, and the flora of eastern Asia to that of India or Indonesia.

The most familiar examples of the similarities are flowering plants. They include common trees and shrubs such as aralias, catalpas, hydrangeas, magnolias, persimmons (*Diospyros*), tulip trees (*Liriodendron*), wisterias, and witch hazels (*Hamamelis*). Some wildflowers concentrated in both regions are astilbes, cohoshes (*Caulophyllum*), Dutchman's-breeches (*Dicentra*), ginsengs (*Panax*), mayapples (*Podophyllum*), partridge berries (*Mitchella*), Solomon's seals (*Polygonatum*), and trilliums. These examples are genera, but only rarely do both regions share the same species.

In contrast, the ferns exhibit many species in common to both regions. Hokkaido, the northernmost island of Japan, has roughly the same number of fern species as northeastern North America: 122 and 116, respectively. Of these, 47 (40%) are common to both regions—an outstandingly high percentage given the distance separating the two regions. Species in common (Figure 110) include the maidenhair fern (*Adiantum pedatum*, Plate 2), silvery spleenwort (*Deparia acrostichoides*), interrupted fern (*Osmunda claytoniana*, Figure 38), and the pubescent variety of the marsh fern (*Thelypteris palustris* var. *pubescens*).

Besides the *same* species, floristic similarity between the two regions is evinced by pairs of most closely related species, what taxonomists call sister species, where one occurs in eastern North America and the other in eastern Asia. An example is the walking fern (*Asplenium rhizophyllum*) of the eastern North America. Its closest relative is Ruprecht's walking fern (*A. ruprechtii*) of eastern Asia. Both species thrive on shaded cliffs and mossy boulders. They differ only by the base of the blade being heart-shaped in the American plants versus rounded to tapered in the Asian ones (Figure 111). Their close relationship is indicated by a

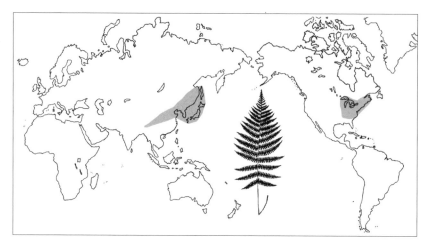

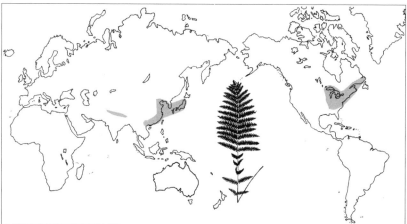

Figure 110 Distributions of the silvery spleenwort (*Deparia acrostichoides*, above) and the interrupted fern (*Osmunda claytoniana*, below).

number of shared characteristics *not* found in other aspleniums: netted veins and long-triangular leaves drawn out into a whip-like tip. When the tip touches the ground, a new plantlet is formed, and when this plantlet matures it repeats the process, as does the plantlet from that plantlet, and so on, forming a connected series of individuals, all produced vegetatively and having the same genetic constitution. By this manner of growth, the plants appear to walk over the rocks (Plate 4). The morphology and growth habit of the walking ferns are so different

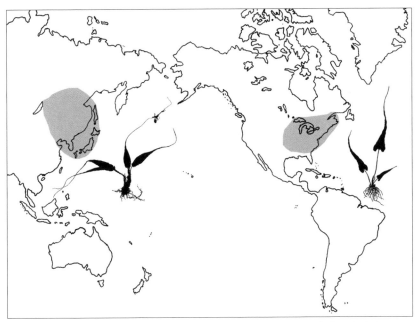

Figure III The walking ferns *Asplenium ruprechtii* (left) and *A. rhizophyllum* (right) are sister species that provide an example of a floristic relationship between eastern Asia and eastern North America.

from other aspleniums that they are sometimes placed in their own genus, *Camptosorus,* to emphasize the distinctness.

Other North American ferns find their next of kin in eastern Asia. The New York fern (*Thelypteris noveboracensis*) is a close relative of the narrow-sorus fern (*T. nipponica*) of Japan. The hay-scented fern (*Dennstaedtia punctilobula*), which is often weedy in New England and parts of the Appalachians, finds its cousins in the two Asian species *D. appendiculata* and *D. scabra,* and the Massachusetts fern (*T. simulata*) shares blood ties with two Asian relatives, *T. glanduligera* and *T. japonica.* The glade fern (*Diplazium pycnocarpon*) of the eastern United States is kin to a remarkably similar Malesian fern, *D. flavoviride,* and both belong to a clan of species concentrated in eastern Asia (Kato and Darnedi 1988).

How did these floristic similarities arise? The answer harks back to the Tertiary, the geological time interval between the demise of the dinosaurs and the onset of the Ice Ages. During the early Tertiary about

189

54 million to 38 million years ago, the earth's climate was the warmest in the history of plant life on earth (Parrish 1987). Warmth-loving tropical and temperate forests thrived around the globe at high northern latitudes. In North America these forests occurred as far north as Greenland, northern Canada, and Alaska. They extended westward across the Bering Strait (which was above sea level for most of the Tertiary) into Siberia and other parts of Asia. To the east the forest crossed two land bridges into Europe (Tiffney 1985a, b). For millions of years this circumboreal forest provided a nearly continuous habitat. Over time, migration resulted in a similar mix of species across the northern hemisphere—a mix that paleobotanists refer to as the boreotropical flora (also referred to as the Arcto-Tertiary geoflora, a name now out of favor among paleobotanists).

Thanks to fossils, we have a glimpse of what this boreotropical flora was like. Two of its well-known members were the coast redwood (*Sequoia sempervirens*) and dawn redwood (*Metasequoia glyptostroboides*), which grew in Asia, Alaska, northern Canada, Greenland, Spitsbergen, and Europe. Today the coast redwood grows only in coastal California, and the dawn redwood in a few isolated valleys in China. Dawn redwood is often called a living fossil because it was first discovered as a fossil in 1941, then living plants were found 3 years later. As for ferns, the sensitive fern (*Onoclea sensibilis*, Figure 52) flourished in North America, Greenland, the British Isles, and Japan during the Tertiary. It is now restricted to eastern North America and eastern Asia (Figure 112).

What reduced the ranges of two redwoods and the sensitive fern? The distributions of many plants (and animals) were reduced during the latter half of the Tertiary as the earth's climate grew more seasonal and cooled—trends that culminated in the Ice Ages. Many warmth-loving species of the boreotropical flora receded southward, severing their ties across Eurasia and North America. Ranges were further fragmented in North America by the uplift of the Rocky Mountains during the middle Tertiary. The mountains cast a rain shadow over the interior of the continent, creating a drier climate that favored grasslands, giving rise to the Great Plains. The expansion of grasslands in central North America restricted much of the boreotropical flora to the east-

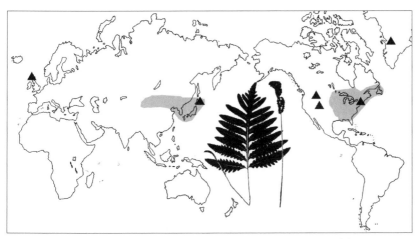

Figure 112 Tertiary (triangles) and present-day (shaded) distributions of the sensitive fern (*Onoclea sensibilis*).

ern United States. In Eurasia the extent of the flora was similarly narrowed by climatic and geologic changes, so that by end of the Tertiary the boreotropical flora had fragmented into three great blocks: eastern North America, eastern Asia, and western Europe.

What about Europe? Its flora resembles that of eastern North America and eastern Asia, but to a lesser extent. It became impoverished during the Ice Ages by glaciers bulldozing their way southward and squeezing the boreotropical flora against the Pyrenees and Alps. These mountains prevented many warmth-loving plants from migrating to milder climates farther south, and as a result, many went extinct in Europe. There were no east–west mountain chains in North America or eastern Asia to impede migration; consequently, far fewer plants went extinct. After the glaciers in Europe receded northward, the land was revegetated by a depauperate flora. Today, Europe has only 150 species of ferns and lycophytes whereas eastern North America has about 350. It is difficult to estimate the number of species in eastern Asia, but Japan alone has more than 600.

Several fern species survived the vicissitudes of the Ice Ages and nowadays occur in all three areas: North America, Europe, and Asia (Figure 113). Examples are the hart's-tongue fern (*Asplenium scolopendrium*),

191

ostrich fern (*Matteuccia struthiopteris*), winter scouring rush (*Equisetum hyemale*), marsh fern (*Thelypteris palustris*), and royal fern (*Osmunda regalis*). Presumably, their success was largely because they were able to grow in the similar climates of all three regions. This ability allows them, and many other species, to grow well if transplanted from one region to another. Some of North America's best-known cultivated plants hail from China and Japan, including camellias, hollyhocks (*Althaea*), forsythias, wisterias, and peonies (*Paeonia*). So do some of North America's worst weeds: Japanese knotweed (*Polygonum japonicum*), kudzu vine (*Pueraria lobata*), and purple loosestrife (*Lythrum salicaria*). Some Asian ferns that enrich gardens in North America include the autumn fern (*Dryopteris erythrosora*), Fortune's holly fern (*Cyrtomium fortunei*), Japanese climbing fern (*Lygodium japonicum*), Japanese painted fern (*Athyrium niponicum* 'Pictum'), and Tsus-sima holly fern (*Polystichum tsus-simense*).

Eastern North America and eastern Asia, especially, and Europe, share a phytogeographical heritage that accounts for the similarities in their floras, one that extends back tens of millions of years to the early Tertiary. In no other group is this similarity as evident as in the ferns.

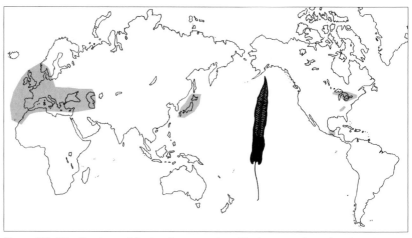

Figure 113 Distributions of the hart's-tongue fern (*Asplenium scolopendrium*) and its varieties: *lindenii* in southern Mexico, *americanum* in North America, and *scolopendrium* in Europe, North Africa, and western Asia. The range of this fern was probably continuous across North America and Eurasia during the Tertiary but became fragmented by the climatic cooling and seasonality that lead to the Ice Ages.

Plate 1 Prothallus of a fern. The archegonia are the dark structures beneath the notch.
Photograph by Gordon Foster.

Plate 2 The maidenhair fern (*Adiantum pedatum*) occurs in eastern North America
and eastern Asia.

Plate 3 The lasagna fern, a widely cultivated form of the bird's-nest fern (*Asplenium nidus*), has thick, wavy leaves.

Plate 4 The eastern North American walking fern (*Asplenium rhizophyllum*), which has its closest relative in eastern Asia.

Plate 6 Prothallus and first leaf (light green, lobed, erect) of the lady fern (*Athyrium filix-femina*). Photograph by Gordon Foster.

Plate 5 The maidenhair spleenwort (*Asplenium trichomanes*), a species that contains diploid (shown here), tetraploid, and hexaploid races.

Plate 7 Tree fern (*Cyathea*) from Colombia. Photograph by Bill McKnight.

Plate 8
Carved tree fern trunks for sale in Mexico. At the base is the hole in the root mantle formerly occupied by the stem. Photograph by Blanca Pérez-García.

Plate 10 *Elaphoglossum hoffmannii,* from Costa Rica, showing gradation from iridescent to green leaves. Photograph by Mauricio Bonifacino.

Plate 9 *Dipteris conjugata,* from Taiwan. Its relatives were abundant, widespread, and conspicuous members of the fern flora throughout much of the Mesozoic. Photograph by S. J. Moore.

Plate 11 *Huperzia talamancana,* a lycophyte from Costa Rica. The yellow structures in the leaf axils are sporangia. Photograph by Mauricio Bonifacino.

Plate 13 A quillwort (*Isoetes*) growing in eutrophic waters and slightly covered by green algae. Photograph by Carl Taylor.

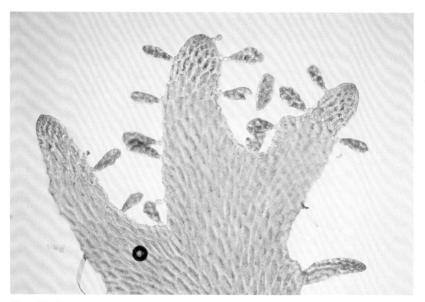

Plate 12 Gemmae along the margin of a gametophyte of *Hymenophyllum tayloriae.* The gemmae provide a means of vegetative reproduction. Photograph by Donald R. Farrar.

198

Plate 14 *Jamesonia,* a distinctive fern genus of the Andean páramos, celebrates William Jameson (1796–1873), Scottish botanist who collected plants around Quito, Ecuador. Photograph by John T. Mickel.

Plate 15 *Matonia pectinata,* from Malaysia. During much of the Mesozoic, relatives (now extinct) of this species were abundant worldwide. Photograph by S. J. Moore.

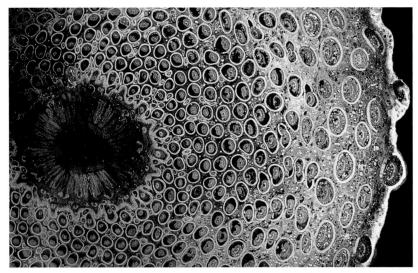

Plate 16 A fossilized trunk of *Palaeosmunda* from the Permian of Tasmania. The stem is the dark area at the center of the trunk; the many small circles represent leaf bases that surrounded the stem. From White (1986), photograph by James Frazier.

Plate 17 The scaly polypody (*Pleopeltis polypodioides*) in dried condition.

Plate 18 The scaly polypody (*Pleopeltis polypodioides*) in hydrated condition.
Photograph by John T. Mickel.

Plate 19 Sori of a polypody (*Poly-podium*) from Costa Rica. The poly-pody family (Polypodiaceae) is char-acterized by sori that lack indusia and by yellow spores.

Plate 20 The flat-branched whisk fern (*Psilotum complanatum*), from Mexico. Photograph by John T. Mickel.

Plate 21 The molesting *Salvinia* (*S. molesta*), showing open growth form. Photograph by S. J. Moore.

Plate 22 The molesting *Salvinia* (*S. molesta*), showing crowded growth form. Photograph by S. J. Moore.

Plate 23 A submerged leaf of the molesting *Salvinia* (*S. molesta*), bearing root-like branches and round whitish sori. Photograph by S. J. Moore.

Plate 24 An iridescent spike moss (*Selaginella willdenowii*) from Thailand.

Plate 25 A potato fern (*Solanopteris brunei*) from Costa Rica. A tuber has been sectioned to show the chambers within, inhabited by ants.

Plate 26 The shoestring fern (*Vittaria lineata*), growing in the leaf axils of a palm in Florida.

FERN GEOGRAPHY

25
Ferns of the Lost World

"South America is a place I love, and I think, if you take it right through from Darien to Fuego, it's the grandest, richest, most wonderful bit of earth upon this planet. . . . Why shouldn't somethin' new and wonderful lie in such a country? And why shouldn't we be the men to find it out?" These words were ascribed to the fictional character Lord John Roxton by his creator, Sir Arthur Conan Doyle, in the science fiction novel *The Lost World* (1912). Such sentiments have been felt by many attracted by South America and its wonders. Doyle set his novel in the table-mountain or tepui region of southern Venezuela and adjacent Brazil and Guyana, a region harboring many unusual ferns, some of which occur no where else in the world. (The word tepui comes from the Pemón Indian language and means mountain. Nearly all the tepuis have pleasant-sounding Indian names such as Auyán, Chimantá, and Sipapo.) There is a curious parallel between these ferns and what happens to the protagonists in Doyle's novel.

At the beginning of the book, the eccentric and dictatorial Professor George Edward Challenger has just returned to London from a journey to Amazonia and claims to have come within range of a "lost world" where prehistoric animals still exist. Confronted by the incredulity of his colleagues, Challenger organizes an expedition consisting of Professor Summerlee, his most outspoken opponent, Lord John Roxton, an explorer and hunter, and Edward Malone, a young journalist who narrates the adventure. After a long voyage and several days' march into the interior, the four arrive within sight of the lost world—a high tepui whose flat top is cut off from the rest of the world by vertical sides. The explorers manage to locate a pinnacle only 40 feet (12 m) away from the main massif. They climb it, then cut down a tall tree to make a bridge to the tepui. But as soon as they reach the other side, the tree trunk falls to the ground through the treachery of one of their porters, leaving them stranded. Alone on the top of the tepui, they encounter dangerous prehistoric animals and cannibalistic ape-people. After several weeks of life-threatening perils, they find a tunnel leading down the tepui. They escape and return to London, where they are lionized and feted, and Challenger's reputation is restored. (Doyle later said that Challenger "has always amused me more than any other [character] which I have invented." No small admission from the creator of Sherlock Holmes!)

In real life, the region where the novel is set contains hundreds of scattered, isolated tepuis ranging from tower-like spires to huge massifs whose summits cover hundreds or thousands of square miles or kilometers. Their heights range from 2100 to 9000 feet (700–3000 m). Typically, these sandstone mountains have nearly flat summits flanked by one to three tiers of sheer vertical cliffs that drop 300–1500 feet (100–500 m) before being broken by forested talus slopes. Overall, they give the impression of a medieval fortress: rock-bound, vertical-walled, impregnable (Figure 114).

Just as Challenger and his band of explorers were stranded on top of a tepui, so too are the ferns that live there, along with the other plants and animals. Each tepui is isolated from others by miles or kilometers of intervening lowland forests or savannas—habitats unfavorable for those ferns adapted to the conditions on top of the tepuis. For these ferns, migration from one tepui to another is only possible by long-distance dispersal (Chapter 23). Biologically, therefore, each tepui is an island.

Isolation exerts a profound effect on populations of plants and animals—it quarantines the population genetically. Rarely, if ever, will its
individuals interbreed with others on nearby tepuis. This allows differences to accumulate in the population without being diluted by genes
from outside. If enough genetic differences accumulate so that the population looks quite different from the original one, then a new species
has evolved.

The tepuis have been an evolutionary cradle for thousands of plant
and animal species. Among the ferns, the family Hymenophyllopsidaceae and genus *Pterozonium* originated there and today are found no
where else in the world (Lellinger 1967, 1987). The Hymenophyllopsidaceae comprises the single genus *Hymenophyllopsis*, which consists of
eight species, all of which grow on or near the tepui summits, usually in
shaded rock crevices or on ledges. All the species have thin leaves with
blade tissue only three or four cells thick between the veins—so thin
that stomata are unnecessary. Their sori are borne along the edge of the
leaf blade, not on the lower surface as in most ferns (Figure 115). In
these two characteristics they resemble the filmy fern genus *Hymenophyllum; -opsis* in *Hymenophyllopsis* is a Greek suffix denoting similarity. But
there the resemblance stops. Evidence from DNA suggests that *Hymeno-*

Figure 114 Cerro Huachamacari, a tepui in southern Venezuela. Photograph by Bruce Holst.

207

phyllopsis is related to—of all things!—the tree fern families Cyatheaceae and Dicksoniaceae, along with some smaller, less well known families: Plagiogyriaceae, Metaxyaceae, and Lophosoriaceae (Wolf et al. 1994).

Similarly, the genus *Pterozonium*, with 14 species, also grows on rocks. It is actually a quasi-endemic because it also occurs at a few scattered sites in Costa Rica, Ecuador, and Peru. Its blades are leathery and either simple or singly pinnate, not delicate and highly divided as in many ferns (Figure 116). Typically, the blades or pinnae have broadly rounded tips, and the sori are arranged in lines along the veins on the lower surface of the blades, collectively forming a band or zone near the margin. The name *Pterozonium* refers to this zone, coming from the Greek *pteris*, an ancient word for fern, and *zona*, zone.

Are *Hymenophyllopsis* and *Pterozonium* ancient relics, like the dinosaurs in Doyle's novel, or have they evolved recently? The latter seems likely, for two reasons. First, geological and palynological studies show that the tepuis have not been static, unchanging places but instead experienced climatic upheavals and vegeta-

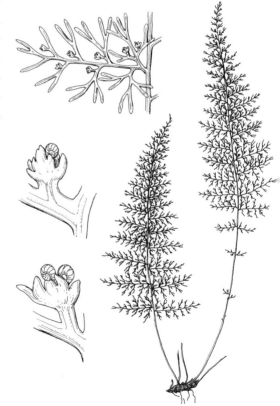

Figure 115 *Hymenophyllopsis hymenophylloides.* The Hymenophyllopsidaceae, with its single genus, is endemic to the tepui region of southern Venezuela. Above left, a pinna. Lower left, two close-ups of the sori.

tional changes during the Ice Ages. Even if the species growing on top of the tepuis were ancient, they have not been growing there since the Age of Dinosaurs. Second, *Pterozonium* belongs to the Pteridaceae, a family whose earliest appearance in the fossil record postdates the extinction of the dinosaurs (*Hymenophyllopsis* has no fossil record). Assuming the fossil record is giving us an accurate estimate of when the family first evolved, *Pterozonium* is too young to have tickled the bellies of the dinosaurs.

The tepuis belong to a geographic region called the Guayana Shield, which extends eastward to French Guiana and westward to Colombia (east of the Andes). The shield consists of Precambrian granite or basalt, which forms the base upon which the tepuis rest. The entire shield region—not just its tepuis—harbors many endemic fern species. Alan Smith (1995), a pteridologist at the University of California, Berkeley, recorded 671 species of pteridophytes from the region, about 145 (22%) of which are endemic. In contrast, flowering plant endemism is much higher, 65%. Why is it lower for ferns?

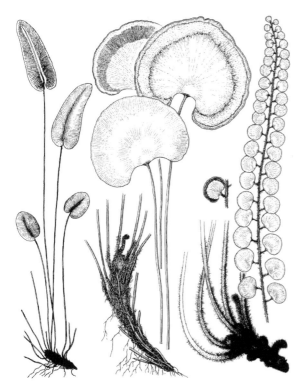

Figure 116 Three species of *Pterozonium* (left to right: *P. scopulinum*, *P. reniforme*, *P. spectabile*), a fern genus nearly endemic to the tepui region of southern Venezuela.

Ferns disperse by dust-like spores that can be carried long distances by winds. But flowering plants disperse by larger and heavier seeds or fruits that are less likely to be carried long distances (Chapter 23). Because ferns are more easily dispersed than flowering plants, they are more likely to occur outside a given area and, consequently, less likely to be endemic.

Nevertheless, endemic ferns *do* occur on the tepuis, and doubtless more occur there but have yet to be discovered. Part of the problem in exploring the tepuis is the risk associated with getting to their tops. Helicopters must often be used to shuttle biologists to and from base camps in the lowlands, and the round-trip can be fraught with difficulties. The most common problem is bad weather setting in, leaving scientists stranded on top of the tepuis for days or weeks. This happened to the only fern specialist ever to visit a tepui, Joseph M. Beitel (1952–1991) of the New York Botanical Garden. He and 12 other scientists were stranded on Cerro de Neblina for 12 days after bad weather set in and the helicopter at their base camp ran out of fuel. With less than an 8-day supply of food, they were forced to forage. The ornithologists set up their mist nets and caught a few birds to eat, and some of the botanists cut palm hearts. Michael Nee, a botanist also with the New York Botanical Garden, gathered fresh blueberries (*Vaccinium puberulum* var. *tatei*) and shared them. Only Joe Beitel refused to eat them; he was once warned never to eat blueberries growing in high mountains. Soon, those who had eaten them were passing out from low blood pressure and slow heart rate. Most were on their backs about 8 hours, conscious but unable to move. Some, like Mike Nee, went temporarily blind. During the ordeal, Joe cared for everyone and took notes on their symptoms. Eventually, everyone recovered and suffered no further ill effects.

Despite the risk of becoming stranded, most scientists would jump at the opportunity to visit the tepuis. They know their chances are excellent for finding new and unusual species—plants and animals that no one has ever seen. As Lord Roxton said in *The Lost World*, "Why shouldn't somethin' new and wonderful lie in such a country?" And why shouldn't we be the ones to find it out?

FERN GEOGRAPHY

26
Ferns, Flashlights,
and Tertiary Forests

Donald Farrar, a professor of botany at Iowa State University, seeks
ferns with a flashlight. This might sound like an unusual tool for a botanist, but the objects of his search are unusual ferns. What Don seeks
are "independent" fern gametophytes, tiny plantlets that never produce
sporophytes. They grow in cool, shaded, rocky places such as beneath
sandstone ledges, under cliff overhangs, and in fissures and crevices—all
habitats with stable microclimates that have not changed much over the
millennia. Don uses his flashlight to peer into these dim places, and the
story he has illuminated is one of the most fascinating in all of pteridology.

Independent gametophytes do not look like the typical fern gametophytes illustrated in botany textbooks. The latter are usually flat,
heart-shaped prothalli. They grow individually, not in colonies, and
typically live less than a year in the wild, dying soon after producing a
sporophyte. Any special means of vegetative (asexual) reproduction is
absent. In contrast, the independent gametophytes are either thread-
like filaments or ribbon-shaped prothalli. They branch profusely, and in-

stead of being short-lived, single individuals, they occur as perennial, evergreen colonies that can carpet as much as several square yards or meters of rock. The colonies reproduce by specialized buds called gemmae, which consist of 2–10 cells that detach and disperse to new locations. By their perennial growth and gemmae, independent gametophytes perpetuate themselves without producing sporophytes.

Don has studied independent gametophytes for about 30 years, primarily in the eastern United States (Farrar 1985–1998). So far he knows of four species that occur there. Two of them—the dwarf polypody (*Micropolypodium nimbata*) and Taylor's filmy fern (*Hymenophyllum tayloriae*, Plate 12)—are extremely rare. They occur only in a small cluster of counties along the border of North and South Carolina, and also, in the case of Taylor's filmy fern, in deep, narrow canyons of northwestern Alabama. But the other two species—the *Trichomanes* gametophyte (*T. intricatum*) and the Appalachian gametophyte (*Vittaria appalachiana*)—are common and widespread in the dissected plateaus and mountains of the eastern United States (Figure 117).

The most widespread is the *Trichomanes* gametophyte, which resembles a small clump or weft of green cotton stuck to the rocks; some describe them as felt-like or resembling tiny pads of green steel wool. When viewed with a hand lens, the colonies resolve into a tangle of multicellular filaments, some of which bear spindle-shaped gemmae at their tips (Figure 118).

The Appalachian gametophyte looks like finely chopped lettuce

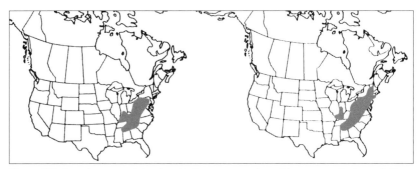

Figure 117 Distributions of the Appalachian gametophyte (*Vittaria appalachiana*, left) and *Trichomanes* gametophyte (*T. intricatum*, right). From Flora of North America Committee (1993).

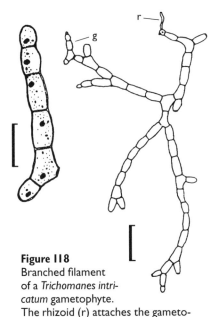

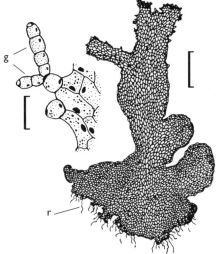

Figure 118
Branched filament of a *Trichomanes intricatum* gametophyte. The rhizoid (r) attaches the gametophyte to the substrate; the gemma (g, enlarged at left) can detach and disperse to a new location. Scale bars: left, 0.1 mm (0.004 inch); right, 0.2 mm (0.008 inch). From Yatskievych et al. (1987).

Figure 119 Prothallus of the Appalachian gametophyte (*Vittaria appalachiana*). The rhizoid (r) attaches the gametophyte to the substrate; the gemmae (g) can detach and disperse to a new location. Scale bars: left, 0.1 mm (0.004 inch); right, 1 mm (0.04 inch). From Yatskievych et al. (1987).

sprinkled over the rocks. It is elongate or ribbon-shaped and branches frequently and irregularly (Figure 119). Some of its branches turn upright along their margins and produce spindle-shaped gemmae (Figure 120). Because of its flattened form, the Appalachian gametophyte might be mistaken for a liverwort, but it differs by being only one cell thick, lacking a midrib and pores, and bearing marginal gemmae.

Despite their unusual appearance, independent gametophytes can be difficult to find in the field. For 2 years as a student at Southern Illinois University at Carbondale, I searched in vain for *Trichomanes* gametophytes in the nearby Shawnee National Forest. I knew that the gametophytes grow there in sandstone canyons, but I had only a vague idea of what they looked like and of the exact combination of shade, temperature, and humidity they seem to prefer. Only after graduating did I see herbarium specimens, which gave me the search image needed to find

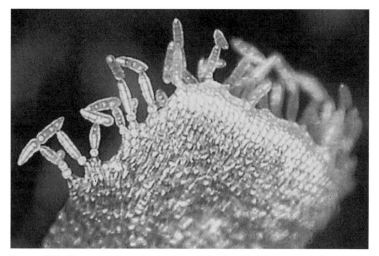

Figure 120 Gemmae along the margin of the Appalachian gametophyte (*Vittaria appalachiana*). Photograph by Donald Farrar.

plants in the field. My first discovery was exciting but embarrassing: they were common in an area I had already searched!

Although occurring widely in the temperate eastern United States, the independent gametophytes are members of tropical fern families. The *Trichomanes* gametophyte and Taylor's filmy fern belong to the Hymenophyllaceae, the filmy fern family, so named because its leaves have a filmy texture from being only one cell thick between the veins. Filmy ferns thrive in wet tropical forests where their leaves do not dry out. The Appalachian gametophyte represents another tropical family, the Vittariaceae or shoestring ferns. Many of the species are epiphytes with pendulous, shoestring-like leaves (Plate 26). A third tropical family, Grammitidaceae, is represented by the dwarf polypody. Nearly all species in this family flourish as epiphytes in cloud forests.

Tropical affinities aside, the most anomalous feature of the independent gametophytes is that which makes them independent: their steadfast refusal to produce sporophytes. Don Farrar has tried coaxing them to do so by growing them under greenhouse conditions that simulate tropical climates—the same conditions in which gametophytes of related tropical species produce sporophytes. Although the green-

214

house-grown independent gametophytes bear sex organs (that is, antheridia and archegonia, which they also produce in the temperate climate in nature), they never develop sporophytes. The gametophytes lack the ability to produce sporophytes—an ability their ancestors must once have had.

What explains this lost ability? How and when did independent gametophytes with tropical affinities become established in the temperate eastern United States? These questions have two possible answers. The first is that independent gametophytes were established (and still are) by spores blown northward from existing sporophyte populations in the American tropics. In other words, they represent present-day tropical species *and* are the result of recent (that is, since the Ice Age) long-distance dispersal. Over time, the sporophytes were lost because they did not tolerate the cold winters. The other answer is that independent gametophytes became established when tropical forests covered the eastern United States during the first half of the Tertiary about 65 million to 35 million years ago. This period was the warmest in the history of plant life on earth, with temperatures at 80° north latitude about 54°F (30°C) warmer than now, and at 30° north, about 9–18°F (5–10°C) warmer (Parrish 1987). This enabled tropical forests to flourish in the eastern United States and warmth-loving plants such as palms, bald cypress (*Taxodium distichum*), and dawn redwood (*Metasequoia glyptostroboides*) to grow as far north as Greenland and Alaska. Just as filmy ferns and shoestring ferns grow in tropical forests today, the sporophyte-producing ancestors of the independent gametophytes grew in tropical forests of eastern North America during the Tertiary. As the climate cooled and grew more seasonal during the latter half of the Tertiary (a cooling that culminated in the Ice Ages), the tropical species in the eastern United States were gradually replaced by temperate ones. The sporophytes of filmy ferns and shoestring ferns could not tolerate the new climate and were lost. The gametophytes, however, toughed it out and persisted to this day as relicts.

Which explanation is correct? It depends on the species of gametophyte. The first answer—recent long-distance dispersal—best explains the origin of the dwarf polypody gametophytes, which occur in the

United States only at a single site in Macon County, North Carolina. Unlike the other species of independent gametophytes, this one still produces sporophytes, although they are extremely rare and never bear spores. This suggests recent dispersal—so recent that the plants have not yet had time to lose their sporophyte-producing ability. This is corroborated by Don Farrar's discovery that some of the rare sporophytes are identical with those of a fern (*Micropolypodium nimbata*) from the West Indies. There, the species regularly produces sporophytes with spores, and it is likely that an errant spore could have been blown from there to the site in North Carolina, perhaps during a hurricane.

But the second explanation—establishment during the Tertiary—best fits the facts for the other species. Don found during his studies of the gametophytes' enzymes, morphology, and development that these characteristics differed from those of related species in tropical America. The differences were strong and numerous enough to indicate that the independent gametophytes are distinct species in their own right (Farrar 1990). Therefore, they could not have migrated from tropical America.

But how can a fern lose the *entire* sporophyte generation? Are there any intermediate steps known that show how this might have happened? Surviving without the sporophyte poses no problem for gametophytes that grow perennially and reproduce by gemmae. Two examples illustrate this: Wright's filmy fern and the Killarney fern. Wright's filmy fern (*Hymenophyllum wrightii*) occurs in an arc around the northern Pacific, from northern Japan to Alaska and south to Vancouver Island. In Canada its gametophytes are widespread, but sporophytes are restricted to the Queen Charlotte Islands. No one knows why the gametophytes elsewhere in Canada do not produce sporophytes, but they easily persist by continuous vegetative growth and by producing gemmae.

The Killarney fern (*Trichomanes speciosum*) grows in the British Isles. During the Victorian fern craze of the middle 1800s (Chapter 32), hoards of enthusiasts descended upon populations of the Killarney fern and plundered them for their lacy leaves, which were pressed and kept as nature memorabilia. This nearly wiped out the sporophytes so that today the species is one of Britain's most endangered plants. The gametophytes, however, small and inconspicuous, went unnoticed and un-molested, persisting to this day at sites where the sporophytes used to grow. In fact, the gametophytes went unnoticed until 1989 when Don found them during a sabbatical leave in Britain. His discovery prompted searches elsewhere in Europe, and today the gametophytes of the Killar-ney fern are known from Luxembourg, France, and Germany (Rasbach et al. 1993, Ratcliffe et al. 1993, Rumsey et al. 1990, 1991). Like Wright's filmy fern, the gametophytes of Killarney fern seem preadapted to inde-pendent existence, thanks largely to perennial growth and reproduction by gemmae. (Although now a means of dispersal, gemmae might have originally served in sexual reproduction by providing the only source of tissue susceptible to antheridiogens—the hormones that stimulate the formation of antheridia and thus promote cross-fertilization. This view is explained by Emigh and Farrar 1977.)

Independent gametophytes illustrate a major theme in plant evolu-tion: the loss of whole structures or organs. Famous examples of this theme are the loss of leaves in desert succulents, of petals and fragrance in wind-pollinated plants, and of chlorophyll in parasitic or saprophytic species. Yet none of these examples is as striking as that provided by the independent gametophytes; they have lost the entire sporophyte gener-ation! Although they have lost the ability to produce big, beautiful leaves, independent gametophytes are enormously satisfying to find in the field. Once I spot them, I like to move in close and take a long look with my hand lens, examining them carefully and trying to find their gemmae. This examination strikes me, a member of a recent, highly tentative ex-periment in evolution, as an instructive event, for these tiny plants have been in eastern North America at least since the middle of the Tertiary some 35 million years ago. And that is a very long time, indeed.

FERN GEOGRAPHY

27

Tropical Diversity

One of the most striking facts in biology is the richness of life in the tropics. As you go from the nearly lifeless ice of the poles toward the equator, the number of species increases dramatically. With few exceptions, the tropics harbor more kinds of organisms—more birds and butterflies, mammals and reptiles, fish and flowering plants—than the temperate zones. This trend, which was also present in the geological past, is called the latitudinal diversity gradient. It is *the* major pattern in the distribution of life on earth, and ferns and lycophytes provide a prime example of it.

If, for instance, you traveled southward in eastern Asia, you would find 42 species of ferns and lycophytes on the Kamchatka Peninsula of Russia, 140 on Hokkaido Island and 430 on Honshu Island of Japan, 560 in Taiwan, 960 in the Philippines, and about 1200 in Borneo. In the Americas, the pattern is the same: 30 species of pteridophytes in Greenland, 98 in New England, 113 in Florida, 652 in Guatemala, and 1250 in Ecuador (Figure 121). In either hemisphere, as you move from high latitudes to the equator, the number of species increases more than 30 times.

This increase makes for some striking comparisons. Costa Rica, a country slightly smaller than West Virginia, has about 1165 species of ferns and lycophytes—nearly three times as many as the United States and Canada. On the Caribbean side of Costa Rica is the La Selva Biological Station. Within its borders lie 9½ square miles (15 km²) of rain forest harboring 150 species of ferns and lycophytes—roughly the same number as in the entire northeastern United States (Grayum and Churchill 1987).

But numbers of species are only half the picture. The tropics also harbor more morphological diversity—more sizes, shapes, and architectures of plants—than the temperate zones. This diversity gets expressed taxonomically by the greater number of families and genera, some of which are nearly or entirely restricted to the tropics. For instance, tree ferns occur almost entirely in the tropics. So do scrambling ferns, which clamber over the surrounding vegetation and rest on it for support, ferns such as *Lygodium* and many species of *Odontosoria* and *Hypolepis*. Epiphytic ferns that festoon the trunks and branches of tropical rain forest trees are rare or entirely absent in the temperate zones. Many common tropical fern families, such as the forked ferns (Gleicheniaceae), dwarf polypodies (Grammitidaceae), and shoestring ferns (Vittariaceae), are largely or wholly absent from the temperate zones. Tropical diversity, therefore, exceeds temperate diversity in two respects: it embraces more species *and* more varieties of life forms.

What causes the latitudinal diversity gradient is one of the big questions of evolutionary biology. Not surprisingly, several hypotheses have been proposed. One of the most frequently discussed is the stability-time hypothesis. It maintains that the rate of new species formation in the temperate and tropical zones is the same, but because the tropics have been more climatically stable for millions of years, the extinction rate there has been lower. The temperate zones, which have been climatically unstable and subject to major episodes of glaciation, present a greater danger of extinction. Thus, over time, more species have accumulated in the tropics.

One problem with this hypothesis is that the tropics have not been static, unchanging places. Evidence from geomorphology, palynology, and climatology reveals that the tropics have experienced climatic changes during the Ice Ages and the preceding geological period, the

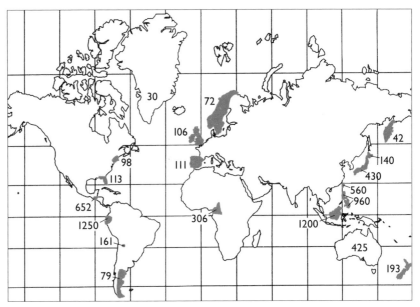

Figure 121 Numbers of fern and lycophyte species in various regions of the world. Note the increase toward the equator.

Tertiary. Just as climatic changes altered the distribution and extent of prairies, coniferous forests, and deciduous woodlands in the temperate zones, so too did they alter savannas, rain forests, and páramos in the tropics. Thus the tropics have been dynamic, not static. If their extinction rate has been lower—an arguable claim—it cannot be attributed to climatic stability alone.

In sharp contrast to the stability-time hypothesis is the Ice Age (Pleistocene) refuge hypothesis. It claims that increased species richness in the tropics was driven by climatic instability during the last Ice Age. During periods of glacial advance in the higher latitudes, the tropics became cooler, drier, and perhaps more seasonal. These climatic conditions favored the spread of tropical grasslands and savannas at the expense of rain forests. Eventually, the rain forests fragmented into forested islands surrounded by a sea of grasslands and savannas. Within these islands, or refuges, populations of plants and animals were isolated from nearby populations and consequently cut off from the homogenizing effect of genes flowing in from the outside. The isolated populations evolved into new species, thus creating areas of increased endemism and species richness.

The Ice Age refuge hypothesis also has problems. Although the tropics have endured climatic instability and vegetation shifts, there is no direct evidence that patches of rain forest were surrounded by grasslands or savannas. Equally problematic is our inability to define the boundaries of the refugia using the criteria of high endemism and high species richness. Our knowledge of the distributions of tropical plants is poor. Moreover, we know little about present-day factors promoting endemism and species richness. Until these factors are better understood, it seems premature to explain tropical diversity solely on the basis of historical factors such as climatic instability and refuges.

That present-day factors influence species richness seems clear. Even within the tropics some regions have more species than others. For example, the Andes harbor more species than Amazonia, which has more species than the llanos (grassland plains) of Colombia and Venezuela. Differences also show up between habitats: rain forests contain more species than dry forests, which contain more species than mangrove swamps. Other factors are clearly at work besides latitude.

One such factor is annual rainfall. In general, tropical regions with high rainfall support more species than those with lower rainfall. Rain forests, for example, support more species than dry forests. Yet the total amount of annual rainfall is not the entire story; also important is how that rainfall is distributed throughout the year. Two regions might receive the same amount of yearly rainfall, but if one of the regions has a pronounced dry season, then it will harbor fewer species than the one with more evenly distributed year-round rainfall. Seasonality makes a big difference, especially for ferns, and in particular fern epiphytes. A good example is provided by the Amazon Basin. Near the mouth of the Amazon River, anytime from June to September, there is a distinct dry season, and the climate there supports only about 100 species of pteridophytes. As you move westward, rainfall becomes distributed more evenly throughout the year, and by the time the Andes come into view, you hardly notice a dry season. This wet, western part of Amazonia, butting up against the Andes from Colombia to Bolivia, hosts the greatest concentration of the region's fern species, perhaps as many as 500. Here, too, ferns form a conspicuous part of the vegetation, abundant on the forest floor and in the treetops.

Topographical diversity is also important. By far the most diverse areas for tropical ferns are the mountains. The Andes harbor an estimated 3000 species of ferns—more than any other region in the American tropics. This contrasts with the roughly 600 species found in the relatively flat Amazon Basin, even though Amazonia occupies a larger area than the Andes. In fact, Amazonia is the most species-*poor* region for ferns in the American tropics; this is also true for liverworts, hornworts, and mosses. If you want to see many different species of ferns, head for the hills.

What mountains offer, I think, are more habitats—habitats created by different combinations of elevation, temperature, cloud cover, rainfall, slopes, exposures, soils, and parent materials. These factors combine to create a mosaic of habitats, each hosting certain species not adapted to grow in others, and this boosts overall species richness. The lowlands are more uniform environmentally, lacking the gradients in elevation, temperatures and other factors that can vary over even short distances in the mountains (Moran 1995). Consequently, the lowlands accommodate fewer species.

Latitude, rainfall, seasonality, and mountains—all these influence species richness, but there are other variables. Additional hypotheses explain tropical diversity on the basis of factors such as solar radiation, niche diversity, and diseases. Probably all combine to form a complex network of physical and biological threads, a web that has been in the making for millions of years. This web is responsible for the rich diversity we see in the tropics today. This diversity draws biologists to the tropics again and again, pulled by the thrill of unexpected discovery and the wonder of seeing different species. Yet when we ask a seemingly simple question about this diversity—Why are there so many species in the tropics?—the answer turns out to be complex. It is a question that admits, after all, no single simple answer.

FERNS AND PEOPLE

28
Serpent's-Tongue Tea

About 100 miles (160 km) off the coast of mainland China lies the island of Taiwan. Although small—about one-third the size of my home state of New York—Taiwan is one of the powerhouses of Asia. Its capital and economic hub is Taipei, a noisy and congested city if there ever was one. Its streets are jammed with traffic—mostly motorcycles—and bordered on either side by tall gray concrete buildings. Power lines hang crisscrossed between the buildings like the rigging of a wrecked ship. But in the middle of the busy city is nestled a peaceful green enclave: the Chiang Kai-shek Memorial Park (Figure 122), an unlikely place for a pteridological discovery.

It is mid-March, and I am visiting the park with my friend and colleague Dr. Shu-miaw Chaw, plant taxonomist at the Institute of Botany, Academia Sinica, Taipei. Shu-miaw has just given me a tour of the Chiang Kai-shek Memorial Hall—an exquisite example of traditional architecture—and as we exit the hall and enter the park grounds, her attention is drawn to an expanse of lawn in front of the hall. It is devoid of people save an elderly woman kneeling in the middle, apparently weeding. Shu-miaw stops and looks at her intently. "I think she's collecting *Ophioglossum*," says Shu-miaw. "What! Here?" I protest, "You gotta be kidding!"

The last place I expect to find *Ophioglossum* is in the middle of a big city. I am used to finding it farther afield along roadsides and in woods and meadows. To satisfy my incredulity, we stride onto the lawn toward the kneeling woman. When only a few steps away, I see two small plastic shopping bags by the woman's side—each completely filled with *Ophioglossum*!

Shu-miaw speaks in Mandarin to the woman, who seems embarrassed by our curiosity. While they talk, I look down and see the pale green, fleshy blades of *Ophioglossum* scattered among the grass. The blades resemble many common lawn weeds, particularly plantains (*Plantago*), but differ by their lack of a midrib. Here and there the erect fertile spikes of *Ophioglossum* poke up above the grass like green pencils stuck in the ground. At the apex of each sit two rows of yellowish spore cases (sporangia). It is from this cluster of spore cases, which supposedly resemble a serpent's tongue, that the plant gets its name.

I pick a plant with a fertile spike and examine it. It is a species I recognize from the southeastern United States: *Ophioglossum petiolatum* (Figure 123). That is also a surprise! Shu-miaw finishes her conversation with the woman and turns to tell me about it. "She says they use the plants

Figure 122 Chiang Kai-shek Memorial Park in downtown Taipei; the large building is Chiang Kai-shek Memorial Hall. Drawing by the author.

in traditional Chinese medicine. The leaves are dried and then ground into a powder and used to make tea. She says the tea is good for general health." "What specifically does she mean by 'general health'?" I ask. Shu-miaw asks the woman again and gets the same enigmatic reply. It seems useless to ask the woman whether the plant is good for colds, arthritis, bronchitis, or a specific illness. I have had the same experience in Latin America upon finding ferns sold at markets or collected in the field for medicinal use. The answers about what maladies they cure are usually enigmatic, almost purposefully so, as if revealing that knowledge will take away the plant's power. We say *syèhsyeh* and *dzìjyèn* ("thank you" and "good-bye") to the woman and return to the sidewalk to continue our stroll.

Shu-miaw says she often sees people collecting *Ophioglossum* around Taipei. In fact, a colony grows in the front lawn of the Institute of Botany and is frequently harvested. Although working at the Institute for a few weeks, I had repeatedly walked past the colony without noticing it. Shu-miaw asks why the plants do not die from overharvesting. I point out that collectors do not dig up the stems and roots; they just pinch off the leaf at the base of its stalk. Because the belowground parts are left in the soil, the plants have a good chance to recover. Also, the stems and roots are infected with a symbiotic fungus that transports water and mineral nutrients from the soil into the plant, so they are

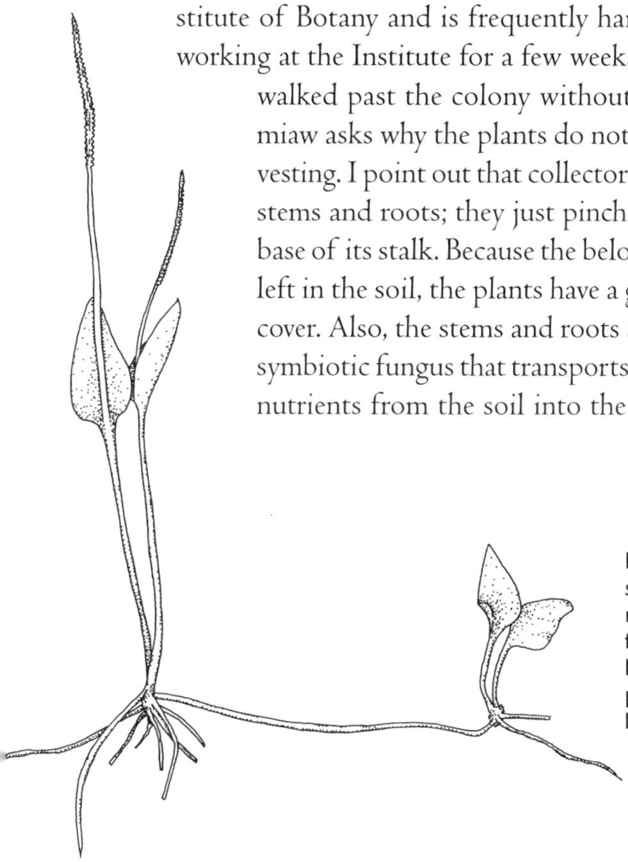

Figure 123 *Ophioglossum petiolatum*, a root running horizontally from the main plant has produced the plantlet on the right. Drawing by the author.

not entirely dependent on the green photosynthetic leaves for nutrition. Recovery is also facilitated by each stem's having three to five nested leaf buds at its apex. If the main leaf is removed, one of the buds grows to take its place.

It is hard to eradicate *Ophioglossum* because it spreads by root buds, forming colonies such as the one on the lawn. Most ferns with buds typically produce them on leaves or on highly modified stems (stolons or runners). *Ophioglossum* is one of the few that bear buds on roots (Chapter 5).

We complete our stroll around the park and hurry to a nearby restaurant to attend a banquet hosted by my botanical colleagues in Taiwan. As we enter the banquet room, I see my friend and collaborator Dr. Chen-meng Kuo of the Botany Department, National Taiwan University, Taipei. Chen-meng, an urbane and soft-spoken man, is the foremost expert on the ferns of Taiwan. I meander toward him through the crowd of botanists and eagerly tell him about finding *Ophioglossum.*

"I am not surprised," he remarks. "*Ophioglossum* is common in northern Taiwan. It even grows in the lawn near where I work on the campus of National Taiwan University. But it is much less common in southern Taiwan where the climate is drier." Chen-meng recounts his observations on the use of *Ophioglossum.* "In my experience, its use as a tea is rare. Most often, it is dried and ground to make a thick paste that is applied as a poultice to skin abscesses. Usually people who collect *Ophioglossum* do it for personal use, but some sell it for profit at open-air markets around Taipei. A 30-gram [1-ounce] bag of dried *Ophioglossum* leaves costs approximately 32 U.S. dollars."

On my return to the United States, I discover that, curiously, *Ophioglossum* once had a similar use in England. John Gerard, a herbalist, wrote in 1597 about "the vertues" of *Ophioglossum:* "The leaues of Adders tounge stamped in a stone morter, and boyled in Oile Oliue vnto the consumption of the iuyce, and vntill the herbes be dry and partched, and then strained, will yeeld a most excellent greene oyle, or rather a balsam for greene wounds, comparable vnto oyle of S. *Iohns* wort, if it do not farre surpasse it by many degrees: whose beauty is such, that very many Artists haue thought the same to be mixed with Verdigrease."

226

In her *Ferns of Great Britain* (1855), Anne Pratt mentioned that Gerard's preparation was still used in some counties in the United Kingdom, especially Kent, Sussex, and Surrey. There it was called the "green oil of Charity" and was sometimes fortified by adding plantain and other herbs.

I hope never to need the green oil of Charity for its purported curative properties. More pleasant is the notion that the tea made with *Ophioglossum* is good for "general health." On my next trip to Taiwan, I plan to buy a bag of dried *Ophioglossum* leaves at an open-air market, brew some serpent's-tongue tea with it, and share it with my friends Shu-miaw and Chen-meng, who have taught me much about the ferns of Taiwan. I also hope to find other unusual species of ferns in completely unexpected habitats or locations. Such unforeseen finds add much pleasure to travel. "Our brightest blazes of gladness," wrote Samuel Johnson, "are often kindled by unexpected sparks."

FERNS AND PEOPLE

29

The Molesting *Salvinia*

Could a small fern threaten the way of life of as many as 80,000 people? Could it cut them off from food, medical care, and schools, forcing them to move from their homes? It is hard to believe, but that is what happened in the early 1980s when a small, floating, aquatic fern began to multiply exponentially in the Sepik River floodplain of Papua New Guinea.

The fern in question was an introduced species of *Salvinia*, one capable of doubling its population size in a little more than 2 days (Figure 124, and Plates 21 and 22). Under the hot tropical sun, it multiplied rapidly and soon carpeted the surfaces of rivers, lakes, and lagoons. It formed extensive floating mats as crowded plants surged over one another and pushed the older plants below the water where they turned brown and slowly decayed. In some instances, these heavy, waterlogged mats were more than 3 feet (1 m) thick, enough to impede travel by dugout canoe, the main method of transportation in this roadless region (Figure 125). No longer could people get to market, attend schools, or seek medical treatment. Fishing was nearly impossible. Even more distressing, they were cut off from their main carbohydrate food, the pith of sago palms (*Metroxylon* spp.), which they harvested from nearby swamps by cutting the trunks and towing them behind their canoes. The dense mats of *Salvinia* obstructed more than travel by dugout canoe. They cut off light to submerged plants, thereby lessening oxygen in the water and killing many mud-dwelling organisms. They clogged irrigation ditches, blocked drainage canals, and jammed water pumps. In some places, the mats harbored schistosomiasis, a human blood parasite. In some places, infestations were so bad that entire villages were abandoned.

This was not the first time that the weedy *Salvinia* had struck. It first became a pest in 1939 in Sri Lanka where it was accidentally introduced by someone from the Botany Department of the University of Colombo. Subsequently, it infested Australia, India, Southeast Asia, and southern Africa.

In 1959 a particularly bad outbreak—one that received a lot of publicity—occurred at Kariba Lake, a reservoir along the border of Zimbabwe and Zambia. There, a small population of *Salvinia* took only 3 years to form a dense carpet covering 390 square miles (1000 km²).

To prevent *Salvinia* from choking more of the world's waterways, something had to be done. On the advice of experts in aquatic weed control, the mats were sprayed with herbicides. This killed many plants, but a few survived and formed outbreaks a year or so later. Spraying with herbicides was also expensive.

Several other remedies were tried. The surface of the water was skimmed with nets to catch and remove the plants, but too many plants escaped. On lakes, long booms were laid across the water in strategic places to control the spread of *Salvinia*, but the booms often broke from the weight of the plants pressing behind

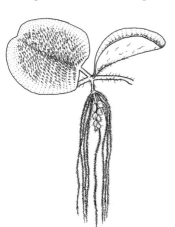

Figure 124 The molesting *Salvinia*, a weedy floating fern. The two upper, rounded leaves are green and rest on the water's surface. The third leaf is submerged, whitish, and resembles a root; attached to it are a cluster of rounded structures, the sori. Drawing by the author.

Figure 125 An infestation of *Salvinia molesta* near Liberty, Texas. The mat is so thick that it supports the weight of the brick cinder block in front of the researcher. Photograph by Philip W. Tipping.

them. Mechanical harvesting did not work either; the machines broke *Salvinia* into small pieces, and those pieces reproduced themselves. Grass carp, which have been successful in controlling certain types of submerged aquatic vegetation, showed no interest in *Salvinia*. Attempts to find a lucrative use for the plants, such as feeding them to cattle, were also unsuccessful. Nothing seemed to work.

Finally, the weed control experts realized that a method of biological control was called for, and they began searching for an insect that could eat *Salvinia* into oblivion. The obvious place to look was in countries where the plant was native. But where was it native?

At the time, researchers thought the offending species was *Salvinia auriculata*, a native of the American tropics. They were optimistic that a suitable control insect could be found there because of a curious fact:

the *Salvinia* was weedy *only* in the Old World. In the American tropics it was not weedy; the plants existed as scattered individuals and never formed extensive floating mats. This suggested that *Salvinia* was kept in check by insect herbivores, whereas in the Old World such insects were absent, apparently not having been present on the plants originally introduced there. Therefore, the researchers reasoned that they would find the right insect, the "magic bullet," within the natural range of *S. auriculata* in the American tropics. In the early 1960s, entomologists traveled to Trinidad and Guyana to learn what insects ate the fern. They found three species that seemed promising: a moth (*Samaea multiplicaulis*), a grasshopper (*Paulinia acuminata*), and a weevil (*Cyrtobagous singularis*).

Before these species could be released on infestations, they underwent stringent host specificity tests to ensure that they did not eat native plants or economically important crops. "This testing is in fact the most labour-intensive and time-consuming part of our job," according to Peter Room, from the University of Queensland, Australia, one of the entomologists. "We did not release the *Salvinia* grasshopper, *Paulinia acuminata*, in Australia because it chewed on strawberry leaves during tests, even though the chances of an aquatic grasshopper encountering strawberries is remote. Nobody wants to be remembered as the entomologist who destroyed a crop-growing industry or caused a native plant to be decimated!" The tests demonstrated that the insects had a high degree of host specificity to *Salvinia*, and hopes were high that one of them would be an effective biological control. But when the insects were released on infestations in Africa, Fiji, and Sri Lanka, they failed to make a significant dent in the *Salvinia* populations.

While the testing was going on, a startling discovery was made about the weedy *Salvinia*. David S. Mitchell, then a doctoral student at the University of London, concluded after careful study that the plant was not *S. auriculata* as all the experts had previously thought. Instead, it represented a previously unknown species, one he named, appropriately, *S. molesta* (Mitchell 1972).

One reason *Salvinia molesta* became widespread is the remarkable adaptation of its leaves to resist waterlogging and sinking. Next time you visit a botanical garden or greenhouse, find the indoor plant pond—

there will probably be at least one species of *Salvinia*. Try to sink the plants by pushing them down. They pop up to the surface, completely dry. This unsinkability is the result of air trapped in the middle layer, or mesophyll, of the leaves. But in *S. molesta* another mechanism is at work: specialized hairs on the upper surface of the floating leaves. These hairs are grouped in threes or fours, united at their tips, and sit atop conical stalks $1/32$–$1/16$ inch (1–2 mm) long called papillae, forming what look like miniature eggbeaters (Figure 126). These hairs are arranged in close rows, forming a second surface above the leaf. When the plants are submerged, the eggbeater hairs trap air beneath, helping buoy the plant back to the surface. Any water remaining on top simply beads up on the secondary surface formed by the eggbeater hairs and rolls off in shimmering, silvery drops.

Another remarkable feature of *Salvinia* is its "roots." What looks like a whitish or brownish mass of roots hanging down in the water (Plate 23) is actually a leaf, bearing sori. It is not a root because roots do not bear sori—only leaves do. The fact is, *Salvinia* has no roots! The function

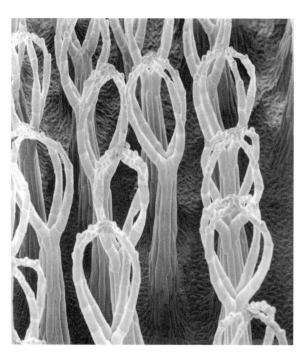

Figure 126 Eggbeater hairs on the upper surface of a floating leaf of the molesting *Salvinia*. Scanning electron micrograph by Gordon Lemmon.

of the root-like submerged leaves has baffled botanists for a long time. No one has experimentally demonstrated that the submerged leaves absorb water and mineral nutrients. Some think that the submerged leaves stabilize the plant by creating drag to minimize drift, and act as a weight to prevent flipping by strong winds. Whatever their function, they are certainly bizarre, un-fern-like fronds.

Mitchell's discovery that the weedy species is different had two implications in the search for a biological control. First, it suggested that the entomologists may have wasted their time searching for insects on *Salvinia auriculata*. What they had to do was look for herbivorous insects on *S. molesta* itself. Second, Mitchell's research provided a clue as to where to look. He had seen only one herbarium specimen of *S. molesta*, collected in 1941 from a lily pool at the botanical garden in Rio de Janeiro. This suggested that *S. molesta* grew natively in southern Brazil. (Botanists rejected the idea that *S. molesta* was native to the Old World because, given its prominence as a terrible weed, it should have been collected there much earlier than the 1930s and 1940s when the first Old World collections were made.)

Hopeful of finding *Salvinia molesta* in its native habitat along with insects that ate it, entomologists traveled to southern Brazil and searched ponds, swamps, and lagoons. In 1978, they were successful. They found numerous populations, all of which were south of Rio de Janeiro and São Paulo, between 24° and 32° south—actually outside the tropics. Although delighted by their discovery, the entomologists were disappointed by their catch of insects. They found what appeared to be the same species of moth, grasshopper, and weevil that had been ineffective in controlling *S. auriculata*. Nevertheless, they thought that another field test might be justified; perhaps these insects represented races specialized to eat *S. molesta*.

A test was begun in 1980 on Lake Moondarra in central Queensland, Australia, which had about 500 acres (200 hectares) carpeted by *Salvinia molesta*. As before, the insects were tested to ensure that they would not harm desirable plants. It was decided not to release the grasshopper because, as before, it chewed on strawberry leaves. The weevil, however, was highly specific to *Salvinia*; it would starve to death rather than eat another plant species (Figure 127). Therefore, only the weevil was released. The researchers periodically visited the lake, and with each visit they noticed the thick carpet of *Salvinia* diminish.

Fourteen months after beginning the test, the researchers considered the infestation under control. Although the weevil did not find and kill all the plants, the populations of both had reached equilibrium. *Salvinia* and weevils coexisted, albeit in low numbers, in a perpetual game of hide and seek with neither dying out. In 1983, the weevils were released in the Sepik River floodplain; 8 months later, the infestation was reduced from 155 square miles to 1 (250 km² to 2) and an estimated 2 million tons of *Salvinia* destroyed. Today, *S. molesta* still causes problems, but at least there is a solution.

A curious consequence of the control efforts is that the entomologists, like the botanists, realized they were dealing with a new species. They christened the new weevil *Cyrtobagous salviniae*.

Experiments have shown that *Salvinia molesta* can survive short periods of subfreezing temperatures, but hard freezes and ice formation kill the plants. But another experiment found that it survived cold temperatures that kill another problematic water weed, the water hyacinth (*Eichhornia crassipes*). Such cold tolerance suggests that *S. molesta* could become a serious pest in the southern United States and southern Europe, and in fact, it already has. From Florida to Texas it has been documented at over 50 sites in 25 drainages, with one of the worst infestations at the Toledo Bend Reservoir in eastern Texas. It has also shown up in southern California and adjacent Arizona.

Salvinia minima is the only other species of *Salvinia* that grows in the southeastern United States. It can be distinguished from *S. molesta* by its smaller floating leaves, with hairs on the upper surface that are free at the tips, not fused into a cage-like structure as in *S. molesta* (Figure 126). *Salvinia minima* was considered native to the southeastern United States, but it is now believed to be introduced from the American tropics (Jacono 1999). It was first collected in the United States in southern Florida in the 1930s. Had the plant been native there, it would almost certainly have been collected before then. Since the 1930s, the fern has spread westward into the Gulf states, where it is now common in swamps and bayous. We know about this introduction and migration thanks to specimens collected by botanists and deposited in herbaria at universities, museums, and botanical gardens. Why, then, if *S. minima* is introduced, does it not become weedy like *S. molesta?* The answer seems to be that since its introduction in the United States, a weevil has been feeding on it, keeping its populations in check—apparently the same weevil (*Cyrtobagous salviniae*) that feeds on *S. molesta*.

Botanists discovered something astonishing about *Salvinia molesta:* the species is pentaploid, with five sets of chromosomes. During meiosis, the type of cell division that gives rise to spores, the fifth chromosome set lacks a corresponding set with which to pair. As a result, the chromosomes from the fifth extra set are distributed unequally to the daughter cells of meiosis, causing abnormal development and resulting in misshapen, nonviable spores, thus destroying the possibility of sexual reproduction (Chapter 6). Thus all reproduction of *S. molesta* is vegetative, by fragmentation of its stems, and all the plants in the world—from southern Brazil to Lake Kariba to the Sepik River floodplain—are genetically identical. The species *S. molesta* is a clone.

The *Salvinia molesta* story is famous, "the most outstanding example of biological control of an aquatic weed." I am particularly fond of the tale because of the pivotal role played by taxonomy, my profession. If David Mitchell had not discovered that the weedy *Salvinia* is different from *S. auriculata*, if he had not provided a clue as to where *S. molesta* grows natively, then entomologists would never have known where or on what to look for a biological control, and many places in the world would still be molested by a serious weed (Room 1990, Thomas 1986, Thomas and Room 1986).

Figure 127 The hero of this story: a curculionid weevil that eats only the molesting *Salvinia*. Drawing by the author.

235

FERNS AND PEOPLE

30
Little Nitrogen Factories

A velvety mat coats the surface of a roadside ditch in the Mississippi River floodplain of northeastern Arkansas, a wine red carpet extending from the cattails on one side to the marsh mallows on the other. Close up, the mat resolves into millions of individual plantlets, these fragmenting and growing so rapidly that they threaten to strand even the whirligig beetles swimming in their midst. Each plantlet, roughly the size of a dime, has 100–200 overlapping leaves less than $1/32$ inch (1 mm) long. This plant is *Azolla*, the world's smallest fern (Figure 128).

Although small, *Azolla* receives big attention from botanists. Each year more scientific papers are published about it than any other fern, and since the 1980s two books have been written about it and several scientific symposia held in its honor. Why all the fuss over such a tiny fern?

Azolla receives a lot of attention because it is the world's most important fern economically. It is used as a fertilizer in the rice paddies of southeastern Asia, especially China and Vietnam, where rice feeds millions of people. *Azolla* makes a first-rate fertilizer because it is rich in nitrogen, a nutrient often in short supply and limiting plant growth. Nitrogen is concentrated in the plant not by the fern itself but by nitrogen-fixing cyanobacteria that live within its leaves (Figure 129). The cyanobacterium, *Anabaena azollae*, takes nitrogen gas (N_2) from the air, a form not usable by the plant, and splits it and combines it with hydrogen to produce ammonium ions (NH_4^+), a form that can be absorbed and used by the plant.

Ammonium synthesis in *Anabaena* takes place in specialized cells called heterocysts, which are easily seen under the microscope. At a magnification of about 100, *Anabaena* looks like a chain of beads, each bead a blue-green photosynthetic cell. The heterocysts stand out as slightly larger, colorless, thick-walled cells interspersed along the chain (Figure 129). The thick walls of the heterocysts exclude oxygen, which disrupts the enzymes of ammonium synthesis inside the cell.

Long, loose strands of *Anabaena* flourish in the water around the tip of *Azolla* stems. When a young leaf, or primordium, starts to form near the tip, it develops a dimple on the side facing the stem (Figure 130). From the surface of this dimple grows a tiny hair, resembling an inflated rubber glove. It entangles the *Anabaena*, dragging it inward as the dimple deepens to form a pocket in the leaf. The pocket eventually seals over, trapping *Anabaena* inside.

Once inside, *Anabaena* develops heterocysts and begins synthesizing ammonium. Meanwhile, *Azolla* develops another kind of hair inside the leaf cavity (Figure 129). These hairs absorb ammonium released by the *Anabaena* and make it available to the rest of the plant (Calvert and Peters 1981, Perkins and Peters 1993).

Both *Anabaena* and *Azolla* benefit from their close relationship. *Anabaena*

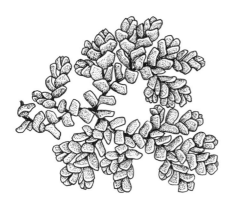

Figure 128 *Azolla*, the world's smallest and most economically useful fern. Each leaf is about $1/32$ inch (1 mm) long. Drawing by the author.

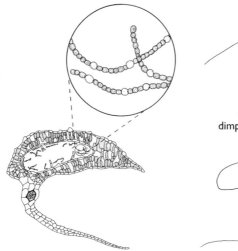

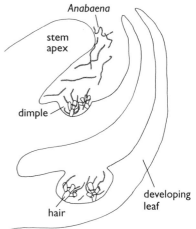

Figure 129 *Azolla* leaf cut lengthwise. The leaf consists of two dissimilar lobes: a thin, colorless, lower lobe that rests on the water, and a thick, green upper lobe, held above the water, with a pocket containing *Anabaena azollae* (shown enlarged in the circle; the slightly larger cells are heterocysts that fix atmospheric nitrogen). Drawing by the author.

Figure 130 *Azolla* cut lengthwise through the stem. Glove-like hairs in dimples of the developing leaves entangle *Anabaena*, dragging it from the stem apex into the deepening cavities. Drawing by the author.

gets a cozy place to grow, and *Azolla* gets a steady supply of needed nitrogen. But the association is apparently not obligatory. It has been reported that wild plants of *Azolla* can grow without *Anabaena*, and vice versa. Nevertheless, the two seem to do best in each other's company.

Rice farmers in China and Vietnam have taken advantage of the *Anabaena-Azolla* symbiosis for centuries. The use of *Azolla* as a fertilizer for rice probably began in China during the Ming dynasty (1368–1644) and in Vietnam during the 11th century. Until more recently, *Azolla* cultivation was monopolized by only a few small villages in which the secret of how to cultivate the plants was known. Each growing season, rice farmers from surrounding areas had to travel to these villages to buy starter stocks for their paddies. In the *Azolla*-producing villages of Thái Bình province, Vietnam, the monopoly was considered so valuable that the secret of cultivating *Azolla* was passed on to the young men during a solemn ceremony after they had married and started farming independently. Women were not told the secret for fear they might marry outside the village and take it away with them. The *Azolla* monopolies were broken during the late 1950s when the governments of China and Vietnam built new *Azolla* farms and funded research on the use of *Azolla* as a fertilizer (Lumpkin and Plucknett 1982, Moore 1969, van Hove 1989).

Why is *Azolla* so difficult to cultivate? The challenge is ensuring survival during the unfavorable growing seasons of winter and midsummer. Winters in the temperate regions of China are too cold for the native Asian species of *Azolla;* even the most hardy varieties are killed by a few hours at or below freezing. On the other hand, midsummer in southern China and Vietnam is too hot. Water temperatures in the paddies can soar to 104–113°F (40–45°C) and parboil *Azolla,* which stops growing at about 95°F (35°C). High summer temperatures also promote the growth of insects and fungi that attack the plants, the most pernicious of which are larvae of a moth that devour the plants and bind them together to make live-in tunnels for protection. Other harmful insects are midges and weevils that devastate the plants by feeding on the roots. But by far the speediest attackers are fungi that can ravage an entire population in a matter of days, causing the *Azolla* to turn black and sink to the bottom of the paddy. Besides insects, high midsummer temperatures promote blooms of algae that absorb most of the nutrients in the water and, if viscous enough, impede the flow of fresh water through the paddies, thereby further increasing the water temperature.

Rice farmers developed several methods to cultivate *Azolla* through unfavorable growing seasons. For overwintering, the traditional method is to irrigate a paddy with water from hot springs; nowadays it is more common to use heated, uncontaminated wastewater from nearby factories. If warm water is unavailable, plants are cultivated in greenhouses 1½ feet (0.5 m) high, built in the paddies, or they are stored in thatched huts sheltered from the wind. The floors of the huts are covered with a reed mat on which the *Azolla* is piled about 1½ feet (0.5 m) high. The pile is then overlaid with 2–4 inches (5–10 cm) of straw ash and periodically moistened to prevent the *Azolla* from drying out. This method is used during the two coldest months of the winter and results in

50–80% of the plants surviving. (Unfortunately, spores cannot be used for propagation because they are not reliably produced in sufficient quantity. Hundreds of thousands of research dollars have been spent trying to coax *Azolla* into producing spores. Researchers have tried different amounts of light, different kinds of light, temperature changes, and hormones. But so far, the plants are not cooperating.)

In southernmost China and in Vietnam, winters are so mild that the plants can remain in the paddies throughout the year. Nevertheless, warm water needs to be maintained in the paddies, and the farmers have a trick for doing this. In the morning, they lower the water level to about 1 1/5 inches (3 cm) so that the water warms up quickly. In the early evening, they raise the water level to about 2 3/4 inches (7 cm) so that it cools off slowly.

During summer, the main problems are fungal attacks and overheating. To minimize these problems, the farmers try to select sites that are breezy, with cool, flowing water. Sometimes they irrigate paddies with cold spring water whose lower temperature reduces fungal growth and insect activity. *Azolla* can also be cultivated in the shade of mature rice plants, but the dim light and high humidity promote fungal attack.

After cultivation during unfavorable growing periods, *Azolla* must be multiplied so that enough plants are available to inoculate the paddies the next growing season. Plants are transferred to flooded fields or canals where they have plenty of room to grow. If the site has the right combination of sunlight, temperature, and nutrients, *Azolla* can double in 3–5 days. Then the plants are taken to the flooded paddies and scattered about. About a month later they will have formed a dense mat, covering the water's surface. Water is then drained from the paddy so that the *Azolla* lies stranded on the mud. A few days later it is mixed into the mud by plowing, harrowing, or by hand. After the plants are partially decomposed (about 4–5 days), the paddy is reflooded and the rice planted.

Azolla can also be grown between rows of rice and allowed to die and sink to the bottom. Death is usually caused by overshading from the dense rice canopy that forms 20–40 days after transplanting. Many farmers combine this method with mixing the *Azolla* directly into the soil.

As it decomposes, *Azolla* releases nitrogen, which is then absorbed by the rice. Fertilizing with *Azolla* yields grains richer in proteins—richer than those obtained when chemical fertilizers are applied.

Agriculturists try to develop new strains of *Azolla* for use in rice cultivation. In Vietnam more than 30 wild races have been selected from *A. pinnata,* the species that has been grown in Asia for centuries. In the Philippines, the International Rice Research Institute maintains a living collection of more than 600 races of *Azolla,* each growing best in different conditions of heat, cold, shade, salinity, and acidity. This allows farmers to select a race fine-tuned to the particular environmental conditions of their paddies.

In China a big advance in *Azolla* cultivation came in 1977 with the introduction of an American species, *A. filiculoides.* Although it decomposed slowly and often died when broadcast into the paddies, it resisted insect attacks. Moreover, it tolerated cold better and started growth earlier in the spring, so it could be grown in northern regions and was better suited for use with the late winter or early spring rice crop. For such use, *A. filiculoides* has almost completely replaced *A. pinnata. Azolla pinnata* is still used for the fall rice crop because it better tolerates high temperatures.

Azolla has several other uses besides fertilizing rice. It is used as a nitrogen source for other aquatic crops such as wild rice (*Zizania aquatica*), arrowhead (*Sagittaria sagittifolia*), and taro (*Colocasia esculenta*). It supplements the feed of cattle, hogs, ducks, chickens, and carp. It is even cultivated as an ornamental in ponds or water gardens. The plants are particularly attractive because they turn brilliant red in the fall before they die and sink to the bottom.

Another use is mosquito control. *Azolla* is sometimes called mosquito fern because it carpets the surface of the water, thereby thwarting adult mosquitoes trying to lay eggs. It is also said to smother mosquito larvae coming up to the surface to breathe. The *Azolla* mats need to be thick and dense, otherwise mosquitoes actually benefit from the cover, which hides them from predators.

Azolla's use as a fertilizer is not without problems. Plants are killed by even the minutest amounts of herbicides commonly sprayed on rice.

Most farmers are unwilling to trade the benefits of weed control for the benefits of *Azolla* fertilizer. Also, not all the world's rice is grown in flooded fields or in paddies where water levels can be controlled, making it difficult to grow *Azolla* and incorporate the plants into the soil. Most important, *Azolla* cultivation is so labor intensive that it is too expensive for countries with high labor costs. In some areas 1000 person-hours are needed to grow *Azolla* for each acre (0.4 hectare) of rice. In these regions it is far cheaper to use chemical fertilizers. For these reasons, *Azolla* is not a panacea for all rice farmers.

Despite its limitations, *Azolla* will probably continue to be cultivated for a long time. Rice covers about 11% of the world's arable land and is the main food for nearly 2.5 billion people. Humanity will need more rice, and it would do well to depend on a fertilizer that is as environmentally safe and energy efficient.

31
Nardoo

On June 26, 1861, William John Wills lay dying under a tree beside Cooper's Creek in central Australia. For weeks he and two fellow explorers had survived on food prepared from the sporocarps of a small fern called nardoo (*Marsilea drummondii*, Figure 132), but the food's quality left something to be desired. Although the men ate heartily, they were emaciated and their legs nearly paralyzed with pain. Wills managed to prop himself up against the tree and, with a pulse of only 48, wrote in his journal: "I have a good appetite and relish the nardoo much, but it seems to give us no nutriment . . . starvation on nardoo is by no means very unpleasant, but for the weakness one feels, for as far as appetite is concerned, it gives me the greatest satisfaction" (Moorehead 1963).

Three days later the two companions set out to find help, leaving Wills behind, at his insistence, to fend for himself. They left him lying on the ground next to firewood, water, and an 8-day supply of nardoo (Figure 131). He was never seen alive again.

Two days after they left Wills, one of Wills's companions, Robert O'Hara Burke, ate an evening meal of nardoo and fell asleep with a full stomach. Early the next morning he died of malnourishment. The third

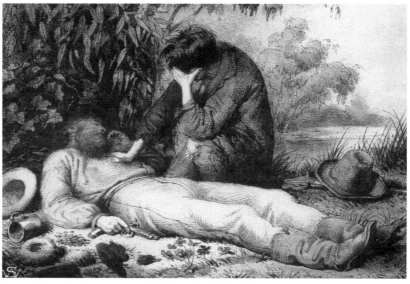

Figure 131 John King mourning William John Wills, left to fend for himself in the Australian outback. Note the nardoo (*Marsilea drummondii*) and its bean-like sporocarps, and the pestle used to grind them, on the ground beside Wills. From a watercolor by William Strutt. Courtesy of the Granger Collection, New York.

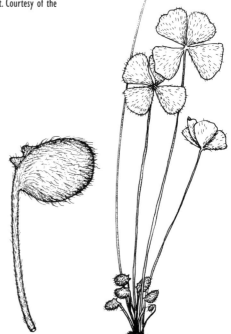

Figure 132 Nardoo (*Marsilea drummondii*), whose sporocarps (enlarged at left) are the black, bean-like structures at the base of the leaf stalk. Drawing by the author.

man, John King, was befriended by Aborigines and eventually rescued by a search party, but he suffered permanent nerve damage in both legs.

King's rescue ended one of the first and most tragic expeditions to the interior of Australia. The explorers were extremely unlucky because they would have been saved had they reached their supply camp only 10 hours earlier. It was then that the camp's garrison departed after having waited 3 months past the rendezvous date. But Burke and Wills, the leaders of the expedition, succeeded in one respect: they were the first to cross the continent from Melbourne in the south to the Gulf of Carpentaria in the north (Figure 133).

Historians have blamed the explorers' sufferings on nardoo's lack of nutrition. But Aborigines had relished nardoo for centuries as one of their main foods along with fish, crow, and mussels. Why would they have continued to eat nardoo if it lacked food value? John Earl and Barry McCleary (1994), two biochemists from Australia, have proposed a different explanation for the explorers' suffering. They believe that the explorers were afflicted with beriberi, a disease caused by a dietary deficiency of thiamine (vitamin B_1), pointing out that Wills's journal is a textbook account of the progression of the disease and is, in fact, the only complete description of it in humans. Yet they also point out that nardoo is not guiltless; it is, in fact, the source of the

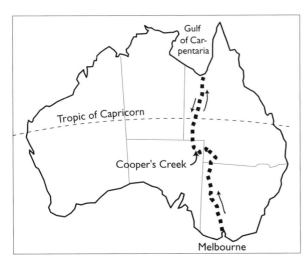

Figure 133 Route taken by the Burke and Wills expedition in 1860–1861. The expedition was the first to cross Australia's uncharted interior, from south to north, in an epic journey of 1650 miles (2640 km).

disease. Why did Burke and Wills succumb to beriberi whereas the Aborigines did not?

The explorers developed the disease because of the manner in which they prepared nardoo. Aborigines pulverized the sporocarps on a flat, hollowed-out stone, then mixed the nardoo flour with water. They showed the explorers how to do this. In his journal, Wills recorded a second step: "The fish being disposed of, next came a supply of nardoo cake and water until I was so full as to be unable to eat any more, when Pitchery [one of the Aborigines], allowing me a short time to recover myself, fetched a large bowl of the raw nardoo flour mixed to a thin paste, a most insinuating article, and one that they appear to esteem a great delicacy" (Moorehead 1963). Then, according to custom as described by a Mr. Benny Kerwin, "They eat it by spooning it into their mouths with a mussel [shell], not with a coolibah [*Eucalyptus*] leaf or with bark, only with a mussel."

But the explorers did not follow the Aborigines' example. They used a different method, preparing nardoo the way Europeans traditionally prepare grains: grinding and cooking. After pulverizing the sporocarps, they mixed the flour with a small amount of water, kneaded it into a dough, and divided it into small cakes that were baked in campfire ashes. The problem with preparing nardoo this way is that thiaminase, the enzyme that destroys thiamine, remains in the sporocarps. This enzyme occurs in high concentrations in nardoo, with the sporocarps containing more than 3 times the amount found in bracken fern (*Pteridium*), a plant well known for its deadly concentrations of the substance (Chapter 21), and the leaves containing about 100 times the amount (McCleary and Chick 1977). Because the explorers prepared their food incorrectly, they poisoned themselves to death. Nardoo also poisons sheep. During the summer of 1974–1975, more than 2200 sheep died from nardoo-induced thiamine deficiency in the Gwydir Basin area west of Moree, Australia (McCleary et al. 1980).

The Aborigines' method of preparing nardoo prevented poisoning by thinning the nardoo flour with water. This diluted the thiamine, the thiaminase, and any organic molecule that could act as a cosubstrate for the thiaminase (a molecule with which thiaminase must combine to be effective). In a dilute porridge of nardoo, the probability that all three molecules will combine at the same time is slight (enzyme activity diminishes by the cube of the dilution; for example, a $1/10$ dilution reduces enzyme activity by $1/1000$). Thus dilution leaves the thiamine intact. Earl and McCleary also believe that the Aborigines' custom of spooning nardoo into their mouths with mussel shells, rather than leaves or bark, also reduced the likelihood that the enzyme would find a co-substrate.

Because cooking destroys most enzymes, it is surprising that baking the nardoo in the ashes of the explorers' campfire did not destroy the thiaminase. Perhaps this resistance of thiaminase to heat is related to nardoo's ability to survive the scorching summer temperatures of the Australian outback. Nardoo's remarkable heat resistance is also shown by its spores, which can germinate after sporangia have been boiled in water for 15 minutes.

I cannot end this chapter without mentioning a few facts about the bizarre sporocarps of nardoo. Australians apply the name nardoo to all their native species of *Marsilea*, which typically grow in ponds that dry up in summer. When the winter rains return and the ponds are flooded, the stems of nardoo send up leaves that resemble long-stalked, four-leaf clovers (Figure 132). At the base of these leaves are borne the sporocarps, which resemble small black beans. Although soft and green when young, the sporocarps harden and darken at maturity. This retards water loss, important during the dry season when sporocarps lie exposed on the ground. Some sporocarps retain moisture so well that they can germinate and produce gametophytes after 130 years (Johnson 1985).

The sporocarp is a peculiar structure, derived from a pinna, or leaflet, that has folded and fused over the course of evolution (Figures 134 and 135). These modifications protect the sori inside, which are attached to a ring of clear, water-absorbing, gelatinous material running around the inner edge of the sporocarp; this ring is called the sorophore.

When the stony walls of the sporocarp crack or decompose with age, water seeps in and is imbibed by the sorophore, which swells. This exerts tremendous pressure on the sporocarp walls, which usually split open 15–20 minutes after the start of imbibition. The sorophore extrudes from the sporocarp and carries the sori with it (Figure 136). The outer cover of the sori (the indusium) soon degrades, and the sporangia release their spores. The spores germinate and grow into mature gametophytes in less than a day, a short time compared to most ferns, which take several months.

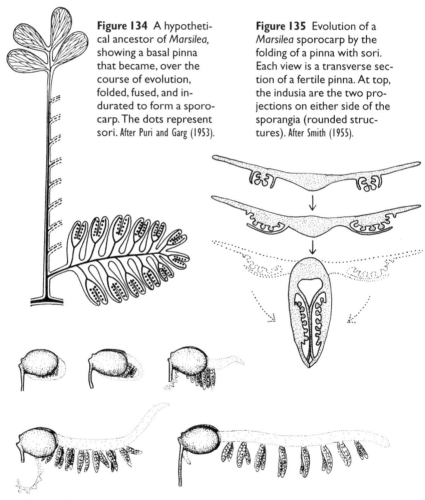

Figure 134 A hypothetical ancestor of *Marsilea*, showing a basal pinna that became, over the course of evolution, folded, fused, and indurated to form a sporocarp. The dots represent sori. After Puri and Garg (1953).

Figure 135 Evolution of a *Marsilea* sporocarp by the folding of a pinna with sori. Each view is a transverse section of a fertile pinna. At top, the indusia are the two projections on either side of the sporangia (rounded structures). After Smith (1955).

Figure 136 A germinating sporocarp, showing the various stages of the protruding sorophore. Sori dangle from the sorophore, which reaches a length of 1 1/5–2 1/2 inches (3–6 cm). After Eames (1936).

The gelatinous material of the sorophore and indusia make up most of the edible part of the sporocarp. It was probably this gelatin that swelled in their stomachs and intestines to produce bloating. Perhaps the swelling alleviated hunger pangs, explaining why Wills wrote that nardoo gave him "the greatest satisfaction." It would also explain his observation that "The stools it [nardoo] causes are enormous, and seem greatly to exceed the quantity of bread consumed."

After the death of Burke and Wills, central Australia was opened up to colonists. Settlers exterminated many plants and animals, and their cattle polluted and destroyed sparse water sources. Many Aborigines could no longer live off the land and were forced to reside near immigrant-run stations where they were weaned onto wheaten flour. Thomas Bancroft, an English botanist on the scene in 1893, observed the change: "The civilised blacks, who were supplied with wheaten flour from the station, were not too proud to make and eat Nardoo damper [cakes]." This attitude fostered the destruction of Aboriginal society, eventually put an end to eating nardoo.

FERNS AND PEOPLE

32
Pteridomania

From 1830 to 1860 an unprecedented passion for ferns swept Victorian England. People flocked to the countryside to collect ferns to plant in their gardens or conservatories, or to press and dry them for their herbarium albums. The influential *Gardeners' Chronicle* reported that glass cases full of ferns "are in much request as ornaments for living rooms." One commentator noted, "almost everyone possessing good taste has made, more or less successfully, an attempt to rear this tribe of plants." It became the rage to own china, textiles, and furniture decorated with fern motifs (Figure 137). In short, ferns were "in." This national enthusiasm for ferns is referred to by British cultural and social historians as the "fern craze," or its Latinate equivalent, pteridomania.

The craze was set off by a simple invention by Nathaniel Bagshaw Ward, a London physician, amateur botanist, and fellow of the Royal Society and Linnean Society. In the late 1820s he began experiments by enclosing plants in almost airtight glass containers, "closely glazed cases" to use his terminology. His containers worked on the principle that during the daylight hours, moisture transpired by plants or evaporated from the soil condensed on the glass, and at night, dripped back into the soil.

If the container was sufficiently sealed, then the soil remained moist and the plants survived for long periods without watering.

Wardian cases, as they came to be called, became extremely popular, especially for growing ferns (Figure 138). Why ferns, instead of flowering plants, is poorly understood, but perhaps it was for no other reason than Ward himself favored ferns. Another reason might be that ferns, which lack gaily colored flowers and fruits, matched the somber mood of the time, when the fashionable color for men's clothing suddenly turned to black. One Victorian writer, perhaps with unconscious irony, recommended cultivating ferns because they "love a dull, quiet atmosphere." Another reason for the popularity of ferns is that they were suited to the Victorian style of decoration, favoring elaborate, profuse designs to create delicate effects. Curved fiddleheads and frilly fern leaves harmonized well with other elements of this style. Whatever the reasons for their popularity, ferns became synonymous with Wardian cases in the minds of most Victorians (Allen 1969).

Dr. Ward's invention provided far more than just a bauble in which to grow ferns as a symbol of elevated status and good taste; it was also a way to transport plants on long voyages. Before Wardian cases, plants rarely survived such journeys. Smaller plants were packed in moss and placed in wooden boxes, which afforded them no sunlight, or larger plants were transported in pots, unprotected from salt spray, desiccating winds, and extremes of temperature. Wardian cases changed all this; plants could survive months at sea. Plants could be shipped between the far-flung colonies of the British Empire, and to and from Britain herself, with reasonable expectation of survival (Barber 1980).

The successful transport of plants played a key role in Victorian commerce and imperial expansion. The British government, through the Royal Botanic Gardens at Kew, shipped millions of plants to and from its colonies in Wardian cases. Under Sir William Jackson Hooker, its director from 1841 to 1865, Kew imported six times as many plants in 15 years as it had done during the preceding century. Quinine and rubber plants, two species native to South America, were shipped in Wardian cases first to England and then to Southeast Asia and Indonesia, where they formed the stock for extensive commercial plantations still in use today. Tea was taken from China to India, giving birth to the Indian tea industry. Bananas, also native to China, were first grown outside that country thanks to Ward's invention. Even many of our common houseplants owe their debut in horticulture to successful transport in Wardian cases. The beneficial effect of Ward's cases for transporting plants in the 1800s is similar to that which refrigeration had on shipping fruits and vegetables in the middle 1900s. Wardian cases continued to be used until the early 1960s when they were replaced by polyethylene bags.

Nowadays we tend to think of botanical gardens as scientific institutions that carry out research on the world's flora or as pleasant places for the public to enjoy and learn about plants. They have always been that, but in the 1800s, botanical gardens played an additional and more pragmatic role, one of promoting commerce and colonialism. One of the main reasons for having colonies was to grow crops to generate income or provide raw materials for the mother country. One responsibility for botanical gardens was to discover what crops could be grown in which colonies and how to plant, care for, harvest, process, and transport them. Just as armies and navies built empires, so too did botanical gardens.

The role of the Royal Botanic Gardens at Kew and its satellite gardens around the world in promoting British commercial interests and

Figure 137 Chamber pot decorated with fern designs. Photograph by John Mickel.

252

colonialism is well documented (Brockway 1979). The scientific and technical knowledge of Kew botanists was critical in developing several highly profitable and strategic crops in tropical colonies. Development of these crops rarely favored the indigenous people, however. In many instances, plants were taken from their countries of origin (such as quinine from Ecuador, rubber from Brazil, and sisal from Mexico), then grown elsewhere on plantations by slaves or poorly paid native laborers. For better or worse, Kew botanists and their Wardian cases helped make the colonies a profitable part of the British Empire.

But back to pteridomania. Victorian book publishers cashed in on the popularity of ferns by producing numerous guides for the amateur. Two

FERN CASES OF THE MOST IMPROVED PATTERNS
Fitted with Ferns of Popular Reputation.

BRONZED OBLONG SHAPE FERNICASE.
Filled with Choice Ferns, Complete.

THE "WINDSOR" ETRUSCAN TERRA COTTA FERNERY.
Filled with Choice Ferns, Complete

Figure 138 Wardian cases from an advertisement by James Carter & Company, 1864.

in particular, George William Francis's *An Analysis of the British Ferns and Their Allies* (1837) and Edward Newman's *A History of British Ferns, and Allied Plants* (1840), sold particularly well and helped fan the early flames of the fern craze. These and subsequent books benefited from advances in printing and illustrating, such as "nature printing," whereby actual fern fronds were inked and pressed onto the paper, resulting in plates of intricate detail, especially the venation. During the 1840s and early 1850s, lavishly illustrated fern books glutted the market. The peak was finally reached in 1854 and 1855, during which 14 new fern books were published, some of which were new editions of previous ones. In 1857 the *Phytologist*, a leading botanical journal, reported, "The literature of ferns . . . surpasses that of all the other branches of botanical science together."

One effect of these books was to stimulate the search for ferns in the field. Many guides listed the distribution of ferns in Britain on a county-by-county basis, and amateurs were keen to "fill in the gaps" by finding ferns in counties where they were previously unrecorded. Information about these discoveries was eagerly communicated to authors for incorporation in subsequent editions. When the second edition of Newman's book was published in 1844, it was three to four times larger than the first edition thanks largely to the flood of new distribution records from fern enthusiasts around the country.

Fieldwork by a host of enthusiastic amateurs also turned up hundreds of new and unusual forms of ferns for the garden. Many of these were abnormal plants, what today we would call a form or a monstrosity. Crested ferns were among the most common abnormalities, that is, plants with their leaf tips or pinna tips (or both) repeatedly forked, creating a frilly, splayed-out effect (Figure 139). Some forms had wavy or plicate leaf margins, such as the lasagna fern, a cultivar of the bird's-nest fern (*Asplenium nidus*, Plate 3). One form still grown today—and one of my favorites—is the 'Victoriae' cultivar, named after Queen Victoria, of the lady fern (*Athyrium filix-femina*). Its pinnae fork widely at the base into two almost equal segments, and these segments, when viewed with those on the opposite pinnae, appear crisscrossed, forming an X shape with the rachis at the center (Figure 140). Victorian gardeners clamored for cultivars such as these and paid high prices for the latest novelties. In

1860 one nurseryman listed in his catalog about 820 species and cultivars, with the hart's-tongue fern (*Asplenium scolopendrium*) accounting for more than 50 of these.

There was, however, a bad effect from all this enthusiasm: ferns were literally loved to death from overcollecting. Throughout Britain, fern fanciers, without thought of conservation, gathered as many ferns as possible from the countryside and brought them home to show their friends, cultivate in their gardens or Wardian cases, or display in arrangements (Figure 141). Sometimes ferns were pressed dry and mounted in an artful way on heavy sheets of paper, often with mosses or lichens around their base for good effect. When enough sheets had been made, they could be collected and bound in book form—a herbarium album—to display in the parlor. Collecting took its toll on native fern populations. In one oft-cited instance, overzealous collectors nearly exterminated a population of the least adder's-tongue (*Ophioglossum lusitanicum*) on Guernsey within 2 years of its discovery.

Figure 139 The 'Cristata' cultivar of the golden-scaled male fern (*Dryopteris affinis*). Photograph by John Mickel.

Figure 140 The 'Victoriae' cultivar of the lady fern (*Athyrium filix-femina*). The pinnae appear crisscrossed and have crested apices. Photograph by John Mickel.

Figure 141 Collecting ferns was popular during the Victorian era, as illustrated in "Gathering ferns" from the *Illustrated London News*, 1871, displayed at the Museum of Barnstaple and North Devon, England.

Worse than individual collectors were the commercial dealers. They sometimes carted away entire populations and bragged about how many tons of ferns they could uproot in a single day. When local ferns inevitably became scarce, some unscrupulous dealers stole them from estates. Whether collected legally or illegally, uprooted ferns were shipped to cities where they were hawked by street dealers or sold in markets. One prominent place for fern dealers in London was outside the entrance to the Bank of England.

By the mid-1860s, many rare species had been nearly exterminated, prompting one collector to write, "It seems cruelty so entirely to destroy the habitat of any Fern: yet, if the present rage continues, I see no hope of any known species being allowed to remain in its old haunts. The poor Ferns, like the wolves in olden times, have a price set upon their heads, and they in like manner will soon altogether disappear. We must have 'Fern laws', to preserve them like game" (Allen 1969). But a few pages later this collector confessed that her first reaction on finding a rare fern was to pack up a hamper full and send it home by rail, and she advised her readers to do the same. Conservation had not yet fully taken root in the minds of many Victorians.

Eventually, the quality of ferns offered for sale diminished. Spindly or sickly plants and bizarre monstrosities doomed to languish or die early were sold to a largely undiscerning public overwhelmed by the variety. It was a sign that the craze had reached its peak.

All fads, however brightly they burn during their heyday, eventually run their course, and so it was with pteridomania. By the late 1860s it came to be what it remains today, a curious and charming chapter in the history of pteridology, and a uniquely British one.

33

The Vegetable Lamb of Tartary

I once received an unusual gift in the mail. It resembled a stuffed animal about the size and shape of a Chihuahua and was covered with golden hair, except for its four long, naked legs (similar to Figure 142). I had not seen anything like it and was not sure what it was made of. After studying it a while, I realized that it was made from a tree fern stem—not the most astute observation because the gift was sent from Chen-meng Kuo of National Taiwan University, Taipei, the foremost authority on the ferns of Taiwan. As far as I could tell, a piece of stem had been cut with four petioles left attached, the petioles twisted downward to form the legs. The ears and tail appeared to be made from dried fiddleheads artfully attached.

A trip to the library soon revealed the fascinating story behind this unusual gift. The tree fern used to make the furry creature was *Cibotium barometz*, a species of the Dicksoniaceae. Assembling these creatures has become a cottage industry in southeastern Asia where the fern is native. They are sold to tourists as souvenirs, often near Buddhist temples, but are also kept in Chinese homes as part of the medicine cabinet because the golden hair is used to staunch bleeding. Several Chinese colleagues have told me that when they were children, their mothers would apply the hairs to cuts and scrapes.

As I read more in the library, the plot thickened. It turned out that dog-like creatures made from the tree fern are called the vegetable lamb of Tartary, about which there is considerable myth. Tartary is the region north of the Black Sea, but *Cibotium barometz* grows only in southeastern Asia. How did this fern artifact acquire such a name?

It all began in the Middle Ages when a myth grew about a half-plant, half-animal called the vegetable lamb. Although the legend had been around for centuries, it gained fame in the 1300s by its description in a book by the great travel-liar of the time, someone calling himself Sir John Mandeville. Mandeville supposedly left on a pilgrimage to the Holy Land in 1322 and returned 34 years later. His book, *The Voyages and Travels of Sir John Mandeville, Knight,* is replete with tales of pygmies, giants and gem-bearing plants—even the first account of circumnavigation of the globe. It caused quite a stir in the medieval world, but whole sections were plagiarized, and much was complete fabrication. It spurred several generations of Renaissance explorers, including Christopher Columbus, who considered it a veritable guidebook and used it to convince the Spanish crown to fund his voyages. Later it inspired writers

Figure 142 A vegetable lamb made in China from the rhizome of the tree fern *Cibotium barometz,* the legs and horns formed from petiole bases. Adapted from Lee (1877).

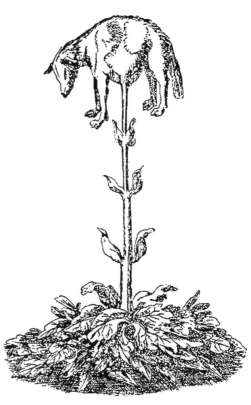

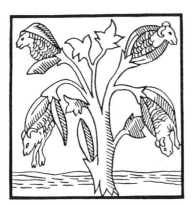

Figure 143 The vegetable lamb, illustrating the earliest version of the legend: a plant that bore little lambs at the tips of its branches. From Lee (1887), redrawn from Sir John Mandeville, ca. 1356.

Figure 145 Another later version of the vegetable lamb. From Lee (1887), redrawn from Johann Zahn, *Specula Physico-Mathematico-Historica Notabilium ac Mirabilium Sciendorum, in Qua Mundi Mirabilis Oeconomia, ...*, Norimbergae, 1696.

Figure 144 A later version of the vegetable lamb. From Lee (1887), redrawn from Claude Duret, *Histoire Admirable des Plantes et Herbes Esmerveillables et Miraculeuses en nature: ...*, Paris, 1605.

such as Shakespeare, Swift, Defoe, and Coleridge (see the fine book about Mandeville by Milton 2001). In any event, one adventure Mandeville described was his visit to the Great Khan of Tartary, during which he saw a strange tree that bore little lambs in pods at the end of its branches (Figure 143); he claimed to have eaten its fruit. The plant seemed fabulous, he admitted, but as he pointed out to his Christian contemporaries, "God is marveyllous in his werkes."

Mandeville's account inspired travelers to search for the vegetable lamb, but none had any luck. They returned only with secondhand accounts of the rare and elusive lamb, usually highly embellished. The legend gradually changed from a plant with lambs at the tips of its branches to a plant with a single stalk that bore a solitary lamb attached by its navel (Figures 144 and 145). The most complete description of this version of the legend comes from one Baron von Heberstein, who wrote in 1549:

> In the neighborhood of the Caspian Sea . . . a certain seed like that of melon, but rather rounder and longer, from which, when it was set in the earth, grew a plant resembling a lamb, and attaining to a height of about two and a half feet [76 cm], and which was called in the language of the country "Borametz" or "the Little Lamb." It had a head, eyes, ears, and all other parts of the body, as a newly-born lamb . . . an exceedingly soft wool, which was frequently used for manufacturing of head-coverings . . . . Further, he told me that this plant, if plant it should be called, had blood, but not true flesh: that, in the place of flesh, it had a substance similar to the flesh of the crab. . . . It was rooted by the navel in the middle of the belly, and devoured the surrounding herbage and grass, and lived as long as that lasted; but when there was no more within its reach the stem withered, and the lamb died. It was of so excellent a flavour that it was the favourite food of wolves and other rapacious animals. [Lee 1887]

Similar accounts of the vegetable lamb trickled in, each one slightly more embellished than the last, until finally the skeptics could stomach no more. The disbelievers arose and, brandishing their pens, attacked the legend and all its absurdities. The indignant true believers responded, and the result was that during the 1500s and 1600s the vegetable lamb legend was polemicized by some of the most celebrated writers of the time. In his *Pseudodoxia Epidemica* (vulgar errors; 1646), Sir Thomas Browne, a famous English physician and scholar, debunked the vegetable lamb:

> Much wonder is made of the Boramez, that strange plant-animal or vegetable Lamb of Tartary, which Wolves delight to feed on, which hath the shape of a Lamb, affordeth a bloody juyce upon breaking, and liveth while the plants be consumed about it. And yet if all this be no more, then the shape of a Lamb in the flower or seed, upon the top of the stalk, as we meet with the forms of Bees, Flies and Dogs in some others; he hath seen nothing that shall much wonder at it.

To which Alexander Ross replied in his *Arcana Microcosmi* (secrets of human nature as an epitome of the universe; 1652):

> That [Browne's claim] the plant animal or vegetable Lamb of Tartaria, is not much to be wondered at, if it be no more than the shape of a lamb in the flower or seed. Sure it must be more then this, if those that write the story thereof deceive us not. For Scaliger (Exerc[ita-tiones]. 182.29.) describes it out of them to be like a Lamb in all the parts of it: instead of horns, it hath long hairs like horns, it is covered with a thin skin, it bleeds when it is wounded, and lives so long as it hath grass to feed on; when that is spent, it dieth. And they write also, that it is a prey to Wolves. All these circumstances may be true: For 1. the shape, why may not this plant resemble a Lamb, as well as that Indian fruit described by Nic. Monardes, resembles a Dragon so artificially painted by nature, as if it were done by a painter [referring here to *Dracaena draco*, the dragon tree]. 2. Why may it not have a Downy, or Wooly skin, as well as Peaches, Quinces, Ches[t]nuts, and other fruits which are covered with a Down, called Lanugo by the Poet? 3. Why may it not bleed as well as that Tree we mentioned but now, called Draco, from the shape of the Dragon which its fruit hath; the juice of this Tree from the resemblance is called the blood of the Dragon, well known in Physick for its astringent and corroborating quality. 4. Why may it not have some animal motions, as well as that plant called Pudica, which contracts its 16 leaves when you touch or come neer it, and dilates them again when you depart? Or that Tree in the Isle of Cimbubon, whose leaves falling on the ground, crawl up and down like

worms: they have (saith Scaliger, Exerc. 112.) two little feet on each side: if they be touched, they run away. One of these leaves was kept alive eight days in a platter, which still moved it selfe when it was touched.

Guillaume de Salluste, Seigneur du Bartas, incorporated the legend in his poem *La Semaine* (1578), which describes the earth and life upon it during the second week of creation. On the first day of this second week, Adam and Eve discovered the vegetable lamb. The poem prompted John Parkinson, an apothecary in London, to illustrate the vegetable lamb in his *Paradisi in Sole Paradisus Terrestris* (1629). The book's frontispiece shows Adam and Eve admiring plants and animals in the Garden of Eden, and there, grazing peacefully in the background, is the vegetable lamb.

The legend was common currency until 1698 when Sir Hans Sloane, founder of the British Museum (the biological part of which is now called The Natural History Museum), received a peculiar specimen from India. Here at last was a specimen of the elusive vegetable lamb. Sloane realized that it was made from a tree fern stem, and, eager to de-bunk the legend, gave a show-and-tell before the Royal Society. The distinguished body of savants nodded their periwigged heads in accord.

Sloane's claim gained further support when a Dr. Breyn, a German botanist from Danzig, independently discovered the same kind of furry animals from India (Figure 142). Like Sloane, he concluded that it was made of a tree fern stem. Sloane's and Breyn's announcements convinced the public that the vegetable lamb was just another legend, a product of the credulity of medieval minds. Linnaeus accepted this explanation in 1753 when he used the Tartarian word *barometz*, "little lamb," as the specific epithet for the tree fern whose rhizome was used to make the furry animals: *Cibotium barometz*. In 1790, João de Loureiro, a Portuguese botanist and Catholic missionary, was likewise convinced. In his *Flora Cochinchinensis* (or, in today's geography, a flora of southern Vietnam; 1793) he wrote, "Many authors have written of the Scythian Lamb, or Borametz—most of them fabulously. Ours is not a fruit, but a root, which is easily shaped by the help of a little art into the form of a small rufous dog, by which name, and not that of a 'lamb,' it is called by the Chinese."

This brings us back to the question about how Tartary became associated with a fern of southeastern Asia. Was Sloane's identification wrong? At least one person thought so. Henry Lee, an English natural historian, argued in 1887 that the cotton plant of India was the source of the vegetable lamb. He wrote a scholarly but little-known book on the subject, *The Vegetable Lamb of Tartary: a Curious Fable of the Cotton Plant.* His arguments are convincing.

First, cotton fits the original version of the legend: a plant bearing little lambs at the tips of its branches. This version, Lee pointed out, is how the cotton plant was described by the ancients. In the Old World, cotton was grown only in India; Greeks used wool for their clothes, Egyptians used flax to make linen, and eastern Asians used silk. Herodotus, the first Greek historian, traveled to India in 484 B.C. and reported, "They have wild trees that bear a fruit that is in beauty like wool and in excellence as good as that which comes from sheep. The Indians wear clothes made from these plants." Theophrastus and several of Alexander the Great's generals also described "trees in India that bore balls of wool out of which the inhabitants made clothes. The ancient Greeks were familiar with sheep and had never before seen a cotton plant. What better way to describe cotton than a plant that bears white, wooly lambs at the tips of its branches? It is probable, Lee argued, that similar descriptions gave rise to the legend of the vegetable lamb. The cotton theory also explains versions of the legend that say the vegetable lamb was cultivated from seeds (Baron von Heberstein's description, for example).

But the cotton theory, like the tree fern idea before it, contains a geographic discrepancy: at the time the legend was current, cotton was grown in India but not in Tartary. How, then, did the cotton plant become associated with Tartary? Lee had an answer. During the Middle Ages, Tartary was part of Scythia, a kingdom that embraced a vast territory from 25° to 116° east longitude (its exact extent varied with the power of the Scythians). Another part of Scythia was Indo-Scythia, which comprised the Sind and Punjab provinces of present-day Pakistan. It was there that cotton was cultivated. In the early Middle Ages, cotton was brought overland to Egypt and Constantinople, where it was traded to merchants from around the Mediterranean. This trade was cut when the Muslims conquered Egypt and Constantinople. In response, the lucrative trade in cotton, spices, and other merchandise from India went northward by caravan across the western Himalaya (that is, the Hindu Kush) to Samarkand in present-day Uzbekistan, at that time part of Scythia. From there the caravans joined others traveling westward, and the goods eventually made their way into Europe.

Along the way, the caravans were joined by Tartarian traders carrying (among other things) the fine wool and skins of their sheep. After the merchandise of countless caravans reached the Western world, the vegetable wool (that is, cotton) from India became associated with Tartary, through which it passed en route but where it did not grow. Similarly, certain spices from India and China became associated with Arabia, through which they were traded but were not cultivated.

Thus the legend of the vegetable lamb is based on the cotton plant, not a fern. In 1991 I was in Taiwan collecting ferns with my colleague Chen-meng Kuo. He told me that the tree fern vegetable lambs cost $4–10 and are easy to find. Fortunately, the tree fern used to make the lambs in Taiwan—*Cibotium taiwanense*—is common and not in danger of becoming rare through exploitation. So, the next time you are in Asia, you might consider buying a vegetable lamb. Don't be sheepish! They make great pets for your fern-loving friends.

GLOSSARY

-aceae Suffix denoting the rank of family in the taxonomic hierarchy.

acrostichoid With the sporangia spread throughout the surface, not in discrete lines or dots; said of sori.

acuminate Tapering to a long point with the margins pinched, or concave, just before the tip.

acute Short-tapering to a point, the margins not pinched or concave just before the tip.

adhesion Attraction of molecules of unlike substances, such as water to glass or cellulose.

aerophore Aerating tissue of the leaf, usually a white or yellowish line running lengthwise along the leaf stalk and sometimes down onto the stem. In some genera such as *Blechnum* and *Thelypteris*, aerophores may occur as short pegs at the bases of the pinnae where they join the rachis. Stomata are abundant in aerophores, thus these structures allow air to diffuse into the leaf. Aerophores are characteristic of fern leaves, being absent from those of other plants.

-ales Suffix denoting the rank of order in the taxonomic hierarchy.

anastomose Interconnect.

angiosperms Flowering plants.

annulus Complete or partial ring or cluster of thick-walled cells on the spore case, functioning to open the spore case.

antheridium Male sex organ, containing the sperm; borne on underside of the prothallus.

apogamy Form of asexual reproduction in which new sporophytes proliferate directly from the tissue of the prothallus instead of from the fertilized egg cell (zygote).

appressed Pressed close to the surface, not spreading.

archegonium Female sex organ, containing the egg; usually flask-shaped
with a swollen base and short neck, and borne on underside of the prothallus.

attenuate Gradually tapering to a very narrow, slender point.

axil Angle between the stem and a leaf.

binomial Species name, which consists of two words, the genus name and
the specific epithet.

blade Thin, broad part of a leaf or leaf, as distinguished from the leaf stalk
or petiole; also called the lamina.

bryophytes Mosses, hornworts, and liverworts—land plants that disperse
by spores and have the gametophyte conspicuous and persistent, and the
sporophyte unbranched and with a single apical spore case.

bud In ferns, usually a lump of tissue that grows into a new fern plant.

bulblet Small bulb-like body borne upon a stem or leaf and serving to vegetatively reproduce the plant.

canopy Uppermost layer of foliage in a forest.

cellulose Carbohydrate that is the chief component of the plant cell wall.

chromosome Structure that carries the genes; in plants and animals, chromosomes are found in the nucleus and become visible only during cell division.

cohesion Mutual attraction of molecules of the same substance.

compound Of a leaf composed of two or more leaflets.

cone Tight cluster of highly modified, spore-bearing leaves borne at the
branch tips.

crested Having forking tips, usually many; usually referring to the leaf, pinnae, or segments. Many fern cultivars are characterized by crested leaves.

cultivar Cultivated variety of plant, generally chosen for a desirable trait or
traits, originating in cultivation or selected from among wild plants.

depauperate Impoverised.

dichotomous Forking regularly by pairs.

dimorphic Having two forms; in ferns, usually referring to the differences
in size or shape of the sterile and fertile leaves (or their segments).

diploid Having two sets of chromosomes, a condition ($2n$) characteristic of
the sporophyte generation. Compare with haploid.

distal Referring to the part farthest away from the main body or leaf axis. Compare with proximal.

elater Strap-shaped, hygroscopic band attached to the spores of horsetails (*Equisetum*).

endemic Confined to a particular geographical area; usually used for species with narrow distributions.

entire With an unmodified margin, that is, not divided, lobed, or toothed.

epidermis Outermost layer of cells on the leaf and young stem and root.

epiphyte Plant that grows on another plant and uses it only for support; it is not parasitic.

euphyll Leaves that developed evolutionarily from three-dimensional branching systems of early (Devonian) vascular plants; also known as a megaphyll.

false indusium Indusium formed by the inwardly rolled margin of the leaf; characteristic of many genera in the Pteridaceae such as *Adiantum, Cheilanthes,* and *Pellaea.*

family Rank in the taxonomic hierarchy consisting of a group of related genera; plant family names end with the suffix -aceae.

fern allies Vascular plants that reproduce by liberating their spores and having a life cycle like that of true ferns but differing in how they bear their sporangia and by having small leaves with simple, unbranched veins. Living families of fern allies are the Equisetaceae, Isoetaceae, Lycopodiaceae, Psilotaceae, and Selaginellaceae. The term "fern ally" is now obsolete because it has been shown that the Equisetaceae and Psilotaceae *are* ferns, and ferns are more closely related to seed plants than to lycophytes (Isoetaceae, Lycopodiaceae, and Selaginellaceae).

fertile In ferns, usually referring to the sori-bearing leaves.

fiddlehead Young fern leaf coiled in bud; the crozier.

flora List of all the species growing in a region, or a collective term for all the species growing in a region; also refers to a book that provides a means of identifying plants within a certain geographical area.

frond Leaf of a fern, usually referring to one that is highly divided.

gametes Sex cells (egg and sperm) that fuse during fertilization; in plants, these cells are produced by mitosis, not meiosis as in animals.

gametophyte In ferns, a small, usually flat plant bearing the sex organs (archegonia and antheridia) that in turn produce the gametes; each cell in the body of the gametophyte has one set of chromosomes, that is, is haploid. Gametophytes grow from spores.

gemma Bud, which see.

gene Unit on a chromosome that determines the inheritance of a particular character.

genus Rank in the taxonomic hierarchy consisting of a group of related species.

glabrous Without hairs or scales, smooth.

globose Spherical.

gymnosperms Plants that produce seeds but lack flowers, including cycads, ginkgoes, and pines.

haploid Having one set of chromosomes, a condition (n) characteristic of the gametophyte generation. Compare with diploid.

heterosporous Having two kinds of spores, male and female, the males being smaller and the two kinds produced in separate sporangia: *Azolla, Isoetes, Marsilea, Pilularia, Regnellidium, Salvinia,* and *Selaginella.*

homology Similarity caused by inheritance of a characteristic from a common ancestor.

homosporous Having one kind of spore.

humus Organic material resulting from the decomposition of forest leaf and branch litter.

hybrid Offspring of two different species; nearly all fern hybrids are sterile, having aborted spores.

indurated Hardened.

indusium Structure covering the sorus. See also false indusium.

internode Portion of a stem between two successive nodes.

land plants Mosses, hornworts, liverworts, lycophytes, ferns, and seed plants; also known as embryophytes. These plants evolved from aquatic, green algal ancestors.

latitudinal diversity gradient Tendency for most taxonomic groups to have most of their species in the tropics, with diminishing numbers of species toward the poles.

leaflet One of the divisions of a compound leaf.

lepidodendrids Arborescent lycophytes that abounded during the Carboniferous; characterized by patterned bark and an unusual rooting system called a rhizomorph.

lycophytes Lycopodiaceae, Selaginellaceae, Isoetaceae, and their fossil relatives (for example, lepidodendrids), characterized by simple entire leaves with a single vein (microphylls) and a single sporangium borne on the upper surface of the leaf or in its axil. Evolutionarily, these plants are the sister group to the ferns and seed plants.

marginal Relating to the margin or edge of a leaf; often said of sori borne along the margin instead of on the lower surface of the leaf.

megaphyll Leaf developed evolutionarily from three-dimensional branching systems of early (Devonian) vascular plants; also known as a euphyll.

megaspore Female spore, so named because it is usually larger than the male spore (microspore).

meiosis Kind of cell division that (in plants) gives rise to spores. During meiosis, the cell replicates its chromosomes once and divides twice. The result is four cells with only half the chromosome number of the original cell.

microphyll Simple entire leaf with one vein and (if fertile) bearing a single sporangium on its upper surface; characteristic of the lycophytes and thought to have a different evolutionary origin than the megaphyll.

microspore Male spore, so named because it is usually smaller than the female spore (megaspore).

mitosis Kind of cell division in which the chromosomes duplicate, then the two daughter chromosomes are pulled apart into separate cells to form two genetically identical daughter cells.

nitrogen fixation Incorporation of atmospheric nitrogen, which is unusable by plants, into compounds that are usable; carried out only by certain kinds of bacteria, such as the cyanobacterium *Anabaena azollae*, which inhabits the leaves of the mosquito fern (*Azolla*).

node Point on a stem where a leaf is attached.

New World The Americas, whose tropics include those parts of the West Indies, Central and South America between 22.5° north and south of the equator.

Old World Europe, Asia, Africa, and Australia.

-opsida Suffix denoting the rank of class in the taxonomic hierarchy.

páramo Shrub or grassland vegetation at elevations above timberline in the mountains of the New World tropics, particularly the Andes.

petiole Leaf stalk, sometimes called a stipe.

phloem Food-conducting tissue in plants, forming part of the veins or vascular bundles.

phyllopodium (plural, phyllopodia) Stump-like extension from the rhizome to which the leaves are attached, usually by a distinct abscission layer.

pinna Primary division of a pinnately divided leaf; a leaflet.

pinnate Having the arrangement of a feather, with a single midvein from which leaflets arise.

pinnate-pinnatifid Referring to a blade that is once-divided with deeply lobed pinnae.

pinnatifid Cut half to three-fourths to the rachis.

pinnatisect Cut almost all the way to the rachis.

pinnule Secondary pinna.

polyploidy Doubling of entire sets of chromosomes.

prothallus (plural, prothalli) Gametophyte, which see.

proximal Referring to the part near or toward the base or point of attachment. Compare with distal.

pteridologist Student of pteridophytes.

pteridophytes Ferns and lycophytes, defined by having a life cycle in which the sporophyte and gametophyte generations grow independently of one another, not attached; the sporophyte is large and conspicuous, the gametophyte inconspicuous and ephemeral.

pups Plantlets arising from root buds on older plants of staghorn ferns (*Platycerium*).

rachis Midrib of a compound leaf.

rain forest Forest that receives more than 100 inches (2500 mm) of rainfall per year; usually lacking a pronounced dry season.

receptacle Tissue upon which the sporangia are borne. In *Hymenophyllum* and *Trichomanes* this is bristle-like; in most other ferns it is flush with the leaf surface or slightly elevated.

refugia Hypothesized areas of shrunken and fragmented rain forests that were scattered in Central and South America during the last Ice Age, so named because the rain forest species found refuge in them, being otherwise surrounded by unfavorable savanna or grassland habitat.

reticulogram Network-like diagram depicting the relationships resulting from hybridization and polyploidy among a group of species.

rhizome Stem growing horizontally and anchored to the soil by roots.

rhizomorph In certain lycophytes (for example, *Isoetes* and lepidodendrids), a rooting system developed from the first dichotomy of the embryonic shoot (because it originates from shoot tissue, it is not a true root). It has the anchoring and absorptive functions of a root but the general morphology and other characteristics of aerial shoots.

savanna Grassland with scattered trees.

scale Outgrowth of the epidermal layer that appears as a small, flat, usually dry structure two or more cells wide; hairs (trichomes) are similar but only one cell wide.

seed plants Gymnosperms (for example, pines, ginkgoes, and cycads) and angiosperms (flowering plants).

segment Ultimate division into which a blade is divided.

sessile Without a stalk.

sinus Space or recess between two lobes of a leaf or other expanded structure.

sister group The most closely related group in an evolutionary tree; when a branch on an evolutionary tree (cladogram) divides, it forms two sister groups.

somatic All the body cells of an organism except those giving rise to the egg and sperm.

sorus (plural, sori) Cluster of spore cases (sporangia).

species Category of individuals usually interbreeding freely and having many characteristics in common; the word is used for both the singular and plural.

species richness Number of species of a given taxonomic group in a given area.

specific epithet Second word in a species name, for example, *cristata* in *Dryopteris cristata.* Not to be confused with the species name (binomial), which is both words.

sperm Male gamete, smaller and motile compared to the larger, nonmotile female gamete (egg).

sporangium (plural, sporangia) Specialized structure within which spores are produced; the spore case.

spore Reproductive cell produced in a sporangium, germinating and developing into a prothallus; the first cell in the gametophyte phase of the life cycle. See also unreduced spores.

spore mother cell Cell that divides by meiosis to give rise to spores.

sporocarp Hard, round or bean-shaped structures that contain sporangia; characteristic of the Marsileaceae (*Marsilea, Pilularia,* and *Regnellidium*). Evolutionarily, the sporocarp represents a folded, sealed, hardened pinna.

sporophyll Spore-producing leaf.

sporophyte Phase of the life cycle that produces spores, in vascular plants the familiar phase bearing roots, stems, and leaves (as opposed to the gametophyte or prothallus). Each cell in the body of the sporophyte has two sets of chromosomes (that is, is diploid).

starch Principal food-storage product of plants, composed of 1000 or more glucose units strung together.

stellate Star-like, having arms or hairs radiating from a central point; usually referring to hairs or scales.

sterile Referring to leaves that do not produce sori, also to hybrids whose spores are aborted.

stipule Basal appendage of a petiole (or stipe), usually two; in ferns, applied to the Marattiaceae and sometimes to the flared leaf bases in *Osmunda*.

stolon Long, slender stem running horizontally along the soil and capable of producing a new plant at its tip or along its length; a runner.

stoma (plural, stomata or stomates) Minute opening bordered by guard cells in the epidermis of leaves and stem. Air passes through the opening, and most of the plant's water evaporates through the pores. Sometimes the term refers collectively to the pore and guard cells.

strobilus Reproductive structure composed of many spore-bearing leaves (sporophylls) attached to a central axis; found in present-day plants such as spike mosses (*Selaginella*), club mosses (*Lycopodium, Huperzia, Lycopodiella,* and *Phylloglossum*), and horsetails (*Equisetum*) and in extinct groups such as the calamites (*Calamites*) and giant lycopods of the Carboniferous (lepidodendrids). Sometimes, strobili are called cones, but true cones are found only in conifers and have a different structure and evolutionary origin.

subgen. Abbreviation for the taxonomic rank of subgenus, for a group of more closely related species within a genus.

synonym Alternative scientific name for a currently accepted one.

tepui One of the flat-topped, steep-sided table mountains in southern Venezuela, not part of the Andes.

terrestrial Referring to plants that grow in the ground, not on trees.

tetraploid Having four sets of chromosomes (4x).

triploid Having three sets of chromosomes (3x); triploids are either sterile because they produce aborted spores, or fertile because they are apogamous.

tuber Short, enlarged, fleshy underground stem, such as that of a potato; in ferns, referring to the rounded fleshy stems produced on the underground stolons of some species of sword ferns (*Nephrolepis*) and the ant-inhabited stems of the potato fern (*Solanopteris*).

unreduced spores Spores that have not had their chromosome number halved (reduced) by meiosis; spores that are 2n, not n.

var. Abbreviation for the taxonomic rank of variety, for a group of more closely related populations within a species.

vascular Pertaining to specialized tissue (xylem and phloem) that conducts water, mineral nutrients, and sugars.

vascular bundle Strand of vascular tissue (xylem and phloem).

xylem Tissue through which water and mineral nutrients are conducted.

zosterophylls Early relatives of living lycophytes, characterized by kidney-shaped sporangia borne laterally (not apically) on green photosynthetic axes; went extinct by the late Devonian.

zygote Single fertilized egg cell, the first cell of a new sporophyte.

REFERENCES

Allen, D. E. 1969. The Victorian Fern Craze, a History of Pteridomania. Hutchinson & Co., London.

André, E. F. 1883. Tour du Monde. Paris.

Andrews, H. N., and E. M. Kerns. 1947. The Idaho tempskyas and associated fossil plants. Annals of the Missouri Botanical Garden 34: 119–186.

Ash, S., R. J. Litwin, and A. Traverse. 1982. The Upper Triassic fern *Phlebopteris smithii* (Daugherty) Arnold and its spores. Palynology 6: 203–219.

Balick, M. J., and J. M. Beitel. 1988. *Lycopodium* spores found in condom dusting agent. Nature 332: 591.

Bancroft, T. L. 1893. On the habit and use of nardoo (*Marsilea drummondii*, A. Br.), together with some observations on the influence of water plants in retarding evaporation. Proceedings of the Linnean Society of New South Wales, series 2, 8: 215–217.

Barber, L. 1980. The Heyday of Natural History, 1820–1870. Jonathan Cape, London.

Boston, H. L. 1986. A discussion of the adaptations for carbon acquisition in relation to the growth strategy of aquatic isoetids. Aquatic Botany 26: 259–270.

Boufford, D. E., and S. A. Spongberg. 1983. Eastern Asian–eastern North American phytogeographical relationships—a history from the time of Linnaeus to the twentieth century. Annals of the Missouri Botanical Garden 70: 423–439.

Brockway, L. H. 1979. Science and Colonial Expansion, the Role of the British Royal Botanic Gardens. Academic Press, New York.

Browne, T. 1672. *Pseudodoxia Epidemica:* or, Enquiries Into Very Many Received Tenets and Commonly Presumed Truths. Sixth edition. Edward Dod, London.

Brownsey, P. J. 2001. New Zealand's pteridophyte flora: Plants of ancient lineage but recent arrival? Brittonia 53: 284–303.

Calvert, H. E., and G. A. Peters. 1981. The *Azolla–Anabaena azollae* relationship, IX. Morphological analysis of leaf cavity hair populations. New Phytologist 89: 327–335.

Campbell, D. H. 1928. The Structure and Development of Mosses and Ferns. Macmillan, New York.

Chiou, W.-l, and D. R. Farrar. 1997. Antheridiogen production and response in Polypodiaceae species. American Journal of Botany 84: 633–640.

Clute, W. N. 1901. Our Ferns and Their Haunts. Frederick A. Stokes, New York.

Cook, T. A. 1914. The Curves of Life, Being an Account of Spiral Formations and Their Application to Growth in Nature, to Science and to Art; with Special Reference to the Manuscripts of Leonardo da Vinci. Constable and Company, London. [reprinted unabridged by Dover, New York, in 1979]

Cooper-Driver, G. A. 1985. Anti-predation strategies in pteridophytes—a biochemical approach. Proceedings of the Royal Society of Edinburgh 86B: 397–402.

Cooper-Driver, G. A. 1990. Defense strategies in bracken, *Pteridium aquilinum* (L.) Kuhn. Annals of the Missouri Botanical Garden 77: 281–286.

Cooper-Driver, G. A., and T. Swain. 1976. Cyanogenic polymorphism in bracken in relation to herbivore predation. Nature 260: 604.

Corsin, P., and M. Waterlot. 1979. Paleobiogeography of the Dipteridaceae and Matoniaceae of the Mesozoic. Fourth International Gondwana Symposium 1: 51–70.

Davies, K. L. 1991. A brief comparative survey of aerophore structure within the Filicopsida. Botanical Journal of the Linnean Society 107: 115–137.

Domanski, C. W. 1993. M. J. Leszczyc-Suminski (1820–1898), an unknown botanist-discoverer. Fiddlehead Forum 20: 11–15.

Dyer, A. F., and S. Lindsay. 1992. Soil spore banks of temperate ferns. American Fern Journal 82: 89–12.

Eames, A. J. 1936. Morphology of Vascular Plants, Lower Groups. McGraw-Hill, New York.

Earl, J. W., and B. V. McCleary. 1994. Mystery of the poisoned expedition. Nature 368: 683–684.

Edwards, D. S. 1986. *Aglaophyton major,* a non-vascular land-plant from the Devonian Rhynie Chert. Botanical Journal of the Linnean Society 93: 173–204.

Emigh, V. D., and D. R. Farrar. 1977. Gemmae: a role in sexual reproduction in the fern genus *Vittaria.* Science 198: 297–298.

Farley, J. 1982. Gametes & Spores, Ideas About Sexual Reproduction, 1750–1914. Johns Hopkins University Press, Baltimore.

Farrar, D. R. 1985. Independent fern gametophytes in the wild. Proceedings of the Royal Society of Edinburgh 86B: 361–369.

Farrar, D. R. 1990. Species and evolution in asexually reproducing independent fern gametophytes. Systematic Botany 15: 98–111.

Farrar, D. R. 1991. *Vittaria appalachiana:* a name for the "Appalachian gametophyte." American Fern Journal 81: 69–75.

Farrar, D. R. 1992. *Trichomanes intricatum:* the independent *Trichomanes* gametophyte in the eastern United States. American Fern Journal 82: 68–74.

Farrar, D. R. 1998. The tropical flora of rockhouse cliff formations in the eastern United States. Journal of the Torrey Botanical Society 125: 91–108.

Farrar, D. R., and C. L. Johnson-Groh. 1990. Subterranean sporophytic gemmae in moonwort ferns, *Botrychium* subgenus *Botrychium.* American Journal of Botany 77: 1168–1175.

Flora of North America Editorial Committee. 1993. Flora of North America. Volume 2, Pteridophytes and Gymnosperms. Oxford University Press, New York.

Fox, D. L., and J. R. Wells. 1971. Schemochromic blue leaf-surfaces of *Selaginella.* American Fern Journal 61: 137–139.

Gastony, G. J. 1988. The *Pellaea glabella* complex: electrophoretic evidence for the derivations of apogamous taxa and a revised synonymy. American Fern Journal 78: 44–67.

Gay, H. 1991. Ant-houses in the fern genus *Lecanopteris* Reinw. (Polypodiaceae): the rhizome morphology and architecture of *L. sarcopus* Teijsm. & Binnend. and *L. darnaedii* Hennipman. Botanical Journal of the Linnean Society 106: 199–208.

Gay, H. 1993. Animal-fed plants: an investigation into the uptake of ant-derived nutrients by the Far-Eastern epiphytic fern *Lecanopteris* Reinw. (Polypodiaceae). Biological Journal of the Linnean Society 50: 221–233.

Gómez, L. D. 1974. Biology of the potato fern *Solanopteris brunei.* Brenesia 4: 37–61.

Gómez, L. D. 1977. The *Azteca* ants of *Solanopteris brunei.* American Fern Journal 67: 31.

Gould, K. S., and D. W. Lee. 1996. Physical and ultrastructural basis of blue leaf iridescence in four Malaysian understory plants. American Journal of Botany 83: 45–50.

Graham, A. 1966. *Plantae Rariores Camschatcenses:* a translation of the dissertation of Jonas P. Halenius, 1750. Brittonia 18: 131–139.

Graham, R., D. W. Lee, and K. Norstog. 1993. Physical and ultrastructural basis of blue leaf iridescence in two Neotropical ferns. American Journal of Botany 80: 198–203.

Grayum, M. H., and H. W. Churchill. 1987. An introduction to the pteridophyte flora of Finca La Selva, Costa Rica. American Fern Journal 77: 73–89.

Hagemann, W. 1969. Zur Morphologie der Knolle von *Polypodium bifrons* Hook. und *P. brunei* Wercklé. Société Botanique de France, Mémoires, 1969: 17–27.

Harris, T. M. 1961. The Yorkshire Jurassic Flora. I. Thallophyta–Pteridophyta. British Museum (Natural History), London.

Haufler, C. H., and C. B. Welling. 1994. Antheridiogen, dark germination, and outcrossing mechanisms in *Bommeria* (Adiantaceae). American Journal of Botany 81: 616–621.

Hirmer, M. 1927. Handbuch der Paläobotanik. R. Oldenbourg, Berlin.

Hodge, W. H. 1973. Fern foods of Japan and the problem of toxicity. American Fern Journal 63: 77–80.

Hoshizaki, B. J., and R. C. Moran. 2001. Fern Grower's Manual. Revised and Expanded Edition. Timber Press, Portland, Oregon.

Ingold, C. T. 1939. Spore Discharge in Land Plants. Clarendon Press, Oxford.

Ingold, C. T. 1965. Spore Liberation. Clarendon Press, Oxford.

Jacono, C. C. 1999. *Salvinia molesta* (Salviniaceae), new to Texas and Louisiana. Sida 18: 927–928.

Johnson, D. M. 1985. New records for longevity of *Marsilea* sporocarps. American Fern Journal 75: 30–31.

Kato, M. 1993. Biogeography of ferns: dispersal and vicariance. Journal of Biogeography 20: 265–274.

Kato, M., and D. Darnedi. 1988. Taxonomic and phytogeographic relationships of *Diplazium flavoviride, D. pycnocarpon,* and *Diplaziopsis.* American Fern Journal 78: 77–85.

Kato, M., and K. Iwatsuki. 1983. Phytogeographic relationships of pteridophytes between temperate North America and Japan. Annals of the Missouri Botanical Garden 70: 724–733.

Keeley, J. E. 1981. *Isoëtes howellii:* a submerged aquatic CAM plant? American Journal of Botany 68: 420–424.

Keeley, J. E. 1987. Photosynthesis in quillworts, or why are some aquatic plants similar to cacti? Plants Today 1: 127–132.

Keeley, J. E. 1988. A puzzle solved for the quillwort. Fremontia 16: 15–16.

Keeley, J. E. 1998. CAM photosynthesis in submerged aquatic plants. Botanical Review 64: 121–175.

Kenrick, P. 2001. Turning over a new leaf. Nature 410: 309–310.

Kenrick, P., and P. R. Crane. 1997. The Origin and Early Diversification of Land Plants, a Cladistic Study. Smithsonian Institution Press, Washington, D.C.

Lee, D. W. 1977. On iridescent plants. Gardens' Bulletin, Straits Settlements, Singapore 30: 21–31.

Lee, D. W. 1986. Unusual strategies of light absorption in rain-forest herbs, pages 105–131 *in* Thomas J. Givnish, editor, On the Economy of Plant Form and Function. Cambridge University Press, New York.

Lee, D. W., and J. B. Lowry. 1975. Physical basis and ecological significance of iridescence in blue plants. Nature 254: 50–51.

Lee, H. 1887. The Vegetable Lamb of Tartary: a Curious Fable of the Cotton Plant, to Which Is Added a Sketch of the History of Cotton and the Cotton Trade. S. Low, Marston, Searle & Rivington, London.

León, B., and H. Beltrán. 2002. A new *Microgramma* subgenus *Solanopteris* (Polypodiaceae) from Peru and a new combination in the subgenus. Novon 12: 481–485.

Lellinger, D. B. 1967. *Pterozonium* (Filicales: Polypodiaceae), *in* B. Maguire, editor, The Botany of the Guayana Highland. Memoirs of the New York Botanical Garden 17: 2–23.

Lellinger, D. B. 1987. Hymenophyllopsidaceae (Filicales), *in* B. Maguire, editor, Botany of the Guayana Highlands. Memoirs of the New York Botanical Garden 38: 2–9.

Li, H.-l. 1952. Floristic relationships between eastern Asia and eastern North America. Transactions of the American Philosophical Society 42: 371–429. [reprinted with foreword and additional references as a Morris Arboretum Monograph in 1971]

Lindsay, J. 1794. Account of the germination and raising of ferns from the seed. Transactions of the Linnean Society 2: 93–100.

Lloyd, R. M., and E. J. Klekowski, Jr. 1970. Spore germination and viability in Pteridophyta: evolutionary significance of chlorophyllous spores. Biotropica 2: 129–137.

Lumpkin, T. A., and D. L. Plucknett. 1982. *Azolla* as a Green Manure: Use and Management in Crop Production. Westview Tropical Agriculture Series, no. 5.

McCleary, B. V., and B. F. Chick. 1977. The purification and properties of a thiaminase I enzyme from nardoo (*Marsilea drummondii*). Phytochemistry 16: 207–213.

McCleary, B. V., C. A. Kennedy, and B. F. Chick. 1980. Nardoo, bracken and rock ferns cause vitamin B_1 deficiency in sheep. Agricultural Gazette of New South Wales 91(5): 1–4.

Madsen, T. V. 1987. Interactions between internal and external CO_2 pools in the photosynthesis of the aquatic CAM plants *Littorella uniflora* (L.) Aschers and *Isoëtes lacustris* L. New Phytologist 106: 35–50.

Menéndez, C. A. 1966. La presencia de *Thyrsopteris* en la Cretácico Superior de Cerro Guido, Chile. Ameghiniana 4: 299–302.

Mickel, J. T. 1981. *Marattia* propagation stipulated. Fiddlehead Forum 8: 40.

Mickel, J. T. 1985. The proliferous species of *Elaphoglossum* (Elaphoglossaceae) and their relatives. Brittonia 37: 261–278.

Mickel, J. T., and J. M. Beitel. 1988. Pteridophyte Flora of Oaxaca, Mexico. Memoirs of the New York Botanical Garden 46: 1–568.

Milton, G. 2001. The Riddle and the Knight: in Search of Sir John Mandeville, the World's Greatest Traveler. Farrar Straus & Giroux, New York.

Mitchell, D. S. 1972. The Kariba weed: *Salvinia molesta*. British Fern Gazette 10: 251–252.

Moore, W. A. 1969. *Azolla:* biology and agronomic significance. Botanical Review 35: 17–35.

Moorehead, A. 1963. Cooper's Creek. Harper & Row, New York.

Moran, R. C. 1995. The importance of mountains to pteridophytes, with emphasis on Neotropical montane forests, pages 359–363 *in* S. P. Churchill, H. Balslev, E. Forero, and J. L. Luteyn, editors, Biodiversity and Conservation of Neotropical Montane Forests. New York Botanical Garden, Bronx.

Moran, R. C., and A. R. Smith. 2001. Phytogeographic relationships between Neotropical and African–Madagascan pteridophytes. Brittonia 53: 304–351.

Moran, R. C., S. Klimas, and M. Carlsen. 2003. Low-trunk epiphytic ferns on tree ferns versus angiosperms in Costa Rica. Biotropica 35: 48–56.

Müller, L., G. Starnecker, and S. Winkler. 1981. Zur Ökologie epiphytischer Farne in Sudbrasilien 1. Saugschuppen. Flora 171: 55–63.

Nasrulhaq-Boyce, A., and J. G. Duckett. 1991. Dimorphic epidermal cell chloroplasts in the mesophyll-less leaves of an extreme-shade tropical fern, *Teratophyllum rotundifoliatum* (R. Bonap.) Holtt.: a light and electron microscope study. New Phytologist 119: 433–444.

Niklas, K. J., B. H. Tiffney, and A. H. Knoll. 1983. Patterns in vascular land plant diversification. Nature 303: 614–616.

Øllgaard, B., and K. Tind. 1993. Scandinavian Ferns. Rhodos Press, Copenhagen.

Page, C. N. 1976. The taxonomy and phytogeography of bracken—a review. Botanical Journal of the Linnean Society 73: 1–34.

Parrish, J. T. 1987. Global palaeogeography and palaeoclimate of the late Cretaceous and early Tertiary, pages 51–74 *in* E. M. Friis, W. G. Chaloner, and P. R. Crane, editors, The Origins of Angiosperms and Their Biological Consequences. Cambridge University Press, Cambridge.

Perkins, S. K., and G. A. Peters. 1993. The *Azolla–Anabaena* symbiosis: endophyte continuity in the *Azolla* life-cycle is facilitated by epidermal trichomes. New Phytologist 123: 53–64.

Perrie, L. R., P. J. Brownsey, P. J. Lockhart, E. A. Brown, and M. F. Large. 2003. Biogeography of temperate Australasian *Polystichum* ferns as inferred from chloroplast sequence and AFLP. Journal of Biogeography 30: 1729–1736.

Perring, F. H., and B. G. Gardiner, editors. 1976. The biology of bracken. Journal of the Linnean Society, Botany, 73: 1–302.

Pessin, L. J. 1924. A physiological and anatomical study of the leaves of *Polypodium polypodioides.* American Journal of Botany 11: 370–381.

Pessin, L. J. 1925. An ecological study of the polypody fern *Polypodium polypodioides* as an epiphyte in Mississippi. Ecology 6: 17–38.

Phillips, T. L. 1979. Reproduction of heterosporous arborescent lycopods in the Mississippian–Pennsylvanian of Euramerica. Review of Paleobotany and Palynology 27: 239–289.

Phillips, T. L., and W. A. DiMichele. 1992. Comparative ecology and life-history biology of arborescent lycopsids in late Carboniferous swamps of Euramerica. Annals of the Missouri Botanical Garden 79: 560–588.

Phipps, C. J., T. N. Taylor, E. L. Taylor, N. Rubén Cúneo, L. D. Boucher, and X. Yao. 1998. *Osmunda* (Osmundaceae) from the Triassic of Antarctica: an example of evolutionary stasis. American Journal of Botany 85: 888–895.

Posthumus, O. 1928. *Dipteris novo-guineensis,* ein 'lebendes Fossil.' Recueil des Travaux Botaniques Néerlandais 24: 244–249.

Pring, G. H. 1964. The bracken in the grove, *Pteridium aquilinum.* Missouri Botanical Garden Bulletin 52(8): 3–5.

Pryer, K. M., H. Schneider, A. R. Smith, R. Cranfill, P. G. Wolf, J. S. Hunt, and S. D. Sipes. 2001. Horsetails and ferns are a monophyletic group and the closest living relatives to seed plants. Nature 409: 618–622.

Puri, V., and M. L. Garg. 1953. A contribution to the anatomy of the sporocarp of *Marsilea minuta* L. with a discussion of the nature of sporocarp in the Marsileaceae. Phytomorphology 3: 190–209.

Raghaven, V. 1992. Germination of fern spores. American Scientist 80: 176–185.

Rasbach, H., K. Rasbach, and C. Jérôme. 1993. Über das Vorkommen des Hautfarns *Trichomanes speciosum* (Hymenophyllaceae) in den Vogesen (Frankreich) und dem benachbarten Deutschland. Carolinea 51: 51–52.

Ratcliffe, D. A., H. J. B. Birks, and H. H. Birks. 1993. The ecology and conservation of the Killarney fern *Trichomanes speciosum* Willd. in Britain and Ireland. Biological Conservation 66: 231–247.

Rauh, W. 1973. *Solanopteris bismarckii* Rauh, ein neuer knollenbildender Ameisenfarn aus Zentral-Peru. Tropische und Subtropische Pflanzenwelt 5: 223–256.

Ritman, K. T., and J. A. Milburn. 1990. The acoustic detection of cavitation in fern sporangia. Journal of Experimental Botany 41(230): 1157–1160.

Room, P. M. 1990. Ecology of a simple plant-herbivore system: biological control of *Salvinia.* Trends in Ecology and Evolution 5: 74–79.

Rothwell, G. W., and R. Roessler. 2000. The late Palaeozoic tree fern *Psaronius*—an ecosystem unto itself. Review of Palaeobotany and Palynology 108: 55–74.

Rothwell, G. W., and R. A. Stockey. 1991. *Onoclea sensibilis* in the Paleocene of North America, a dramatic example of structural and ecological stasis. Review of Paleobotany and Palynology 70: 113–124.

Rumsey, F. J., E. Sheffield, and D. R. Farrar. 1990. British filmy-fern gametophytes. Pteridologist 2: 39–42.

Rumsey, F. J., A. D. Headley, D. R. Farrar, and E. Sheffield. 1991. The Killarney fern (*Trichomanes speciosum*) in Yorkshire. Naturalist 116: 41–43.

Sand-Jensen, K., and J. Borum. 1984. Epiphyte shading and its effects on photosynthesis and diel metabolism of *Lobelia dortmanna* L. during the spring bloom in a Danish lake. Aquatic Botany 20: 109–119.

Sand-Jensen, K., and M. Søndergaard. 1981. Phytoplankton and epiphyte development and their shading effect on submerged macrophytes in lakes of different nutrient status. Internationale Revue der Gesamten Hydrobiologie 66: 529–552.

Schneider, H., K. M. Pryer, R. Cranfill, A. R. Smith, and P. G. Wolf. 2002. Evolution of vascular plant body plans: a phylogenetic perspective, pages 330–364 *in* Q. C. B. Cronk, R. M. Bateman, and J. A. Hawkins, editors, Developmental Genetics and Plant Evolution. Taylor & Francis, London.

Schneider, H., E. Schuettpelz, K. M. Pryer, R. Cranfill, S. Magallón, and R. Lupia. 2004. Ferns diversified in the shadow of angiosperms. Nature 428: 553–557.

Simán, S. E., A. C. Povey, and E. Sheffield. 1999. Human health risks from fern spores?—A review. Fern Gazette 18: 275–287.

Slosson, M. 1906. How Ferns Grow. Henry Holt & Co., New York.

Smith, A. R. 1972. Comparison of fern and flowering plant distributions with some evolutionary interpretations for ferns. Biotropica 4: 4–9.

Smith, A. R. 1995. Pteridophytes, pages 1–334 *in* J. A. Steyermark, P. E. Berry, and B. K. Holst, general editors, Flora of the Venezuelan Guayana. Volume 2. Missouri Botanical Garden, St. Louis, and Timber Press, Portland, Oregon.

Smith, G. M. 1955. Cryptogamic Botany. Volume II, Bryophytes and Pteridophytes. Second Edition. McGraw-Hill, New York.

Spruce, R. 1908. Notes of a Botanist on the Amazon & Andes; Being Records of Travel on the Amazon and Its Tributaries the Trombetas, Rio Negro, etc. . . . during the years 1849–1864. Macmillan & Co., London.

Stearn, W. T. 1957. An introduction to the *Species Plantarum* and cognate botanical works of Carl Linnaeus [prefixed to facsimile of Volume 1]. Ray Society, London.

Stevens, P. S. 1974. Patterns in Nature. Little, Brown & Company, New York.

Stewart, W. N. 1947. A comparative study of stigmarian appendages and *Isoëtes* roots. American Journal of Botany 34: 315–324.

Stewart, W. N., and G. W. Rothwell. 1993. Paleobotany and the Evolution of Plants. Second Edition. Cambridge University Press, New York.

Stuart, T. S. 1968. Revival of respiration and photosynthesis in dried leaves of *Polypodium polypodioides.* Planta 83: 185–206.

Tessenow, U., and Y. Baynes. 1975. Redox-dependent accumulation of Fe and Mn in a littoral sediment supporting *Isoëtes lacustris* L. Naturwissenschaften 62: 342–343.

Tessenow, U., and Y. Baynes. 1978. Experimental effects of *Isoëtes lacustris* L. on the distribution of Eh, pH, Fe and Mn in lake sediment. Internationale Vereinigung für Theoretische und Angewandte Limnologie, Verhandlungen 20: 2358–2362.

Thomas, B. A. 1966. The cuticle of the lepidodendrid stem. New Phytologist 65: 296–303.

Thomas, B. A. 1981. Structural adaptations shown by the Lepidocarpaceae. Review of Palaeobotany and Palynology 32: 377–388.

Thomas, P. A. 1986. Successful control of the floating weed *Salvinia molesta* in Papua New Guinea: a useful biological invasion neutralizes a disastrous one. Environmental Conservation 13: 242–248.

Thomas, P. A., and P. M. Room. 1986. Taxonomy and control of *Salvinia molesta*. Nature 320: 581–584.

Thompson, D. W. 1942. On Growth and Form. Second edition. University Press, Cambridge, England.

Thompson, J. A., and R. T. Smith, editors. 1990. Bracken biology and management. Australian Institute of Agricultural Science Occasional Publication 40: 1–341.

Thomson, J. A. 2000. New perspectives on taxonomic relationships in *Pteridium*, pages 15–34 *in* Bracken Fern: Toxicity, Biology and Control. International Bracken Group Special Publication 4.

Tiffney, B. H. 1985a. Perspectives on the origin of the floristic similarity between eastern Asia and eastern North America. Journal of the Arnold Arboretum 66: 73–94.

Tiffney, B. H. 1985b. The Eocene North Atlantic land bridge: its importance in Tertiary and modern phytogeography of the northern hemisphere. Journal of the Arnold Arboretum 66: 243–273.

Tippo, O., and W. L. Stern. 1977. Humanistic Botany. W. W. Norton & Co., New York.

Troop, J. E., and J. T. Mickel. 1968. Petiolar shoots in the dennstaedtioid and related ferns. American Fern Journal 58: 64–69.

Tryon, A. F., and B. Lugardon. 1991. Spores of the Pteridophyta. Springer-Verlag, New York.

Tryon, A. F., and R. C. Moran. 1997. The Ferns and Allied Plants of New England. Massachusetts Audubon Society, Lincoln.

Tryon, R. M. 1941. A revision of the genus *Pteridium*. Rhodora 43: 1–31, 37–67.

Tryon, R. M. 1970. Development and evolution of fern floras of oceanic islands. Biotropica 2: 76–84.

Tryon, R. M., and A. F. Tryon. 1982. Ferns and Allied Plants with Special Reference to Tropical America. Springer-Verlag, New York.

van Hove, C. 1989. *Azolla* and Its Multiple Uses, with Emphasis on Africa. Food and Agriculture Organization of the United Nations, Rome.

von Hagen, V. W. 1949. South America Called Them; Explorations of the Great Naturalists: Charles-Marie de la Condamine, Alexander Humboldt, Charles Darwin, Richard Spruce. Scientific Book Club, London.

Wagner, W. H., Jr. 1972. *Solanopteris brunei*, a little-known fern epiphyte with dimorphic stems. American Fern Journal 62: 33–43.

Walker, T. G., and A. C. Jermy. 1982. The ecology and cytology of *Phanerosorus* (Matoniaceae). Fern Gazette 12: 209–213.

Wallace, A. R. 1886. The Malay Archipelago. Macmillan, London.

White, M. F. 1986. The Greening of Gondwana. Reed Books, Frenchs Forest, Australia.

Wium-Andersen, S. 1971. Photosynthetic uptake of free CO_2 by the roots of *Lobelia dortmanna.* Physiologia Plantarum 25: 245–248.

Wolf, P. G., S. D. Sipes, M. R. White, M. L. Martines, K. M. Pryer, A. R. Smith, and K. Ueda. 1994. Phylogenetic relationships of the enigmatic fern families Hymenophyllopsidaceae and Lophosoriaceae: evidence from *rbcL* nucleotide sequences. Plant Systematics and Evolution 3: 383–392.

Wolf, P. G., K. M. Pryer, A. R. Smith, and M. Hasebe. 1998. Phylogenetic studies of extant pteridophytes, pages 541–556 *in* D. E. Soltis, P. S. Soltis, and J. J. Doyle, editors, Molecular Systematics of Plants II, DNA sequencing. Kluwer Academic Publishers, New York.

Yatskievych, G. 1993. Antheridiogen response in *Phanerophlebia* and related fern genera. American Fern Journal 83: 30–36.

Yatskievych, G., M. A. Homoya, and D. R. Farrar. 1987. The fern genera *Vittaria* and *Trichomanes* in Indiana. Proceedings of the Indiana Academy of Science 96: 429–434.

INDEX

Pellaea, 39, 92
  atropurpurea, 40
  glabella, 41, 42
Permian, 103, 130, 131
Pessin, Louis, 155–157
Phanerosorus, 120, 121, 123
Phegopteris, 89
  connectilis, 40
  decursive-pinnata, 53
Philippines, 206
Phlebodium aureum, 35
Phlebopteris smithii, 120
phyllopodia, 90
phyllotaxy, 108
Pilularia, 34, 82
pine, princess, see *Lycopodium digitatum*
Pityrogramma, 92
Plagiogyriaceae, 82, 208
plankton line, 125
Platycerium, 52, 53, 91
Pleopeltis, 96
  polypodioides, 154–159, 176; Plates 17, 18
pneumatophores, 72
polynomials, 85–86
polyploidy, 40, 55–61, 235
Polypodiaceae, 130
Polypodiales, 83, 130
polypodies, dwarf, see Grammitida-ceae
Polypodiopsida, 63
Polypodium, 90, 94
  virginianum, 17
polypody
  golden, see *Phlebodium aureum*
  scaly, see *Pleopeltis polypodioides*
polypody family, see Polypodiaceae
Polystichum, 94
  tsus-simense, 192

Posthumus, Oene, 119, 124
potato fern, Amazonian, see
  Solanopteris bifrons
Pratt, Anne, 227
princess pine, see *Lycopodium digitatum*
Pring, George, 166
prothalli, 19, 39, 43, 73, 211–217; Plates
  1, 12
prunasin, 171
Prunus, 171
prussic acid, 171
Psalixochlaenaceae, 130
Psaronius, 75, 130
Psilotaceae, 62, 63; see also *Psilotum*,
  Tmesipteris
  characteristics, 73–75
  phylogenetic relationships, 69, 73,
  75
Psilotopsida, 63
Psilotum, 50, 62, 69, 75
  complanatum, 64; Plate 20
  complanatum × *P. nudum*, 61
Pseudodoxia Epidemica, 262
ptaquiloside, 172
Pteridium, 166–171, 246
  aquilinum var. *latiusculum*, 166, 168–169
  cuadatum, 168
pteridomania, 216, 250–257
Pteridophyta or pteridophytes, 63, 69
Pteris, 39, 87
  cretica var. *albolineata*, 40
Pterozonium, 207, 209–210
pulvini of Marattiaceae, 75
purple cliff brake, see *Pellaea atropurpurea*
Pyrenees, 191
Pyrrosia, 92
quartz, shocked grains, 126
Queen Charlotte Islands, 216
Queen Victoria, 254

Tryon, Rolla M., 89, 166
Tryonella, 89
Tsus-sima holly fern, see *Polystichum
  tsus-simense*
type specimens, 100–101
Vancouver Island, 216
Vanuatu, 143
variegated brake, see *Pteris cretica* var.
  albolineata
vegetable fern, see *Diplazium esculentum*
vegetable lamb of Tartary, 258–265
vegetative reproduction, see asexual
  reproduction
Venezuela, 181, 205–210, 221
Vietnam, 236, 238, 263
vitamin B$_1$, 170, 245–247
Vittaria, 91, 219
  appalachiana, 212–213
  gametophytes, 212–214
  lineata, Plate 26
  root buds, 52
*The Voyages and Travels of Sir John Mande-
  ville, Knight,* 259–261
Wagner, Warren H., Jr., 89, 101, 145
Wagneriopteris, 89
Wallace, Alfred Russell, 121, 123

Ward, Nathaniel Bagshaw, 250–251
Wardian cases, 250–253
water
  adhesion, 25
  cavitation, 26, 27
  cohesion, 25
  polarity, 25
water sprite, see *Ceratopteris pteridoides*
weevils, curculionid, 231, 234, 235
Wells, James, 148
whisk ferns, see *Psilotum*
Wills, William John, 243
winged beech fern, see *Phegopteris decursive-pinnata*
wood ferns, see *Dryopteris*
  Goldie's, see *D. goldiana*
  shaggy, see *D. atrata*
Woodward, Thomas J., 89
Woodwardia, 89
  orientalis, 46
Zambia, 229
Zimbabwe, 229
zosterophylls, 66
Zosterophyllum myretonianum, 67
zygote, 21, 38, 39, 57